Increase and Multiply

*In the plenitude of Creation we meet with
multitudes of things, abundances and prolifera-
tions; but in the words of Scripture where there
is increase and multiplication in such a way that
one thing is expressed in many ways, and one
expression is understood in many ways, we find
multiplicity only with things which signify
concretely and with things interpreted spiritu-
ally. . . . And therefore we believe you, Lord, to
have said about both representation and interpre-
tation, "Increase and multiply" (Gen. 1:22). By
this blessing you allowed us the means and
ability to express in many ways that which we
have in our understanding as one and to
understand in many ways that which we read
obscurely put in one particular way.*

AUGUSTINE

Increase and Multiply

ℳ ARTS-OF-DISCOURSE PROCEDURE
IN THE PREACHING OF DONNE

by John S. Chamberlin

The University of North Carolina Press
Chapel Hill

Library of Congress Cataloging in Publication Data

Chamberlin, John S
Increase and multiply.

Includes bibliographical references.
1. Donne, John, 1572–1631—Prose. 2. Preaching
—History. I. Title.
PR2248.C48   252'.03   76-6998
ISBN 0-8078-1266-8

CONTENTS

Acknowledgments / ix
Introduction / xi

PART I: THE ARTS OF DISCOURSE

Chapter 1. Grammar
Section A / *Grammar and Grammatical Commentaries* / 3
Section B / *Augustine on Grammar and on How the Mind
Comes to Know through Discourse* / 12
Section C / *Augustine's Exegesis and Preaching* / 18
Section D / *The Medieval* Distinctiones *Compilations and
Their Use* / 34

Chapter 2. Dialectic
Section A / *The Scholastic* Ars praedicandi / 44
Section B / *A Sermon by Bonaventure* / 59

Chapter 3. Rhetoric
Section A / *Renaissance Treatises of Ecclesiastical
Rhetoric* / 67
Section B / *Protestant Preaching of the English
Reformation* / 84

PART II: DONNE'S PREACHING

Chapter 4. Procedure
Section A / *The Reaction of the High Church Party* / 95
Section B / *Donne on How the Preacher Should Deal with His
Text* / 102

Chapter 5. The Sermons
Section A / *The* Divisio / 109
Section B / *Multiplying the Words of Scripture* / 122
Section C / *Donne's Sermon on Ps. 32:1–2* / 136

Chapter 6. Conclusion / 155

Abbreviations / 161
Notes / 163
Selected Bibliography / 179
Index / 193

ACKNOWLEDGMENTS

This book is the development of interests I pursued in
Toronto's program in Medieval Studies, in which I had
the opportunity to cross the usual lines of demarcation
between disciplines and historical periods. I owe much
to Millar MacLure's enthusiasm for my subject and his
gracious and sensible counsel. I have benefitted greatly
from the erudition and goodwill of Father J. Reginald
O'Donnell of the Pontifical Institute of Medieval
Studies during the entire course of preparing this
volume. Also, I have had the privilege of spending
years with the resources of the Pontifical Institute
Library and am grateful for the Woodrow Wilson
Fellowship that enabled me to consult the libraries of
the British Museum and Lambeth Palace.

My wife Anna has shown uncommon patience and
good sense both in bearing with me during the last two
years and in going over and over the manuscript to
weed out flaws. I am grateful also to the editorial staff
and readers of The University of North Carolina Press
for the care they have taken in considering and
preparing my work.

All translations of the Latin and Greek are mine,
unless credit is specifically given in the notes to
another's English. However, for the passages quoted
from Augustine, I have depended heavily on the
excellent French translations in the Bibliothèque
Augustinienne. Citations of the Psalms are according
to the Vulgate enumeration for patristic, medieval, and
Tridentine authors.

INTRODUCTION

The Word of God is made a Sermon, that is, a text is dilated, diffused into a Sermon.

JOHN DONNE,
from a sermon preached at
Lincoln's Inn (?) on Whitsunday
ca. 1620

John Donne here[1] considers a sermon to be composed of the scriptural verses upon which it is preached: the words of the sacred text actually comprise the preacher's discourse. In his speaking, then, the preacher expands the divine words so that they acquire a fuller meaning and open into an abundantly rich signification. Just how the speaker in the pulpit takes up the text and proceeds to his invention from it will determine the shape and character of his discourse.

Several factors influence the way the preacher *dilates* the scriptural text into a sermon. He must have made some assumptions concerning such matters as: What is the nature of sacred language? Scripture admits of what procedures for developing its meaning? Of what does reading consist? By what means is the significance of God's Word to be understood and conveyed to others?

The church has had various sources upon which it might draw in answering these questions. The Old Testament authors themselves assumed a certain attitude toward the records of the Law and the written account of the history of God's care for His people. The New Testament writers inherited from the Jewish community a long tradition of reading and teaching from the sacred book. The apostolic preachers read the old writings in the new light of their faith in Christ and thus developed certain of their own procedures for scriptural exposition. Also, the early church, as it came to gain upon the pagan world, assimilated the achievements of classical culture and adapted those resources to serve its own purposes in the cause of the Gospel.

To consider this source of the preacher's assumptions concerning his elaboration of the meaning of the scriptural text, we shall examine classical learning as formulated particularly in the three arts of discourse: grammar, dialectic, and rhetoric.

The particular group of subjects that came to constitute the liberal arts seems first to have been set out in Latin in the *Disciplinae libri IX* of Marcus Varro (116–27 B.C.). From the nine disciplines, Martianus Capella in the fifth century A. D. subtracted two, medicine and architecture, because he considered their subject matter too earthly.[2] Capella's presentation of the remaining seven arts, the *De nuptiis,* was the first of several such compendiums that late antiquity bequeathed to the medieval school tradition. The more learned would, of course, turn to the great ancient propounders of the respective arts, if accessible— to Donatus for grammar, to Aristotle for dialectic, and to Cicero for rhetoric.

Through most of the church's history, her preachers have received the fundamentals of their education in the liberal arts tradition. Their assumptions concerning discourse have been influenced accordingly. As learned fashions in the subjects of the trivium changed, so too did the procedures by which the preacher developed his text into a sermon. Thus Augustine worked out the signficance of sacred Scripture by means different from those of the scholastics, and the scholastic *ars praedicandi* differed from the ecclesiastical rhetoric of the Renaissance. Donne quite deliberately drew on all these several distinctive traditions in dilating his text, and his sermons thus can serve as a vantage point from which the application of arts-of-discourse procedures to preaching can be viewed. On the other hand, an account of the precedents for Donne's means of invention, considered in the broad context of the doctrines of the trivium, makes possible a fuller reading of his own sermons.

Scholars have often drawn attention to the affinities between the procedures of patristic and medieval scriptural expositors and certain aspects of Donne's preaching. M. P. Ramsay, in making her case for Donne's Neoplatonism, remarks that seventeenth-century "wit" is in part but the persistence of the old allegorical method.[3] W. Fraser Mitchell, too, regards one distinctive feature of the "metaphysical" fashion in preaching to be the imitation of the rhetorical devices of the Fathers and the Schoolmen.[4]

What may be called the "Wisconsin School of Donne Studies," under the inspiration of Ruth Wallerstein, has pursued most fully the direction suggested by these earlier scholars. In her book, *Studies in Seventeenth-Century Poetic* (1950), Wallerstein made the point that Augustinianism contributed much to the modes of Donne's symbolic expression,[5] and in the completed portion of her projected work on Platonism in seventeenth-century England, she writes of "Donne's sacramental interpretation of the Bible"[6] in which the scriptural words themselves seem to take on an emblematic reality. Both Dennis Quinn[7] and Joan Webber[8] come to these same insights from different points of view: Quinn from a survey of the history of exegesis and Webber from the literary perspective of prose style. Others of the Fathers whose influence on Donne is taken to be appreciable are Tertullian, Gregory, and Bernard. While the patristic element in Donne's preaching has thus received considerable attention from literary critics, his relation to other theories of ecclesiastical rhetoric, both medieval and Renaissance, has not been pursued to a similar extent.[9]

These achievements of the "Wisconsin School" have been furthered by Winfried Schleiner in *The Imagery of John Donne's Sermons.*[10] In his third chapter Schleiner places several of the most frequent of Donne's figures within the context of their scriptural and patristic "fields of imagery," and in his fourth chapter he considers how certain of Donne's exegetical and rhetorical procedures work together. Janel M. Mueller, also, in the introduction to her edition of the five prebend sermons,[11] has emphasized the patristic contribution to Donne's preaching, particularly the importance for him of the Augustinian notion of memory. Several of these insights will be more thoroughly developed here by relating Donne's means for dilating his text to the arts-of-discourse traditions from which they derive.

Where others have spoken of the "emblematic" or "sacramental" reality that words seem to have for Donne, Gale Carrithers, author of the most recent study of his preaching, speaks of an "iconic" view of language in which words partake of the nature of the things to which they refer.[12] But he mentions this "iconicism" primarily to deny its importance in Donne's case.

While such a way of thinking about language was widely current in former times—Augustine, however, is excepted—Donne was typical of other Renaissance authors in his "shyness" toward this idea. Instead, words acquire their meaning by the shared conventions of the religious community. This and the redemptive function that they have in the church account sufficiently for their validity and reliability. Such an analysis is in keeping with the "theocentric relativism" that, Carrithers argues in the course of his book, is central to Donne's existentialist philosophy. The present study will offer a different view of Donne's assumptions concerning language.

This volume will consider the several most notable procedures in the church's preaching up to the time of Donne for developing a scriptural text into a discourse by relating doctrines of the trivium with particular theories and techniques for homiletic invention. A sermon will then be closely analyzed to illustrate how these principles work in practice. The intention is to accumulate a critical vocabulary with which to discuss Donne's sermons in terms of the traditions upon which he drew.

Part One includes three chapters, each devoted to one of the arts of discourse. For grammar, the basic principles of the art—as formulated in treatises on the subject and as assumed by the ancient commentators—will be considered. Augustine's views on the arts of language and the manner in which the mind comes to know through discourse are relevant to his procedures for exegetical invention that he sets out in *De doctrina Christiana*. Those procedures are seen to be essentially grammatical in nature. An analysis of a part of his sermon on Psalm 103 (Vulgate) will show that his expository preaching is quite in keeping with his own precepts. A later, codified version of the results of this improvisatory invention is the medieval *distinctiones* collection, whose use particularly characterized preaching in the twelfth century. This will be illustrated by the reading of a sermon by Alan of Lille.

For dialectic, the complex and intricate procedures for the text's division that are prescribed in the *ars praedicandi* will be related to the dialectical doctrines from which they derive. The apparently arbitrary rules in accordance with which the scholastic preacher is to handle his *theme* are more understandable when regarded in the context of certain implied notions concerning scriptural statements. A detailed analysis of a section of a sermon by Bonaventure on Psalm 106 (Vulgate) shows how these principles work in practice.

For rhetoric, the topical approaches characteristic of the two main schools of Renaissance rhetorical doctrine, the Ciceronian and the Aristotelian, will provide a basis for the consideration of the procedures of invention commended by several sixteenth-century preaching treatises. One of these treatises is that of Puritan William Perkins. After briefly surveying the course of Reformation preaching in England, Perkins's series of sermons on Matthew 5–7 will be analyzed to demonstrate his method of developing the text.

Part Two will show how Donne used the arts-of-discourse procedures to dilate a text into a sermon. Here the terminology and doctrines of the trivium—as established by the precedents of the Fathers, of the Schoolmen, and of the Renaissance ecclesiastical rhetoricians—will provide the means for investigating Donne's own theory and practice. Chapter Four will make the case that his procedures of sermon development were adopted in reaction to Puritan methods of reduction by topical logic. The ecclesiastical history of the late sixteenth century provides the setting in which the High Church reaction in preaching can be viewed. In this context Donne's own attitudes toward the methods of the Puritans, of the Fathers, and of the Cabalists will then be adduced.

Chapter Five examines how Donne develops a text into a discourse and in what terms he refers to his procedure. The division of the text—the point at which the words of Scripture are made into the structure of the preacher's discourse—is set out in the *divisio* of each sermon. This structure can then be filled out by grammatical means for multiplying the signification and consignifications of words, a means that Donne characteristically uses. The means by which the procedures for the division of the text and for the multiplication of its words and figures come together into a single complete discourse are considered by an analysis of Donne's sermon on Psalm 32:1–2.

The effort has been made to read Donne's sermons with a carefully prepared awareness of how he is reading Scripture and elaborating on its meaning. Since preaching is a form in which reading and creative literary expression meet, such a study as this perhaps has the particular usefulness of suggesting how authors of the past might have expected to be read. It may be fallacious to assume that writing is but reading in reverse and so is likely to proceed according to something of the same patterns. But in any case, the medium is the same, viz., language; and a writer's assumptions concerning how language is significant can well have bearing upon how he uses it.

PART I

The Arts of Discourse

CHAPTER I *Grammar*

SECTION A / GRAMMAR AND GRAMMATICAL
COMMENTARIES

> ℈ *Not being learned in the art of poetry, you would
> not think of taking up Terence without an
> instructor. Asper, Conutus, Donatus, and
> countless others must be consulted in order for
> anyone to be able to appreciate a poet whose
> verses seem to have gained approval among the
> theater crowd. And yet you, without any guide
> whatsoever, rush into those books, the
> Scriptures, which, whatever else they may be, are
> professed by nearly the whole human race to be
> sacred and full of holy subjects; but you dare to
> interpret these works without any teacher.*

> A U G U S T I N E,
> De utilitate credendi
> 391 A.D.

In the fourth century the *poetica disciplina* mentioned here[1]
would be the art of grammar—the close study of certain greatly
admired texts that had come down from a former, and by then
much-venerated, age. Grammatical commentators such as those
Augustine cites helped the student to read the words of the
text by offering observations on the usage of language and
brought him to a fuller appreciation of the author's vast knowl-
edge by explaining allusions. How much more valuable and
indeed indispensable in the new Christian age would be an art
helpful to the believer in reading and appreciating Scripture. It
was Augustine above all who adapted the classical arts of dis-
course to serve the purposes of a redeemed culture. The inter-
pretive precepts that he formulated, the philosophy of language
he proposed, and the exegetical techniques that he practiced in
his many sermons derive especially from the literary, or gram-

matical, learning of his time and his profession. Augustine's essentially grammatical procedures for expounding Scripture were to prove enormously important in the later church and were to provide in the seventeenth century influential precedent for another of her great preachers, John Donne. Much of Donne's most imaginative development of biblical language in his sermons relies on Augustine's way with words.

The elements of grammar as one of the trivium, its assumptions concerning language, and its function as a discipline are fundamental to the scope and procedure of the grammatical exposition of a text. The epistemological status of the study of words and of the art of persuasion was problematical, since it was dubious what in these pursuits might qualify as first principles and how conclusions might be scientifically drawn from them. The mathematical disciplines of the quadrivium, perhaps geometry in particular, best served to define what an art should be, that it should reason about a subject, proceeding from as few basic precepts as possible to a full, orderly elaboration of their consequences. Only in such a way could any subject be truly *known*.

For this reason Plato will not grant to Gorgias that rhetoric is an art (τέχνη), since "it has no need to know the truth about how things really are, but merely to discover contrivances of persuasion" (*Gorgias*, 459C). It is a routine (ἐμπειρία) acquired empirically rather than theoretically, a knack (τριβή) one picks up by going over and over the same material (*Gorgias*, 463B).

Grammar presumably has these same shortcomings; for although it may not depend on influencing people's preferences as rhetoric does, still grammar's givens are also social phenomena. The particular word that designates a certain object and the patterns by which inflectional endings vary must be learned by experience and practice; such details of language seem not to be consistently determined by any self-evident truths. Plato may have been trying to grasp such principles in the *Cratylus*, but in the end he apparently abandons these attempts. The study of words does not seem to lead to knowledge of intelligible reality (*Cratylus*, 439B).

Accordingly, grammar was pulled simultaneously in two directions. Plato was correct in regarding the tabulation and formulation of observed phenomena of language use as empirical and descriptive. Dionysius Thrax defines grammar in Plato's own terms as "the knowledge by experience [ἐμπειρία] of the language of poets and prosewriters as generally current."[2] And yet the attraction to practice the grammatical art as a true τέχνη was irresistible. Its precepts and structures were assumed to be determined by the ways things actually are and its investigations were taken to furnish true knowledge about real objects. Grammar had both its empirical and its theoretical or ontological aspects, and although seemingly in opposition both continued to have a place in the art's pursuits.

For Hellenistic scholars and their Latin successors, "knowledge by experience" meant the scholarly preservation, analysis, and veneration of the ancient authors' practices of language. Much of what the grammarian presented in a treatise on his art relied on the empirical investigation of the words in the precious texts received from the past. Thus Donatus's *Ars grammatica*, after some discussion of the alphabet and syllabic quantity, sets out the parts of speech, their categories, and the inflectional patterns that were formulated from the accumulation, comparison, and arrangement of instances of use in the works of the venerable old writers.

He then lists the meanings of certain technical terms useful in the analysis of texts. The names for figurative expressions come under the headings *"De schematibus"* and *"De tropis."* Citations, taken especially from Vergil, illustrate the various turns of phrase. A trope is "a term transferred [*translata*] from its proper signification to some nonproper analogical uses [*ad non propriam similitudinem*] by reason of ornamentation or the need for euphemism," as in Vergil, "Mount Atlas, whose pine-covered *head*, constantly wreathed with dark clouds" (*Aeneid* 4. 248–49).[3]

The divergences from regular usage (*"vitia"*) are also carefully identified under *"De barbarismo"* and *"De soloecismo."* Among the vitia there is *amphibolia* ("ambiguity"), which, says Donatus, "occurs for these reasons: on account of confusion in the construing of an object or on account of a deponent verb, when it is not clear if the noun is object or agent. Also on account of homonyms, as someone would say '*aciem*,' and not clarify whether he means 'keen glance' or 'battle line' or 'knife.'"[4] Servius, in his commentary on Donatus's treatise, adds the further remark that "those words are synonyms which are various expressions in language, but have one meaning. Those words are homonyms which are just the contrary [i.e., are one expression in language but have various meanings]."[5] This understanding of ambiguity and tropes is the point of departure for Augustine's conception of translated ambiguous signs in the *De doctrina Christiana*.

However, as the grammarian's formulation of the usage in the literary canon proceeded, the discipline articulated prescriptive patterns of its own on the basis of usual occurrence and internal consistency and, in doing so, moved away from a strictly descriptive investigation of its subject. Consequently an exceptional use in an authoritative text posed the problem of whether the grammarian should simply take note of this use or whether instead he should regard it as a violation of a rational pattern inherent in language. The anomalists favored the first alternative; the analogists, the second. The controversy was already of long standing by the time Varro discussed it in his *De lingua Latina*. Though the grammarian may profess to allow scrupulously for exceptional word forms, establishing general patterns was too basic a part of his endeavor for him always to resist the temptation to extend and connect analogy further than evidence allowed. "And certainly so it is," says Servius, "that grammar is said to be an art [*ars*] because it encompasses everything within strict precepts [*artis praeceptis*]."[6] *Ars, ratio,* and *regulae* are terms Servius uses to refer to the principles that rationally order the phenomena of language in a coherent system. The distinction seems not to have been clearly drawn between general rules that *take into account* many particular instances and a rational structure that *accounts for* the shapes language takes and that stands behind all comprehensible discourse.

There were other opportunities that allowed grammar to shift its ground from a strictly experiential basis. Aristotle had proceeded in his investigation of logical reasoning by considering how people make statements about what things are. By analyzing in what terms such statements are meaningfully made, he arrived at certain all-inclusive categories under which all subjects of discourse fall. Defining a thing places it within such a class and then successively differentiates it from others in that class. Thus, man is in the animal class but uniquely differentiated by his rationality. A word's meaning consists of such a definition.

In some sense, then, a word is an instrument by which something's essential nature is made known. Marius Victorinus, in a commentary on Cicero, observes that "a term goes with a thing;

in fact, never is a thing without a name. . . . The thing in question has about it a particular form of its own and a species with respect to knowledge. Therefore if the species of the thing is known, there must be a name whereby it is known."[7] A word may by convention stand for one sort or another of the things the mind perceives, as the word *man* evokes the notion *rational animal*. Or, on the other hand, a word may by its own formal character provide information about the very nature of what it designates, as *ollo*, the Hungarian word for "scissors," has the configuration of a pair of scissors or as the words *flow* or *river* contain liquid sounds. Only on the basis of the latter assumption can the investigation of words qualify as a true art. If the study of the shapes and relationships of words is to be an art in the Platonic sense and so afford true knowledge about reality, then there must be a correlation between the nature of the signifier and the nature of the signified. Grammatical research is also an investigation of the content and form of substantial being. Language and the real world, standing over and against each other in reflecting networks of interrelationships, are mutually informative.

Servius offers this derivation of *noun*: "'noun' [*nomen*] is so called because it renders things known [*notas*] to us."[8] By investigating the lines of association among words, we can come to know something true about what those words designate. Called etymology, this is one of the principal pursuits of the grammatical art. A Greek commentator on Dionysius Thrax explains that etymology "is the explication of words whereby the truth [τὸ ἔτυμον] is made plain," and so it is a study of the truth about things (ἀληθολογία).[9]

The many strands that relate words by derivation also afford rhetoricians the means of elaborating a speech. Cicero, in commending grammar's resources to the orator, shows his familiarity with its assumptions: "Many arguments are gathered from *notatio*. This is what is used when an argument is developed out of the meaning of a word. The Greeks call this ἐτυμολογία. . . . But to avoid using a new word that is not suitable enough, we call this study *notatio*, because words are the means whereby things are known [*notae*]."[10] The rhetorician might well avail himself of the possibilities that word study offers for multiplying lines of argument. However, he is indifferent to the epistemological assumptions that allow for such elaborations and to the limits that such assumptions might impose on the possibilities for copiousness. Strictly on the basis of the assumed necessary correlation between word and thing, one might expect the word to be uniquely determined by the thing's nature, but in fact any number of etymologies seem to be acceptable for the same word. *Woman* may be derived from *wife-man* or from *woe-man*, depending, apparently, on the context. There seem to be several lines of correlation possible between a word and what it signifies, according to the various respects in which the object is taken. A woman is a mate to her husband (wif-man) and also the cause of original sin (wo-man). One or the other but not both etymologies can reveal woman's essential nature. What is gained in convenience for the rhetorician is lost in scientific rigor.

Another grammatical investigation that furthers our knowledge of things is the study of distinctions among words, an exercise that helps to match each term to the particular thing it designates. To distinguish a word's proper sense by contrasting it with what it does not signify need involve differentiating it only from as many things as are sufficient to avoid confusion. The fact that this procedure became a common grammatical practice can perhaps be attributed to Prodicus, who gained some notoriety in the ancient world for his habit of making such distinctions.

The grammarians compiled lists in which the meanings for words of similar appearance were differentiated in such a way.[11] These *differentiae verborum* frequently provided some substantiation for the distinctions drawn by way of etymology or of precedent in the ancient authors: "Between *'nullum'* and *'neminem'* there is this difference [*hoc interest*], that *'nullus'* can be referred to anything, *'nemo'* just to a man; and that because *'nemo'* is from *'nec homo.'*" "Between *'coarguere'* and *'arguere'* there is this difference [*hoc interest*], that *'coarguere'* means to surround or to confine, *'arguere,'* to reveal or to disclose; as Vergil says (*Aen*. 4. 13), 'Fear revealed [*arguit*] their base minds.' "[12] Such collections of *differentiae* were to be adapted to the special purpose of differentiating transferred significations in the exegesis of Scripture and so were to serve as an important basis for rhetorical invention in medieval preaching.

Not only in its lexical studies—etymology and differentia— does the art of grammar yield knowledge concerning the world but also in its classification and arrangement of the forms words take in sentences. The various categories of the parts of speech and the inflectional paradigms they manifest correspond with the actual classes of things sorted according to their various natures. The prescriptive patterns generalized from usage thus find their justification in reality. In this fashion, Donatus distinguishes nouns into "two kinds according to their character [*qualitas*], for they are either proper or common."[13] Common nouns are broken down further into corporeal and incorporeal, grammatical classes that match categories of substance. Servius elaborates on these distinctions, commenting that

grammarians define a noun as corporeal or incorporeal this way, that whatever is seen and touched is corporeal, for example, stone; while what is not seen or touched is incorporeal, for example, dutifulness. He [Donatus] further distinguishes the noun by another feature, that is, whether it is proper or common. Now proper is of what is unique, as Hector; common, of what is among many, as man. We should know that proper names are frequently found which come from common nouns, as Felix, and this makes sense. We should know this by thinking about it, since, if what is unique is a proper noun, it is declined only in the singular. It is not possible for a particular thing [*res unius*] to fall into plurality of form. . . . However, a common noun, since it is one thing among many, is declined in the plural, but also in the singular, for the one is contained in the many.[14]

The classes and grammatical behavior of words parallel the way things are in the world, and so, by exercising reason concerning reality, we should be able to reach a conclusion concerning the ways in which language is actually used.

So far was the grammarian from considering there to be discrepancies among the assumptions that underlay the various aspects of his art that he regarded the empirical and the ontological pursuits of grammar as substantiating each other. The analysis of the language in the ancient texts revealed a word's natural meaning, or, vice versa, the meaning of a word that could be ascertained by etymological reasoning was just the signification to be found in the old authors. In *Saturnalia*, Macrobius attributes to Servius the opinion that the ancient writers, by expressing themselves so exactly and with such a profound knowledge of a term's actual meaning, preserved in their usage "the true sense and nature of a word."[15]

All these various resources of the art of grammar were at the disposal of the scholar of late antiquity when he annotated the old authors. The means by which Donatus and Servius helped the student interpret and appreciate Terence and Vergil indicate the procedures of careful reading that Augustine thought Scripture also warranted.

A grammatical commentary is meant to provide assistance in the process of reading as the reader, coming upon each word one at a time, moves successively through a work. Thus the text is treated as a series of discrete units of language whose form, signification, and appropriateness are to be explained. However far afield the commentator may seem to depart from the matter at hand, the information he introduces is intended to be relevant to the elucidation of a word.

With the formula *"sensus hic est,"* Donatus paraphrases and construes difficult passages or supplies ellipsed words with *"deest."* Certain expressions are identified by technical terms from the arts of discourse, such as "syllepsis" or "conjectural argument reasoned from the contrary."[16] Uncommon words are defined, and several etymologies for a single word may be offered. "We say 'sepulcher' by way of negation," explains Donatus, "because it is a thing without anything pretty about it [*sine pulchra re*]. . . . 'Sepulcher' is so called from the verb 'to bury' [*sepeliendo*]."[17]

Differentiae sharpen our sense of a word's exactness by contrasting what the poet chose to write with what he did not. Servius commenting on Vergil observes, "Between *'penus'* [provisions] and *'cellarium'* [food] there is this difference [*hoc interest*], that *'cellarium'* is groceries to last just a few days, and so grain that has been requisitioned is said to go into the pantry [*in cellam*] [cf. Cicero, *Div. in Caecil.* 10. 30], but *'penus'* is to last for a long time."[18] *Hoc interest* is the formula the grammarians commonly use in drawing such distinctions.

Sometimes the scholiast brings to the reader's attention the appropriateness in a given context of a particular connotation of a word. Other possible nuances are identified, and illustrative passages, sometimes under the headings of good sense and bad sense, are cited for them. Servius remarks that *fetus* ("full") is a word that can by itself be taken either favorably to mean fruitful or unfavorably to mean frought, just as *venenum* ("drug") can mean either medicine or poison (*"bonum venenum et malum venenum"*).[19] This is another procedure from the grammarian's resources that served Augustine in his exposition of Scripture.

The commentator found opportunities to show the vastness of his author's learning by explaining obscure allusions to all sorts of arcane matters. The old poets, especially Vergil, were thought to have known everything and to have most artfully incorporated this erudition into their writing. When the brash and ill-mannered Evangelus of Macrobius's *Saturnalia* challenges Vergil's vaunted reputation, the other guests shudder at this blasphemy, but then all graciously agree to contribute to exonerating the poet's good name. One will show Vergil's rhetorical brilliance, another his familiarity with the pontifical and augural law, still another his knowledge of astronomy and philosophy. As Symmachus rather extravagantly promises, "But we, who are not supposed to be dull-witted, we will not suffer the inmost reaches of this sacred poem to remain concealed, but by searching out access to its secret meanings, we will reveal its shrines, thrown open for the veneration of the learned."[20]

Servius on Vergil, more than Donatus on Terence, has the occasion to draw upon various sorts of specialized learning in his comments on a word. Like Macrobius's guests, he attributes to Vergil vast learning and a predilection for the obscure. Aeneas, it seems, was keeping to certain fine points of the augural law regarding headgear when he went off to explore the Carthaginian coast (*Aen.* 1. 305). And so you see, adds Servius, that "in Vergil's case, by having in the course of his story one thing mean also something else [*aliud significare aliud ponere*], such details as these are enough to indicate his knowledge of all branches of learning."[21] Much of classical philosophy and science were transmitted to the Middle Ages in commentaries like Servius's that were essentially grammatical in their procedure but bristling with ancillary erudition.

Such were the procedures by which a grammatical commentator helped the student read the old authors and the means by which Augustine believed the Bible also deserved to be read. Scripture too was a venerated text from the past; its author was more than learned, He was omniscient; biblical language also was sometimes obscure and spoke beyond itself. If the study of ordinary words could lead to true knowledge about naturally intelligible reality, then the study of the words of Scripture by similar means could further our understanding of divinely revealed reality and the mystery of redemption. It is the preacher who helps the faithful in reading the sacred text.

The founders of the new Christian culture need have had none of the misgivings Plato had had about literary studies. God had revealed Himself in words for men to read, to take delight in, and to proclaim to others. Augustine had the advantage of centuries of work by grammarians and rhetoricians, and he regarded these pursuits as yielding knowledge about the world and God's presence in it.

Augustine did not complete his projected exposition of all the liberal arts. However, his scattered remarks about grammar[1] display the same mingling of theoretical and empirical elements of the art that the school tradition had passed on. On the one hand, one of the grammarian's services to culture is the preservation and tabulation of the usage of ancient authors. In explaining how the musician treats syllable length differently, the Master in the dialogue *De musica* reminds his student:

And yet you know, I'm sure, that that whole science which the Greeks call *"grammatica,"* the Romans *"litteratura,"* is said to keep the past under its custody. . . . The grammarian, that keeper of the past, would find fault [with a syllable length], alleging no other reason why it ought to be shortened than that they who lived before us and whose books—commented on by grammarians—have come down to us, have established the usage as short, not long. . . . The grammarian prescribes emendation . . . according to the precedent of the venerable ancients [*secundum majorum auctoritatem*], as they are called whose writings he preserves.[2]

On the other hand, Augustine holds extremely Platonic notions concerning how subject matter must be ordered into a rationally coherent body of knowledge so that it can be regarded as an art and be properly taught. Certain formalities arise out of the procedures of the art itself. To pursue the study of literature by the grammatical method, the grammarian "teaches and takes a stand in the exposition of literary texts according to a certain valid plan [*ratio*]."[3] *Ratio*, as Augustine defines it elsewhere, is "the faculty of the mind able to distinguish and associate among those things which we come to know."[4] The grammarian in the exercise of his art should, then, analyze differences and similarities in the material and relate it into a logically arranged whole for clear, systematic presentation. That study cannot be regarded as a true discipline (*disciplina*) "in which there are not definitions, divisions and logical procedures, where not everything is taken into account, where there is any confusion of the parts and they are not properly related to the whole, where anything essential is left out and anything alien is brought in."[5]

In the *De ordine*—an early treatise in which the author, a recent convert from Manichaeism, is struggling to understand what seems to be out of keeping or merely random in God's providential order—Augustine deals most fully with grammar as a discipline. Here he gives an account of the hypothetical genesis of the arts of discourse, not to be taken as his version of the historical development of language, but as an explanation of how reason meets the needs of people to communicate: "For that which is rational in us, that which makes use of reason and does things or follows through in a reasonable way . . . that faculty recognizes that words, certain designating [*significantes*] sounds, should be assigned to things, so that, whereas people could not sense directly each other's thoughts and feelings, still they might resort to perceivable expression to communicate with each other through some sort of medium."[6] To provide the means whereby men can convey to others their own experience, reason contrives a system of signifiers representing things, and that is what language is. The principle of rationality itself serves the function of Plato's "namegiver" (ὀνοματουργός) (*Crat.* 389A) but with this difference: the particular way by which a given thing can be signified does not seem to be a matter of any necessary reason but only of arbitrary convention. "A single configuration of a letter (X)," says Augustine, "means one thing among the Greeks, another among the Romans, not because of its nature, but because of agreement and consent about what it signifies."[7]

Augustine is unlike Plato also in that he finds in the disposition of language some of the same intelligibility so apparent in mathematical subjects. Because grammar is a discipline that studies by methodical analysis material constructed by the operations of reason, the art instructs us in more than just the practical matter of communication. Its exercise acquaints us with the forms of logical and coherent order and so enables us to recognize the disposition of all things according to immanent rational principles. Those disciplines most effective in bringing us to a greater awareness of such principles are dialectic and mathematical studies. In fact, the purpose of the seemingly aimless and unproductive progress of the *De ordine* may be to insist that "no one ought to strive for an understanding [of God and the soul] without some knowledge of that twin subject, how to argue well and how to use the resources of numbers."[8] The principle of order so informs the arts of the quadrivium that "if anyone would wish to see the very source and center of reality he will find it in these studies or thereby will be led to it unfailingly."[9] Yet insofar as grammar also conduces to a fuller realization of intelligent order in things, Augustine attributes to it a "nature and power almost divine."[10]

Besides its value in assisting the mind's apprehension of the intelligibility of things, the practice of the art is delightful. Creative expression executed according to precepts formulated by the disciplines is pleasing to the artist in his fulfillment of ordered forms and to the spectator or listener in his perception of design. As the liberal arts themselves dispose their subject rationally, so what is done according to their principles manifests a proportional coherence that men enjoy. "As I see it," says Augustine, "there are two ways in which the power and force of reason can be brought to the apprehension of the senses, in men's works which are seen, and in words which are heard."[11] In both artifacts and discourse, it is not the sensation that pleases but the recognition of the absolute and immutable sense of order that informs the work.

Intrinsic to language, however, is a rationality that does not consist in just the disposition of the subject. A term designates a particular thing for necessary reasons, and the way that words relate together represents something true about the world. Augustine cannot keep to his own theory of the conventional origin of speech because he, like the other grammarians, is intent on finding by rational procedures the tokens of reason's immanence in language.

It is a common idea among the grammarians that, as Marius Victorinus said, "Never is a thing without a name," and vice versa. If there must be for clear understanding a single term to match each particular sort of thing, then the Hebrew parallelisms of the Old Testament pose certain difficulties for the

the word *tree* if we had never come upon one before? Yet what is the nature of our previous encounter with incorporeal things? How are intelligibles present in our minds when we express or understand something about them in discourse? The answer lies in Augustine's concept of the faculty of memory that not only retains objects from without but also keeps ideas conveyed through man's inmost contact with the divine: "But as for all the things which we come to know, it is not that we give attention to someone beside us speaking out loud, but to someone presiding within the mind itself, although we may be advised by the means of words to pay attention. And he to whom attention is given, who is said to dwell in the inner man, he teaches us, and he is Christ, the immutable power and everlasting wisdom of God."[20] If words are the traces of an inward relation to a god who speaks, then the study of words can help us realize more fully the meanings of that discourse within us.

The memory, however, is more than a mere storehouse. It gives shape to what it holds. By keeping the contents of past experience sorted, related, and arranged intelligibly, the memory makes it possible for the mind to make sense out of what it apprehends and to make itself understood. There man "finds the measure and proportion of all the forms in terms of which he thinks, having them present to his mind."[21] Thus, the memory not only retains the sensual and emotional experiences of the past, as well as the incorporeal ideas divinely present to it, but it also seems to shape its contents to render them intelligible and available for discourse. It does so in accord with certain principles of rational order somehow found within itself.

In the *De ordine*, Augustine thought the various phenomena that the liberal arts take as their subjects to be ordered by these same principles of rationality that he finds inherent in the soul. In the case of language, the informing of sound with intelligibility involved man's attribution of certain arbitrary, conventional associations between things and signs. Man's creation of language was not, however, a piece of legislation but the outcome of the presence of the Inward Teacher, who is also the Creator and Sustainer of all of reality. Augustine, perhaps, has better reason than had the grammarians to suppose that language and the world correlate with each other. Because of God's existence, discourse is intelligible in just the same way that the world is intelligible. Augustine might well assume, as he does in discussing *mortuus*, that God would shape the character of language, particularly the language of Scripture, according to the nature of things.

The memory has a peculiar importance in teaching, then, for Augustine, since it is only because of this faculty that anything can be discovered by discoursing. Words can either recall in us our experience of past encounters with things corporeal and incorporeal or urge us to listen to the Inward Teacher. Donne also gives great importance to memory in our understanding of God, and this he owes to Augustine's ideas.

"Certainly there is a sense, then," says Augustine speaking especially of remembering the emotions, "in which the memory is the stomach of the soul [venter animi]. . . . Perhaps it is like chewing over [ruminando] cud from the stomach, when feelings are brought forth from the memory for recollection."[22] This metaphor is apt to describe the grammarian's function of reminding the reader of the full and proper significance of words in his commentary on a text or the preacher's task of expounding Scripture.

SECTION C / AUGUSTINE'S EXEGESIS
AND PREACHING

Augustine's De doctrina Christiana is a treatise on the arts of grammar and rhetoric that instructs the Christian reader and orator in considering the text of the Bible and presenting the import of his interpretation persuasively. As an exposition of these disciplines, it proceeds in an orderly way according to "definitions, divisions, and logical procedures." Distinguishing the two skills necessary to discourse on Scripture, Books I–III deal with invention (de inveniendo) and Book IV with presentation (de proferendo).[1]

Invention for the Christian speaker is not what it was for the classical rhetorician. It does not consist in the search for many various arguments to be turned to account in the courtroom but, instead, in the explication, or exegesis, of the sacred text. It is for Augustine an especially exalted exercise of the grammarian's art.[2] Yet Scripture cannot be approached as just another venerable text from the past, for its authority lies, not in the precedent of its usage, but in the belief that God has revealed Himself through His Book.

In the *De ordine*, Augustine explains the preliminary importance of authority for the student's progress in the disciplines: "Because there is not anyone who becomes knowledgeable who has not come out of a state of ignorance, and yet because no ignorant person knows how he ought to conduct himself towards his masters nor by leading what sort of life will he become better enabled to learn, it is the case that only authority [*auctoritas*] can open the way to all who want to learn about the good, its greatness and mystery."[3] This receptive disposition to authority is crucial in expounding the Bible, for it is only in holding by an act of faith to the teaching received from the church that the reader can apprehend the significance of the words. The tenets of Christianity provide the precedents by which sense is conveyed. There should be full accord between the interpreter, the author, and the text's truthful meaning. "When we share with the author whom we read what he is saying," Augustine says in *De utilitate credendi*, "and it is conducive to leading a good life, then is the truth of the text most fully realized, and no place is left open to error from elsewhere. But I am quite sure that in texts about difficult subjects this sort of success in reading is rare; and it seems to me that in such instances it is not possible to know distinctly, but only to believe."[4] Scripture is often of such obscurity that it calls for faith in its meaning to open the way to understanding.

To be attentive to the true meaning of the Bible's words, one must believe that "whatever is in Scripture is exalted and holy. All truth is there, and doctrine perfectly suited to renew and restore souls; it is so appropriately cast that there is no one who cannot draw from it whatever he needs to satisfy himself if he approaches to do so with devotion and a proper sense of awe [*devote ac pie*], as true religion requires."[5] The reader must first agree that the sacred text constitutes a sufficient and completely consistent set of meaning and admits nothing unworthy. To break into it he must consult "the rule of faith [*regulam fidei*], which is to be found in the more open places of Scripture and in the authority of the Church."[6] The belief must also be held that there is no doctrine in obscure passages not to be found clearly stated elsewhere.[7] The reader has another, though less trustworthy, recourse: "Where some meaning is being elicited whose difficulty cannot be resolved by clear places in Scripture, it has to be explained by resort to reason [*ratione*]."[8]

The grammarians formulated the elements of their art by the tabulation, comparison, and arrangement of language use into classes and patterns of analogy. The intelligibility of discourse depends on the consistency and uniformity of the grammatical forms that words take. In a similar way, there is an "analogy of faith" by which Scripture must be read for it to be intelligible. Christian doctrine provides the consistency, not of form but of meaning, that makes possible an understanding of the Bible. It is only proper, then, that the study of Scripture has "certain precepts or rules, and, as it were, letters of the alphabet" by which it is to be read.[9]

Because there must first be this belief to read by, the first book of *De doctrina Christiana* develops the fundamental doctrine of the love for God and for others. The reader has grasped the true meaning of the Bible if he has accepted any or all possible readings that foster love and has excluded any reading that does not do so.[10]

The treatise's next books, in which Augustine proposes in detail how to discover this meaning in the text, are ordered by distinctions, categories, and terms that come directly from the art of grammar. Here the resources that served the grammatical commentator are adapted for the preacher. The second book deals with "proper" and "transferred" expressions whose significance is *unknown* and the third book with "proper" and "transferred" expressions whose significance is *ambiguous*.[11] Because, however, we are to consider here the means by which the procedures of grammar are adapted to serve as procedures of interpretation, elaboration, and multiplication of the meaning of Scripture, we shall first take up the simpler types of interpretive, grammatical problems, then the more complex. So, we shall deal first with unknown and ambiguous *proper* expressions and then with unknown and ambiguous *transferred* expressions.

I. Proper signification: Augustine first specifies that the words of Scripture are conventional, deliberate, lingual, and written signs.[12] Within this particular type, the proper signification occurs when words "are attributed to the things for which [*propter quas*] they were instituted. For example, we say '*bovem*' when we have in mind a head of cattle, because all men who speak the Latin language as we do call it by that name."[13] He then proposes certain procedures for interpreting words that designate things properly.

A. Unknown proper signs: To understand words whose significances are unfamiliar, Augustine commends a knowledge of the Bible's original languages[14] and the consultation of various translators' renderings of a particular passage, "for often a look at many other versions clarifies obscurities."[15] However, in so doing the exegete is not just concerned with determining the exact sense of a word's use but with enlarging on its meaning for the reader. In a sermon on Psalm 87, Augustine allows a reading of a phrase in the Septuagint for which, as he himself admits, there is no basis in the Hebrew; yet the version "is not by any mistake, but by the opportunity which the words offer."[16] Here the rhetorician's concern for copious invention is already apparent.

B. Ambiguous proper signs: As there can be no confusion, presumably, in the instance of a proper word that designates just what is meant, the ambiguity here lies in construing the sentence.[17] Augustine suggests that the reader consider the context (just as the rhetoricians had advised the court orator to take up what precedes and follows the disputed point in a legal document)[18] and then judge the alternative syntaxes by the "regula fidei." Then, if there are still several meanings possible, the use of any or all of them is "in the power of the reader."[19] Even proper signs, then, may offer the preacher the occasion for multiplying the meanings of the sacred text.

II. Transferred signification: There are important consequences to the fact that Augustine treats tropes in the *De doctrina Christiana*, not as a rhetorical way of speaking, but in terms of the grammatical doctrine of signifier and signified.

It is a case of transferred signs when the things which we signify by the proper words themselves are made use of to signify something else. For example, we say 'bovem,' and by these two syllables we understand an ox, because that is what is conventionally called by that name; but taken again, we understand the ox to signify the evangelist, for that is what Scripture means by it according to the apostle's interpretation, when it says, "Thou shalt not muzzle the mouth of the ox that treadeth out the corn" [Deut. 25:4; 1 Cor. 9:9].[20]

Language thus acquires a second register. Words are signs of things, but the things signified are also signs of other things; if words correlate with the natures of the things they signify, the signifying things will correlate with the natures of what they signify. If language can be said to reflect the network of reality, a second mirror has been added in which reality is reflected also in itself. The grammatical procedures that can be used to analyze the relationships of the one register can also be used in the other. The Jews mistook things that were, in fact, signs of other things as merely things; their idolatry can thus be said to be a grammatical error.[21]

When places of transferred sense are taken up according to grammatical procedures, it is not so much the force of the whole figure taken together that is considered for the direction of interpretation but rather erudition concerning the discrete words and things that make up the expression. In the same way that grammarians deal with words in their commentaries, so the exegete deals with words and things in the tropes of Scripture. As one who proceeds through the text in the same way a reader does, the commentator may look for indications of the correct understanding of a figurative passage by examining the context: on one level, the place of a word among other words in the sentence (there may be significance in their very order); on another level, the place of the signifying thing among other things and events of the narrated episode. Also, in the particularly characteristic manner of the grammarian, the exegete considers on one level, the word *ox*; on another level, the signifying thing, the animal ox by itself. And he looks for indications of how to interpret those signs by integrating them with the disciplines of learning to which they belong. The word itself is placed in the patterns of language formulated by the art of grammar. The signifying thing is placed in the natural world as understood by natural history.

Thus, suppose we were without the help of 1 Cor. 9:9 and we wanted to understand the Deuteronomical injunction "Thou shalt not muzzle the mouth of the ox that treadeth out the corn." Looking first to the context of the words, we might find it significant that the phrase that tells what the ox is doing comes last. Or, considering the context of the signifying thing in the circumstances of the episode, we might find it important that here the ox is preparing the corn for baking into bread. Taking the word by itself, we might find meaning in the fact that *ox* has, as the grammarian informs us, an exceptional plural form. Or taking the signifying thing by itself, we might think it of consequence that oxen, as the naturalist tells us, are the only animals that graze while walking backward (Pliny, *Historia naturalis*, 8. 70. 178). Whether or not all the possible sources of meaning will necessarily prove significant in every instance is a matter of indifference. The procedures are a means of invention for the preacher. As long as the meaning ascertained has its place in the whole network of Christian doctrine, then the interpretation is valid.

A. Unknown transferred signs: "If transferred signs," says Augustine, "should cause the reader difficulty because of his ignorance, he ought to look at some information about language as well as at some about things."[22]

1. Language: A knowledge of the biblical languages is again helpful in understanding those unfamiliar words carried over from the original Hebrew and Greek as proper names. This particular etymological study, *onomastica sacra*, was pursued by Philo and adopted by Origen and Jerome, following New Testament precedent.[23] Thus, the word *Siloa*, which properly designates by name a pool in Jerusalem, also carries in Hebrew the meaning "delivered" (*Missus*, John 9:7). "It has the sense of something else by way of analogical use [*ad similtudinem*]," says Augustine, "and I have no doubt it implies some religious mystery," such as baptism.[24] Here then, the grammarian's knowledge concerning the word has helped to determine the meaning.

2. Things: "Ignorance of natural history," says Augustine, "makes for difficulty in expounding obscure figures, for then we do not know the natures of animals or rocks or plants or those other things which often are introduced in Scripture to serve in some similitude."[25] Once having acquired such knowledge, the reader is able to consider the possible associative meanings indicated by the things that relate to the object in the natural world.

For example, how is the exegete to go about reading the evangelist's phrase "wise like serpents" (Matt. 10:16)? The word *serpent* signifies properly an ophidian, a kind of reptile. Natural science provides the information that a snake will expose its body to protect its head and will shed its skin in narrow places and so be renewed. These facts give the interpreter some direction in his search for the meaning. Now the martyr, too, exposes his body to persecution in order to keep his head, Christ, intact;

when he passes through the straights of death, he, too, is renewed. The information that helps the interpreter arrive at a plausible signification contributes also to a full and edifying development on the figure. By drawing several lines of correlation between the nature of the sign (the snake) and the nature of the signified (the martyr), this allegorical elaboration of what the signifying thing means is analogous to the grammatical procedure of etymology, in which the several aspects of the thing named are correlated. Since nothing is said obscurely that is not stated plainly elsewhere in Scripture, straightforward passages can be cited to confirm the doctrinal meaning (Eph. 4:22–25; Matt. 7:13).[26]

For this reason, it is possible for Augustine to commend to Christian uses all classical learning that can be relevant to things in nature and the arts, which are signified by the words of Scripture: numerology, music, history, dialectic.[27] The faithful may spoil the Egyptians of their treasures.[28] However, the task of mastering all the content of the ancient disciplines could be dispensed with if exegetical manuals were compiled. "If someone able to do so would be willing to undertake the job for the benefit of his fellow Christians," remarks Augustine, "I think it possible for a person to put down in writing descriptions, arranged in entries by class, of unfamiliar geographical places, animals, herbs, trees, rocks, and metals, any sort of thing which comes up in Scripture."[29] It is a suggestion not lost on the medieval encyclopedists.[30]

B. Ambiguous transferred signs: Ambiguity offers opportunities for alternative meanings, several of which may conform to the *regula fidei*; elaboration on any of three congruent levels— words, things, or doctrine—can be matched by elaboration on the other levels. Instances of ambiguous transferred signification, then, afford the preacher a great many possibilities for multiplying and developing the meanings of a text, possibilities he must be willing to admit. "But because things are similar to other things in many ways," says Augustine, "we must not be too strict, and think that because in one place a thing signifies in a transferred sense [*ad similitudinem*] a certain thing, it must always signify just that same thing."[31]

Meanings for the same sign may be different in various ways, even to the point of being contrary to one another, and still be conformable to the rule of faith, as "when the same thing is taken in a transferred sense [*per similitudinem*] in one place to represent something good [*in bono*], in another, something bad [*in malo*]."³² This is very like Servius's procedure with the various connotations of words. The common illustration here is the significations of *lion*. In the Book of Revelation, the lion is Christ ("The lion of the tribe of Juda has prevailed," Rev. 5:5); in the First Epistle of Peter, he is the Devil ("Your adversary the devil, as a roaring lion, goeth about seeking whom it may devour," 1 Pet. 5:8). Things have various characteristics, any one of which may make them appropriate to bring out by analogy a feature of something else; the possibilities are practically limitless and certainly include contraries. "It also happens," explains Augustine, "that in transferred senses things very different are called by the same name. What are so widely dissimilar from each other as Christ and the Devil? Yet Christ is called a lion, and so is the Devil. . . . And one is a lion in strength [*propter fortitudinem*], the other in fierceness [*propter feritatem*]."³³ Things that figuratively signify several other things in Scripture can be thought of as homonyms, or even as letters of the alphabet capable of forming various words: "A figurative expression may have various meanings, just as a letter's value is understood according to where it is placed. If you would hear the first letter in the name of God [*Dei*] and would decide it ought always to be put there and only there, you will scratch out the first letter of the devil's name [*Diaboli*]."³⁴ The exegete's differentiation of the homonymous meanings of signifying things is analogous to the grammatical procedure of distinguishing the various connotations of one word or the various meanings of similar words in *differentiae*.

As a homonymous figure may represent many meanings, so a meaning may have many synonymous representations.

In parables and figurative expressions, it is possible for one thing to be called by many names. And so it is not inconsistent if I say to you that the wayside, the stony places, the thorny places (Matt. 13:18ff.) are all Christians who have failed, and, too, they are tares. Is not Christ both a lion and a lamb? In the jungle or the flock, a lamb is a lamb, and a lion a lion, just that; but Christ is both. They are what they are by their particular nature [*per proprietatem*], he is both by transferred meaning [*per similitudinem*].³⁵

The exegete's reading of a text is diversified and extended, then, as reason (*ratio*) distinguishes significations, draws associations, and traces the complication of meaning through various levels while measuring the validity of its interpretation by the rule of faith, much as reason formulates the art of grammar by disposing language into patterns of analogy and difference. The preacher in his task of invention, his search for matter on which to speak, need only avail himself by grammatical procedures of abundant meanings and images in that world of the sacred text that God has created. Augustine sees a parallel with a verse from Genesis:

> In the plenitude of Creation we meet with multitudes of things, abundances and proliferations; but in the words of Scripture where there is increase and multiplication in such a way that one thing is expressed in many ways, and one expression is understood in many ways, we find multiplicity only with things which signify concretely and with things interpreted spiritually. . . . And therefore we believe you, Lord, to have said about both representation and interpretation, 'Increase and multiply' (Gen. 1:22). By this blessing you allowed us the means and ability to express in many ways that which we have in our understanding as one and to understand in many ways that which we read obscurely put in one particular way.[36]

Discourse depends on the memory's recollection of what things are designated by what words. Likewise, Scripture must be so familiar to the exegete that all the texts that convey the same doctrine or make use of the same representation in a figurative expression are at his command to extend and confirm his understanding of a passage. In reading the Bible, says Augustine, "memory is of great value, for if it fails, it is no use trying to apply rules."[37]

In this sense, too, Augustine speaks of the act of remembrance as "rumination," when connections and correspondences are drawn, differences discerned, and our understanding enhanced as the expressions, representations, and doctrines of Scripture are tumbled (*revolvendo*) together in the memory. In a passage in the *Confessiones* derived from an old reading of Ps. 28:9—"The voice of the Lord, He who exalts the stags, will reveal the forest"[38]—Augustine addresses his Lord: "Not in vain have you had written so many dark secrets in Scripture, nor are all the forests without their stags refreshing themselves and recovering among the trees, roaming and grazing, at their ease, chewing the cud [*ruminantes*]."[39]

The recitation and exposition of a text should accomplish the fuller realization of meanings in Scripture, which have been turned over in one's mind and meditated upon. Augustine explains at the beginning of a sermon on Psalm 46 what he expects the effect of his preaching to be.

The Lord our God has poured out for us with multiplicity and variety [*multipliciter varieque*] through the means of Scripture the faith in which and by which we live, varying the mysteries of the words [*sacramenta verborum*] but conveying one faith. One and the same thing is said in many ways, so that by the manner of expression there is variety to overcome disdain [*propter fastidium*], but unity is maintained by conformity to doctrine [*propter concordiam*]. And so on this Psalm which we have heard sung and to which we sang a response, things will be said which you know already. But perhaps, with God's help, we will have given you some delight as you, when reminded of those things which you know from elsewhere, ruminate on them. Now chewing the cud is a God-given sign identifying clean animals, whereby the meaning is intended that every man ought to take to his heart what he hears, so that he be not negligent in thinking about it afterwards and so when he hears, he be like one chewing things over. When he recalls what he has heard to his memory and considers it with sweet meditation [*cogitatione dulcissima*], let him be as one ruminating. The same things are said in another way and thereby they cause us to consider pleasantly [*dulciter*] things we already know and to listen willingly to the same again, and that because the manner of speaking is varied and the familiar thing is renewed [*renovatur*] by the manner of expression.[40]

Presumably the congregation has been catechized. The preacher does not teach new things but causes the faithful to realize more fully for themselves what they already know. To do this he opens and elaborates obscure scriptural figures, mingles the familiar with the strange, and causes his listeners to marvel at the pervading network of meaning within the diversely worked cover of words. Each person can rediscover in his own memory the truth of previously accepted doctrine by following a procedure of reading that freshly engages his own experience of things and his own psychological life and that meets with and exercises the principles divinely present within him.

The delight of meditative reading consists in this meshing of recognition and discovery. "Those things we learn," says Augustine, "which are stated openly and evidently in other places of Scripture, when these same things are extracted from hidden places, in a certain way they are renewed for us in our understanding; and renewed, they become delightful."[41] The preacher can further the efficacy of God's Word by delighting his congregation with a renewed sense of having realized the truth, but his discourse is beautiful also because his listeners' faculties of apprehension discern in it certain proportional relationships that order the work. The correlations among the reflecting networks of language, things, and doctrinal significance are pleasing in the way they put in ratio things alike yet different. There is delight, too, in following procedures for ascertaining meaning, which are derived from the ordered methods of the arts and are analogous to each other at different levels. The art of the sermon must be but a projection of the eloquence of Scripture. As a successor to the grammatical commentator, the preacher is in a sense only verbalizing the process of reading. In this life we cannot encounter the Word except through intermediaries: "through letters, through sounds, through books, a reader, an expositor."[42]

Scripture is not merely a table of laws and propositions that we are told to take or leave, but its reading calls on us to do something that the preacher can only guide us to: we must be humble enough and receptive enough to let our faculties participate in this interplay with divine truth within the intricate network of signification. It is above all, then, disdain (*fastidium*) and lassitude (*languor*) that hinder reading.[43] The figurative language of Scripture was meant to overcome indifference by offering incentive to those persistent in their search for meaning and by enhancing the beauty of expression. Cicero commended the effectiveness of "transferred and unusual wording" to the orator,[44] and Augustine was at pains to demonstrate to cultured pagans that the Bible, too, had its elegancies.[45] Most important, the difficulty and eloquence of figures engage the reader in an activity, an activity in which mystery, art, and his own mind all come into play, play that is delightful and redemptive. Augustine speaks of a verse from the Song of Songs (4:2), "Your teeth are like a flock of shorn ewes, that have come up from the washing, all of which bear twins and not one among them is bereaved." He says, "I do not know why, but I contemplate righteous men more pleasantly when I see them as teeth of the Church, cutting men off from error and assimilating them into its body as if what had been hard, was now softened up, bitten off and chewed. And I consider with great enjoyment the sheep, clipped of the burdens of the world as if of their fleece and ascending out of the washing, i.e., baptism; I see them all give birth to twin lambs, the two commandments of love, and none sterile of the holy fruit."[46]

It seems likely that most of the sermons by Augustine and others of the Fathers were prepared only by a brief period of meditation and were delivered extemporaneously.[47] The spontaneous presentation allowed the preacher to be responsive to the activity and promptings of thought deep in his memory (not just to what had been committed to it for the occasion) as he proceeded with his reading and responsive also to the reactions of the congregation as it participated in that reading. Augustine conceives of the Ciceronian "grand style"[48] as an impassioned delivery caught up by the force of the text's truth. "Powerful owing to the soul's feeling. . . . It is carried along by its own forcefulness, and if it possesses beauty of expression, it is because of the power of the things talked about, not because of care in embellishment."[49] Since the preacher strives above all to bring his hearers to act (*flectere*),[50] he must be ready to evoke and intensify their response.

Art need not interfere with this spontaneity. The system of invention presented in Books II and III of *De doctrina Christiana* furnishes the exegete with a network along which he can elaborate extemporaneously the Scripture's resources of meaning. This is not the virtuosic improvisation of the Second Sophistic but a set procedure that, rather than providing a technique for the skillful manipulation of themes and embellishments, extends the eloquence of Scripture to homiletic discourse.

The transmitted versions of Augustine's sermons seem to have been put in writing by professional stenographers present in the congregation.[51] Whether their author himself ever edited the transcriptions is a disputed point.[52] If any did receive his subsequent attention they would likely be among the *Enarrationes in Psalmos*, for Augustine dictated commentary on those Psalms for which there were no homilies so that the series might circulate complete.[53]

Augustine's *enarratio* on Psalm 103 explicates a text "almost wholly woven [*contexitur*] out of the figures and mysteries of things."[54] The four sermons were preached at Carthage probably not more than five years before 415 A.D.[55] Compared with the *Sermones*, these addresses to an urban congregation are more artful in style and exposition.[56]

The third of these four sermons explicates verses 11–24 of the Psalm. It consists of a beginning, a middle, and an end. In the opening section (3. 1; 3. 2. 1–12) Augustine remarks that he will dispense with the usual proem since it is evident from his hearers' attentiveness that the Spirit has well prepared them "for understanding the prophetic mysteries with all eagerness."[57] As he did in the two previous sermons, he notes the prevalence of figurative language in the text: "It has pleased God to conceal his wisdom by means of transference in such things, not to withdraw it from the assiduous, but to close it off from the indifferent and to open it to those who knock. . . . In all these things which are said as if about material, visible creatures, let us seek something spiritual hidden there which we might enjoy having found."[58] Also, he reviews the preceding verses of the Psalm in order to locate the point at which the text is to be taken up.

At the sermon's conclusion the Psalm's praise of the Creator leads into a prayer of thanksgiving (3. 25–26). The last sermon on Psalm 103 ends by imploring each of the hearers to "let working things through in your mind bring up your nourishment, ruminate on what you have taken in so that it does not pass into the bowels of your forgetfulness."[59]

The central portion of the sermon is articulated through certain allegorical spans, a series of expansions and contractions of the meaning read by Augustine in a section of the text. Often in the *Enarrationes* the matter bears on the Church's stand against the world.[60] The third sermon on Psalm 103 falls into four such thematic spans: (1) Christ is for all people (3. 2–7); (2) generous works are important (3. 8–14); (3) Christ is a refuge (3. 15–18); (4) Christ's Passion was necessary, but His absence was not long (3. 19–24).

The third span (Christ is a refuge) takes in verses 16–18 of the Psalm. Augustine's procedure in the exposition of each of these verses can be analyzed into three steps: (1) collecting from the sermon's preceding passages the relevant significations of things, (2) investigating the natures of things in the world as a means of finding out the doctrinal meaning they signify, (3) reading the whole clause taken together again.

"The woods of the plain will be satisfied, and the cedars of Lebanon which he planted."[61] It has already been explained that plants growing in the earth should bear fruits of generosity (3.

9–10) and that the wine, bread, and oil of Christ are graciously given to satisfy men (3. 13–14). Now trees on the plain stand low; they represent the humble masses. They are mentioned first because they are the first to be cared for. It is lowliness, a quality shared by both flatland trees and the many lowly people of this world, that makes it appropriate that the "woods of the plain," signify other things, the humble masses. Here too, Augustine finds the very order of the words meaningful.

The cedars of Lebanon are mighty trees that tower high; they represent men powerful in temporal affairs. As a transferred ambiguous figure in Scripture, the cedars can be taken either *in bono* to represent prominent men who use their wealth and influence beneficially or *in malo*. The proper name itself displays this same ambivalent meaning in Hebrew: *Lebanon* means "shining," whether "resplendent" in glory or "gaudy" in ostentation. Warning of the judgment to come for the wicked, several texts concord here to illustrate the acceptation of the figure *in malo*: "the Lord breaks the cedars of Lebanon" (Ps. 28:5); "the tree which my Father has not planted will be rooted up" (Matt. 15:13). Augustine has, then, given some development by *onomastica sacra* and by a recollection of other places in Scripture to both possible contrary senses of the figure. But this text, when the meanings are read back together, conveys the promise that both the humble and the powerful who, owing to divine care, are not barren of generosity toward others will be satisfied by Christ's giving.

"There the sparrows will build their nests." We are reminded that birds represent persons who pursue an exalted spiritual life (3. 5) and cedars, the rich and influential of the world (3. 15). Sparrows are small birds that soar high; they are monks, unencumbered by material wealth, who reach the heights of meditation. The complete sense, then, is that those with means and generosity support and protect those in the religious life.

Augustine then proceeds to take up the subject of holy poverty; he cites Christ's words to the rich young man and commends apostolic example. The Christian must renounce even the desire for worldly possessions. Almost imperceptibly he returns to the language of the Psalm text in the course of developing the topic: "Many do as Peter did, give up what they have; they do so who have little to relinquish, they come, and become worthy sparrows. They may seem a paltry sort, because they have not the prominence of worldly renown; they build their nests in the cedars of Lebanon."[62] The exposition of a verse, then, may circulate away from the text to elaborate one theme by examples and return again to the words.

"Their leader is the house of the coot!" Again certain significations for things must be carried forward. Birds represent persons of high spiritual attainment (3. 5); Christ is a rock ("and the rock was Christ," 1 Cor. 10:4) (3. 6); the cedars of Lebanon are a figure for the powerful who sustain those in the religious life (3. 15–16). Natural history tells us that coots are water birds that nest in rocks along the shore. The rock is Christ, who bore the afflictions that dashed against him while on earth; He affords a refuge to all those who suffer want. The religious must not look to their benefactors to lead them in the spiritual life but to Christ; if they should lose their patronage, Christ will shelter them against the world's vicissitudes. But as for those who might be unwilling to share their means with those who have wholly devoted themselves to religion, "Woe to the cedar standing without nests of sparrows in its boughs."[63]

"The highest mountains are a refuge for the stags, the rocks for hedgehogs and rabbits." Previously in the sermon Augustine determined from the text that Christ provides for the needs of all—for rabbits as well as for wild mules (3. 4); that rocks, the base and peaks of the mountains, are solid precepts (3. 5); that Christ is a rock (3. 6, 17); that the rocky home of the coot is Christ, shelter for those who have been abandoned (3. 17). Stags inhabit the upper slopes of the mountains; they are the righteous who keep to God's high principles. This signification is confirmed by its use elsewhere in Scripture: "He makes me sure-footed as the deer and establishes me upon high places" (Ps. 17:34).

But as if his mind turns naturally to a concern for those who fail in what God asks of them, Augustine wonders what care is taken for the little creatures—the rabbits (timorous persons) and the hedgehogs (those stuck all over with many small, but hurtful, sins). The rest of the verse, in fact, provides a reply: Christ does establish the well founded moral injunctions by which the virtuous live; yet He offers the assurance of forgiveness to sinners. He is, then—both in the sea and on land—protection for the dependent who are without support (home of the coot), a solid foundation for the righteous (mountains of the stag), and a refuge for sinners (rocky crannies of the rabbit and hedgehog).

Augustine has followed through the network of exegetical invention presented in *De doctrina Christiana* in his exposition of these verses. Knowledge of the etymology of proper names and of natural science has opened figures that signify how Christ's love extends to various conditions of men. Yet reading does not consist in just deciphering a series of separate designations but is a process sustained by a continuity of meaning. The course of the sermon moves in thematic spans through the continuum of the text sometimes to consider the very order of the words and certainly to celebrate with David Him who made those creatures that inhabit the landscape.

The coherence and energy of this rapid movement is quite distinctive in Augustine's exegetical preaching. The interconnection of the text is held in mind with such expressions as "next there follows in the fabric [*contextione*] of the Psalm" and "from here we begin to weave [*ordiamur*]."[64] Care is taken to recapitulate and anticipate the commentary's development. The preacher seems almost carried along, as he extemporizes, by the force of the text's succession, but he may find himself brought up short. Upon taking the sun to signify justice, Augustine has to admit he is confounded; he then succeeds in working through a coherent meaning for the verse by understanding the sun's signification to be Christ.[65] The preacher's leadings in the play of his own mind upon the text must not violate the discipline of a valid reading. The exposition is elaborated by reason's activity in distinguishing and associating things into patterns that are somehow proportional (e.g., trees on the plains, cedars in the mountains) and by the introduction of other scriptural texts to concord words or figures or to adduce examples illustrative of a topic.

Our delight in such a sermon cannot consist merely in the disposition of the parts of the whole into beginning, middle, and end. We find it pleasing to follow the preacher's repeated casting of the thread of coherent meaning in the intricate networks of language and objects without its breaking. We admire his art in extending the compass of each allegorical span until the accumulated sense is fuller than would seem possible, and we wonder that such multiplicity and diversity hold together at all. The pattern is not one of parts of a whole but of the coil and span of intelligible and true meaning. That the web does show pattern bears out our belief in the doctrine developed by the text. Also, our recognition of truth by the play of the mind in reading figures of language delights us and confirms our belief in the sense that this very pleasurable comprehension is a manifestation of Christ's dwelling within us.

SECTION D / THE MEDIEVAL DISTINCTIONES
COMPILATIONS AND THEIR USE

The scholars of late antiquity compiled manuals and compendiums that sufficiently conserved the essential skills of discourse to maintain some educational and cultural communities in continuity with the classical past. Isidore of Seville, whose works served for encyclopedic reference in the Middle Ages, was such a compiler. The pervasiveness of grammar in the studies of this period is apparent in Isidore's adoption of grammatical procedures in his investigation of everything.[1] All knowledge can be organized into a catalogue of derivations, such as his *Etymologiae sive origines*, since "knowing etymology furthers an inquiry into anything"[2] or into a set of *differentiae*, such as his *De proprietate sermonum*, since "when a differentiation is made between two like things, we come to know what each one is."[3] Thus, moral or theological understanding can be gained in the course of distinguishing between *amor* and *cupiditas* or between *trinitas* and *unitas*.[4] The range of matter susceptible to grammatical procedures is limited only to what can be designated by words, which includes everything we know. The ontology of language incipient in ancient grammatical doctrine, whereby the system of verbal representation of the natures of things was thought necessary, persisted into the medieval period. It came to have greater consequence then, due to the prominence of the discipline of reading, particularly that of reading Scripture.

The work of Cassiodorus contributed importantly to the realization of Augustine's program for a literary culture founded upon Christian writings, for he saw that texts of Scripture and of many ecclesiastical authors were collected in the library at Vivarium and copied. It is above all upon the sacred page that the practice of the arts finds its fulfillment. Scripture veritably sparkles with the disciplines (*disciplinis irrutilans*): "They are sure and without fault when they shine in the Scriptures; but when the arts are put to use in foolish issues involving men's opinions, then they are shaken by the confused vacillation of strife, so that what in Scriptural studies is always most certainly valid, is, when misused in such ways, frequently rendered dubious."[5] By Cassiodorus's time patristic commentaries provided authoritative examples of the way to use the arts in reading the Bible: "Undoubtedly we ascend to holy Scripture by way of the reliable expositions of the Fathers as if by the ladder of Jacob's dream."[6] Here are the elements for the formation of new traditions for that "interim age" anticipated by Augustine:[7] the arts exalted for a sanctified use and a text already richly endowed with scholia.

In the ninth century Smaragdus of St. Mihiel commented on the *Ars grammatica* of Donatus; he took for precedent of usage, not the classical authors, but the sacred language of Scripture. By "expounding the eight parts of speech with authoritative examples from the Bible," he intended that the art of grammar be presented with the more "spiritual benefit and truthfulness."[8] In respect both to the usage tabulated and the absolute structures thought to stand behind language, the resulting formulation of the patterns of expression was somewhat different from that of the classical grammarians. "We hold that to be acceptable Latin usage because we find it in holy Scripture," says Smaragdus, vindicating what would have been considered a solecism.[9] Forms that do not occur in the Bible were omitted,[10] and new grammatical terminology, such as the imperative of prophecy, was introduced to cover special constructions.

However, grammatical categories are not just descriptive of language use; they conform to the distinctions among natures—corporeal and incorporeal, animate and inanimate[11]—and also, as Smaragdus would have it, to the configuration of the things held by belief. Augustine's "analogy of faith" by which the sacred text is to be read intrudes into the art of grammar itself. Exegetical method is assimilated into the arts when the study of language takes for authoritative usage a text as it has been interpreted by patristic commentators. Thus, scriptural numbers, accepted by exegetes to be doctrinally significant, order language into grammatical categories: "The Latin language is completed and perfected by having eight parts of speech. . . . Because it is above all through a knowledge of Latin that the redeemed come to know the Trinity and by its leading that they hurry on, ascending the royal way to heaven, and travel to our native land of heavenly bliss, it was necessary that the Latin language have a certain perfection about it. Now eight is a number frequently found in Scripture to have a sanctified meaning."[12] Several passages that associate the number eight with surviving destruction (Noah's family of eight survived the flood, 1 Pet. 3:20–21) and finding blessedness (the eight Beatitudes, Matt. 5:3–10) are then adduced. Thus, the association of the number eight in Scripture with the means of gaining salvation corresponds with the ultimate function of language, the publication of the Gospel of redemption. Accordingly, language has eight sorts of words, the parts of speech.

It is where Donatus deals with ambiguity that Smaragdus's grammar of sacred language has affinities with Augustine's grammatical exegesis. The abbot of St. Mihiel defines homonyms as "nouns which convey several species of things under the sound of one term; or . . . those are called homonyms which signify many things by a single name, i.e., one term. Homonyms have one expression and signify many things."[13] In addition to Donatus's example of *acies*, biblical instances are cited in which the word *horn* (*cornu*) is seen to have various connotations or figurative senses.

'Horn' is said of an animal, "if an ox gore with its horn [*cornu*]" (Exod. 21:28); or of an army, "Bachides was in the right wing [*cornu*]" (1 Macc. 9:12); or of glory, "and the face of Moses was horned [*cornuta*] from his interview with the Lord" (Exod. 34:29), "his horn [*cornu*] will be exalted in glory" (Ps. 111:9); or of power, "through you we brandished a horn [*cornu*] at our enemies" (Ps. 43:6); or of royalty, "and the horn [*cornu*] of his anointed will be exalted" (1 Kings 2:10); or of pride, "I have said to the hurtful, do not wish to act unjustly, and to transgressors, do not wish to raise the horn [*cornu*], do not wish to lift your horn [*cornu*] on high" (Ps. 74:5–6), and so blessed Gregory says, "Therein does the judge set apart from the humble those who exalt themselves proudly with the horns [*cornibus*]."[14]

Augustine had explained that in instances of transferred ambiguous signs the same thing could represent various meanings in different places in Scripture, as the figure of a lion does. Smaragdus has listed and sorted out with the help of patristic interpretation the various senses a homonymous word assumes in the sacred text. It would seem inevitable that grammarians, who compiled glossaries and *differentiae* defining and distinguishing the meanings of words, would take up Augustine's suggestion to provide exegetical reference works as aids for the memory for the Christian reader and would catalogue the various significations that the things in Scripture have. Such were the *distinctiones* collections.

A work of the fifth century, *Formulae spiritualis intelligentiae*, sets out the various significations of things in Scripture. Its author, Eucherius, was a bishop of Lyons renowned for the eloquence of his preaching and "celebrated especially for his many literary and grammatical studies."[15] The compilation cites the differentiated meanings that context and interpretation require: "As for the expressions like the above [*millstone*] when they occur in the sacred text, or when especially, as we say, they are taken as understood in clearer places, it is acceptable that they branch out into diverse significations according to person, time, or place, branch out in figures fitting for the places according to the rationale of allegorical interpretation."[16]

Although Eucherius explains the doctrine of threefold scriptural interpretation in the Preface,[17] the various senses are not distinguished as historical, tropological, or anagogical but instead as *in bono* or *in malo* according to the contraries of Servius and Augustine. The instances are catalogued by species of things. *"Aqua"* and *"flumina"* are two entries under the heading "things of this world."

Aqua: people or temptations; in the Psalm, "it was as though the water [*aqua*] had swallowed us down" (Ps. 123:4); again, *in bonam partem* in Jeremiah, "they left me, a fountain of living water [*aquae*]" (Jer. 2:13); and in the prophet, "you who are thirsty, go to water [*aquas*]" (Isa. 55:1), i.e., to doctrine.

Flumina: faithless people; in the Psalm, "by the rivers [*flumina*] of Babylon" (Ps. 136:1); again, *in bonam partem*, "the rivers [*flumina*] of living water will flow from his belly" (John 7:38), i.e., spiritual favors.[18]

The *Formulae* was commended to readers of Scripture by Cassiodorus[19] and evidently was widely used as an exegetical aid during the Middle Ages.[20]

The *distinctiones* collection attributed by J. B. Pitra in 1855 to a second-century writer, Melitos of Sardis, must in fact have first been compiled in Latin, perhaps in the eighth century.[21] The citations for each entry are more numerous than Eucharius's, but the format, more abridged. There are twenty-three significations enumerated for *aqua*, but nothing more is supplied than the equivalent gloss and the scriptural phrase: "(1) *Aquae*, angels: 'the waters [*aquae*] above the heavens praise the name of the Lord' (Ps. 148:4); (2) [*Aquae*,] people: 'the water [*aquae*] which you have seen are people and nations' (Rev. 17:15)."[22]

At the end of the twelfth century there seems to have been a remarkable proliferation of such catalogues in both the monasteries and the schools. With the compilation of the Cistercian Garnier de Rochefort,[23] there circulated a prologue now attributed to Adam the Premonstratensian[24] that seems to have had wide currency.[25] Adam provides some basic instruction in how to read, including "by what and how many ways we can take the things about which a scriptural passage treats." His precepts are clearly in terms of Augustine's grammatical exegesis.

Certainly one and the same thing can sometimes have in Scripture not only a diverse but even an opposed signification [*non solum diversam sed adversam significationem*][26] as in these three examples offered here out of countless possibilities. There is water [*aqua*] whose streams flow from the belly of the believer (John 7:38), and water [*aqua*] against which the Psalmist prays lest its turbulence overwhelm him (Ps. 68:15–16). Again, there is the camel [*camelus*] which goes through the eye of a needle (Matt. 19:24), and the camel [*camelus*] down from which Rebecca in the sight of Isaac dismounted (Gen. 24:64). Also there is the lion [*leo*] which overcomes the tribe of Juda (Rev. 5:5), and there is the lion [*leo*] which roams about seeking whom it may devour (1 Pet. 5:8). Who does not know how far apart the one thing signified in each of these three pairs is from the other although the thing is one and the same that does the signifying. And so when we hear Scripture tell about things, let us examine attentively the characteristics of those qualities naturally inherent in those things; and we then from the evidence will be able to know in what way we ought to take those things, whether in a good or bad signification [*sive in bona sive in mala significatione*] as the narrative thread which binds together [*contexit*] the continuity of the passage requires it.[27]

Here are procedures for working through, with the help of natural science, the meanings of things in Scripture that signify homonymously.

The core of the medieval *distinctiones* compilations is still the listing of the significations of things in various places with the scriptural citation, which is perhaps paraphrased to bring out the figure's appropriateness; but around this there could grow layers of elaboration. Alan of Lille sometimes expands a gloss into an exposition in his *Distinctiones dictionum theologicalium*. He enters under *aqua*, "By that, people are signified, as in the Apocalypse, 'the many waters [*aqua*] . . . (Rev. 17:15?), i.e., a great many people, because a crowd actually makes a roaring noise from the commotion of bodies, and also, every day mankind ebbs and flows because of its mortal flaw."[28] The compilers have various means of enumerating and distinguishing the citations, some more elaborate than by the simple distinction of *in bono* and *in malo*.

The various particular meanings that things assume in Scripture are received from the authority of the commentators. To the medieval reader the Fathers were another Adam, for they had discovered and assigned certain meanings for certain signs and so had created out of scriptural things a conventional language. The *distinctiones* collections, because they codified patristic exegesis, were glossaries of that language and so aided the memory in reading. Referral to the compilations would dispel any ambiguity that homonymns might cause, but the procedure of differentiating meanings was also a way of pursuing knowledge about doctrine. "He who does not know," said Peter the Cantor, "the differences among similar things cannot properly be said to see the Lord, nor can it be said of him who does not know the similarities among different things."[29] Such a practice of the grammarian's discipline serves well Augustine's conception of a Christian cultural tradition.

This was schoolwork with immediate uses in the church's ministry. At the end of the eleventh century, Guibert de Nogent advised preachers to consult such compilations of scholiastic material on Scripture. The competent exposition of transferred meanings depends on a facility in grammatical studies:

No one except those learnedly instructed in literary studies [*litteris sagaciter imbuto*] should presume to understand in his teaching a variety of meanings under the same things and names. For example: rock and foundation, water and sky, grass and wood, sun and moon, and countless others; since they mean many things in the Scriptures, the one who is handling some obscure passage should notice, when he meets one of these words, in how many senses it is usually taken in the Scriptures. For instance, "gold" [*aurum*] means divinity, "gold" means wisdom, "gold" means brightness of life; and when all things have been considered, he may with safety use what he sees to fit better that particular place.[30]

This example could have been taken from the "Melitos of Sardis" collection, where the first three meanings given under *gold* are: "the splendor of divinity; wisdom; the splendor of holiness."[31] The preacher must be well versed in this conventional language of interpretation to adopt it into his own discourse.

At the end of the twelfth century, the masters at Paris seem to have turned much attention to pastoral studies. The Fourth Lateran Council of 1215 gave impetus to these interests, particularly by urging on the clergy certain standards in their preaching and confessional ministry. Many penitential and preaching manuals—digests of the university's achievements in theology, canon law, and exegesis—were composed. Peter the Cantor distinguishes three exercises in the master's study of Scripture—reading (*lectio*), disputation (*disputatio*), and preaching (*praedicatio*)[32]—but there seems to have been little difference between the *lectio* and the sermon.[33] The glosses given in university lectures by Peter the Cantor and Stephen Langton show indications that they were meant to instruct in homiletic practice.[34] The extended expositions of Peter of Poitiers and Prepositinus on the Psalms seem to be a series of sermons developed by the *distinctiones* method of invention.[35] Peter of Cornwall explicitly intends his compilation of multiple meanings collected from patristic commentaries to aid the preacher, "so that now it won't be necessary for someone who composes sermons to toil over finding out [*inventionem*] what should be said, but rather all he need do is to bring together what's worked out here, material already found, set out and explained before your eyes, instead of having to create a sermon all on his own."[36]

Some of the sermons by Alan of Lille on a scriptural text illustrate the result of following such a procedure of invention. The homily has settled down to investigate thoroughly a section of text and does not move rapidly through a whole lesson as the Fathers did. The version of Alan's sermon on Matt. 16:19 in a Munich manuscript[37] is likely only a *reportatio* but is full enough for our purposes here.

"And I will give to you [Peter] the keys of the kingdom of Heaven" (Matt. 16:19). Alan supposes there to be two keys, each with its own function. In keeping with the nature of keys, each key's function involves both locking and opening. One key is the power of binding and loosing (punishment and reward in the afterlife), the other is the office of discerning between leprosy and leprosy (Deut. 17:8), i.e., between sins. The different significances for the two keys are thus each confirmed by scriptural use.

The *distinctiones* procedure (the two keys have different functions) and the consideration of the nature of the signifying thing (keys both lock and open) have multiplied the meanings of the one word *keys* to four. Reason, particularly by its study of canon law, adds an additional factor of three. The power to help determine how the soul will fare in the hereafter is like a key in three respects. Each of the three respects holds in corresponding ways for both uses, binding and loosing. Thus, the priest is said to bind with a key because (1) he indicates by the ritual gesture of excommunication that someone is bound; (2) he imposes acts of self-mortification as satisfaction; (3) he calls on God to condemn. The priest likewise is said to loose with a key because (1) he indicates by ritual gesture that someone is free; (2) he remits satisfaction; (3) he calls on God to forgive.[38] This threefold sense of *bind* follows closely the entry for *bind* in Alan's own *distinctiones* catalogue, but the senses there under *loosen* have been adjusted to match the pattern. The second key represents the judgmental discretion needed to decide how to use this power rightly in various cases.

Alan develops the words *kingdom of heaven* by an elaborate array of its meanings in various places in Scripture. The kingdom of heaven is (1) Christ himself (Luke 17:21); (2) Scripture (Matt. 13:24); (3) the church (John 18:36); (4) eternal life (Matt. 3:2). Each of these four significations is a kingdom, in the sense of a realm or ultimate seat, of a particular divine good for which we yearn. Thus, as Alan sets it out with paromoion, in Christ resides power (*potentia*); in Scripture, understanding (*intelligentia*); in the church, grace (*gratia*); in eternal life, glory (*gloria*).

By the *distinctiones* procedure we have here added a factor of four to our multiplication of the senses of the whole phrase *keys of the kingdom of heaven*. Each key, in each use (binding and loosing), in each respect (ritual gesture, imposition or remittance of satisfaction, petition to God in prayer) can be taken with each sense of *kingdom of heaven*, to give a total of forty-eight possible acceptations of the phrase. But in fact, the powers of the two keys are exercised together, so there are only half that number.

For example, if one takes one of the uses of the one key—the power to loosen the soul's condemnation to eternal punishment

—in the sense of the priest's remitting satisfaction, adds the discretionary function of the other key, and understands the kingdom of heaven as Scripture (the place of understanding), one can say that the way to the second kingdom—Scripture—is kept with the keys of the kingdom of heaven, for because the priest loosens the penitent from punishment, remits the amount of sin, shows there to be a likeness and also a difference among sins, he opens the way to an understanding of the sacred text. The priest helps the faithful to a fuller comprehension of Scripture by delivering them out from under the strict letter of the law.

Alan ends by exhorting the clergy to fulfill the various functions of their office responsibly. The preacher waxes eloquent with wordplay. Wicked churchmen put the keys to scandalous uses by taking illicit advantages with their powers out of a love for worldly gain and by seducing others to everlasting death. They change their keys into clubs, *"claves mutant in clavas,"* and follow, not Peter, but Simon Magis, *"Simonem Magum imitantur in simonia, non Simonem Petrum in sanctimonia."*

The elaborate system of correspondences and varied combinations in the sermon's development may owe something to such rhetorical devices as the preceding. A characteristic feature in the sermon style of both Augustine and Bernard is antithetical parallelism stated with isocolon, parison, and paromoion;[39] a habit of such expression might tend to work itself out in matching patterns of overall structure. However, more fundamental to the sermon's procedures are the *distinctiones*. In drawing different senses out of a single word, in setting out those distinctions in corresponding sets so that they display congruent patterns, in reading out a single verse in multiple combinations of ways, Alan is making apparent "the differences among similar things . . . and the similarities among different things" as Peter the Cantor commends. The procedures derive ultimately from Augustine's discussion of transferred ambiguous signs in the *De doctrina Christiana* but with some differences. Methods for reading adapted from the grammatical commentators, which served the extemporaneous preacher as a means of invention, have here hardened into a system. The sermon as we have it is in very compressed form, but it is clear that it does not move in dynamically sustained allegorical spans but traces out the various parts of a static structure.

Different, too, are the further distinctions, not of signification, but of substance drawn by reason in the subject matters, such as canon law, studied in the universities. The prominence of dialectic among the arts in the scholastic period would result in major innovations in the manner in which the preacher set his text.

It was the grammatical procedures of the Fathers, and particularly of his beloved Augustine, that were to be most congenial to Donne. Augustine's delight in words and his ardent involvement in the experience of reading perhaps made him particularly attractive to the poet. But neither was Donne untouched by scholastic and Renaissance procedures for developing the scriptural text into a sermon discourse.

CHAPTER 2 *Dialectic*

SECTION A / THE SCHOLASTIC
ARS PRAEDICANDI

> ⟩ℂ*There is another way of preaching, that followed
> by the venerable Fathers, which did not consist in
> setting out a theme and schematizing everything
> with distinctions and divisions. And so they
> avoided excessive ingenuity and were not so
> punctilious about dividing the theme and
> subdividing the members; but they, taught by the
> Holy Spirit, passed on to us their divine
> inspirations all together in one piece. And now,
> for good reasons, the present-day academicians
> do not follow the former way of preaching . . .
> but they must divide, subdivide and concord a
> theme from the biblical text so that it is clear how
> the words of the sacred writers confirm and
> substantiate each other. But the sacred writers
> and the Fathers spoke inspired by the same
> Spirit.*
>
> JEAN DE GALLES,
> *Thirteenth Century*

Jean de Galles here[1] recognizes what is certainly the most dis-
tinctive contrast between the preaching of the Fathers and the
Schoolmen—the extemporaneous, continuously moving devel-
opment of the patristic homily, as opposed to the elaborately
articulated, static structure prescribed for the university ser-
mon. Jean, himself an author of an *ars praedicandi* treatise in the
scholastic manner, admits the unfortunate intricacy of his proce-
dures but cites as justification the necessity for churchmen of his
day to preach without the immediate inspiration of the Spirit.
Instead, human reason is left to its own devices, but its opera-

tions must be checked against authority each step of the way and its analysis confirmed, part by part, by accepted precedents.

However, the more formal reason for these characteristic features of the scholastic sermon is the new dialectical procedures of invention that had emerged in the schools. At the centers of learning after about 1050, the ascendancy of Aristotelian dialectic presented in the translations and commentaries of Boethius exercised pervasive influence in philosophical, theological, and homiletical endeavors. The multiplication of meaning out of the scriptural text no longer depended on words themselves as natural signs of things, things that may in turn serve as signs of other things, but on real distinctions drawn directly by reason as the means for distributing the text into a discourse. Instead of considering the interrelationships and possible ambiguities of a single word's nature, the scholastic preacher considered the nature of universally valid statements for development of his text. And somehow his sermon seemed the uniquely necessary and true one for that verse, so successfully did he validate his procedures by reason and authority.

The forms of university preaching certainly influenced the vernacular English sermon in the later Middle Ages,[2] and its prescribed techniques most likely continued to be taught at Oxford and Cambridge into the sixteenth century. Donne certainly knew the details of these procedures, whether from his years at the universities or from his extensive reading of the Schoolmen. He almost always takes deliberate care in the division of his text and occasionally avails himself of intricate elaborations by restatement and subdivision characteristic of the scholastic sermon.

The "modern" type of sermon construction was described by Jean de Galles and others in the *ars praedicandi* treatises of the thirteenth and fourteenth centuries. Certain of their procedures can be recognized as incipient in the homily of Alan of Lille on the keys of the kingdom of heaven. Here the means of invention has become the structure of the discourse with place made for all its associations and differentiations. Corresponding members are extended in matching patterns of development. Distinctions that have their basis in reality are drawn by reason. However, the *ars praedicandi* writer eschews relying on the sameness and difference that lies merely in the homonymy of terms. The unit of language proper to his procedures is not the word, as it had been for Alan in drawing out various significations by *distinctiones*, but the statement. The statement is divided, and then the division is confirmed by concording texts.

In choosing a text that will serve as his theme to be divided, the preacher is expressly told not to consider less than a complete statement. "When a particular sentence of Scripture is not included all the way to its end, but only part is taken up as the text for a sermon," says Thomas Waleys, "it should certainly not be chosen unless it consists of a complete idea [*sententiam aliquam completam*]."[3] And Robert de Basevorn advises likewise, "The second requirement is that the text produce a whole concept [*plenum intellectum*], so that its meaning is not suspended or unintelligible, lacking a verb, as would be the case if one were to take as a text for a sermon on St. Catherine, 'Virgin, daughter of Zion' (Lam. 2:13)."[4] There is nothing that would have prevented Augustine or Alan from elaborating such a text according to procedures of invention that are grammatical. But the scholastic preacher must develop a complete statement, a *plena sententia* or *oratio perfecta* in the technical terminology of the arts of discourse, consisting at least of subject and verb.

The practitioner of the *ars praedicandi* then divides his theme according to rules that seem quite inappropriate to the handling of a statement. Robert de Basevorn speaks of three ways of dividing: (1) into parts of a composite whole (e.g., good works, purity, and genuine tranquility are the foundation, walls, and roof of the knowledge of truth), (2) into parts of a universal whole (e.g., faith, hope, and charity are the three species of theological virtue), (3) into virtual parts of a whole (e.g., reason and will make up the soul).[5] Thomas Waleys follows suit exactly:

I distinguish three ways a preacher may develop his text, viz., by *divisio, distinctio* and *pluralitatis acceptio*. I call that *divisio* when some single composite whole is broken down into its constituent parts. . . . I call that *distinctio* when something is in common generally with what we speak of, and then is sorted out into its particular aspects [*specialia*] . . . (e.g., justice to God and justice to neighbor are the species of justice in general). I call that *pluralitatis acceptio* when I work out multiplicity in a way other than by *divisio* or *distinctio* (e.g., justice consists in avoiding evil and doing good).[6]

Each of the parts resulting from these divisions of a logical whole goes with a section of the partitioned statement. Thus, the statement "Wisdom rests in the heart of the discerning" (Prov. 14:33) might be divided by the three species of theological virtue: *in corde prudentis*, charity of heart; *requiescit*, hope of eternal rest; *sapientia*, faith that, in the knowledge of truth, leads to wisdom. The reiterations of the division make clear the reason for including what was included and for excluding what was excluded. These restatements of parts are therefore called "keys . . . because they disclose the reason why the division was made as it was, and they encompass everything that should be there [*sufficientiam claudunt*]."[7]

Such divisions, which find their justification in the text itself, are said to be done "intrinsically." A sermon that takes its text up intact and divides the body of the discourse by some whole into its parts is said to be done "extrinsically."[8] The latter means is appropriate to popular preaching, but the former is de rigueur in the university.

To subject a statement to the procedures of dividing a substantial whole into its parts seems to be an inappropriate way of developing that statement's meaning. Why should a set of words constituting a syntactical whole and a logical predication be thought to lend itself to such operations? These procedures are less implausible considered in the context of the arts-of-discourse doctrines from which they derive.

Richard of Thetford in his *"Octo modi praedicandi"* specifically mentions Boethius's *De divisione* when he sets out the ways for the preacher to divide his text.[9] In the middle of the twelfth century, John of Salisbury remarked that this little work "has acquired special favor . . . owing to its succinct wording and judicious insight."[10] In it, Boethius identifies six ways of distinguishing parts within wholes. There are three ways according to accidents, which will be dispensed with here. The other three ways are: (1) a genus is divided into its species (e.g., animal into rational and irrational), (2) a constituent whole into its parts (e.g., house into foundation, walls, roof), (3) an equivocal verbal expression into its several meanings (e.g., dog into four-footed, barking animal, constellation of the dog, and dogfish).[11]

The first two types of this set of the three nonaccidental ways correspond with the *distinctio* and *divisio* of Waleys's and de Basevorn's divisions of the universal and the composite wholes. Although these two treatises count other less distinct means of dividing as a third way, Richard of Thetford explicitly disallows

Boethius's third—by sorting out significations of an equivocal expression—as inappropriate to the preacher's purposes. After all," he says, "not every way of dividing should be used in preaching. What does it matter to the layman to know the multiple senses of some word? Therefore, the division of a word into its significations ought not to be used here. But other ways of dividing, by the genus into its species, or the inclusive into what is subsumed under the overall, or the whole into its integral parts, we can use in preaching."[12] Richard may well be condemning here the *distinctiones* procedure of his predecessors. Boethius observes that the division of an equivocal expression or grammatical ambiguity into several significations has a basis only in locale and convention, not in nature.[13] The *ars praedicandi* writers thus tend to insist on divisions in the order of reality that hold universally.

Boethius has the occasion to enumerate these same six ways of dividing, the three "according to the thing itself" (*secundum se*) and the three "according to accidents" (*secundum accidens*),[14] in his commentary on Porphyry's *Isagoge*. Porphyry's *Isagoge*, a brief introduction to the five predicables—genus, species, difference, property, and accident—was intended as an aid to the reading of Aristotle's *Categories* and (in Latin translation) was an elementary logical text used in the schools. The doctrine of the ten categories provides one context to the scholastic preacher's procedures of division.

A reader of the *Categories* is beset immediately by the dilemma of how to take Aristotle's attention to predication. Consider the statement *man is a rational animal*, which predicates the genus (animal) and the differentiation (rational) of the substance (man). Do Aristotle's conclusions about such statements primarily involve their formal validity as determined by the way people seem to talk sensibly about such things? Or if not, how and to what extent are the ramifications of his investigation of statements ontological? How do the several ways that being is manifested in reality determine what can be said to be of or in other things? Does the meaninglessness of some sentences lie in words or in things? Boethius pondered such questions and offered this opinion, "This work, the *Categories*, deals not with things, nor with classes of things, but with words which signify classes of things."[15] In the analysis of terms of predicative statements, Aristotle's *Categories* has its grammatical aspect, but the purpose of this attention to language is to sort out how real things signified by words can be thought to relate to each other. The doctrine of the categories is, then, susceptible to being taken either grammatically or ontologically, and therein lies its ambiguity.

The relevance of Boethius's "division of division" to such matters as these is clear. Rational is said to be in or of animal in a different way than wall is said to be in or of a house. The differences that can distribute a whole into its parts are present in things in various ways, whether accidentally, essentially, or materially. And the same ambiguity that Aristotle lends to his subject can also be found in the medieval understanding of division. Boethius may seem to be distinguishing the ways in which wholes are actually related to their parts; but Abelard understands him to mean that division *is* a certain kind of disjunctive statement, one in which "the character of a certain thing is shown by predicating alternates of it"[16]—e.g., "some animals are rational, some irrational."[17] Division is not an apprehended real relation but a particular kind of statement. Here Abelard comes down on the grammatical or predicative rather than on the ontological side of the doctrine of the categories.

In just the same way, the *ars praedicandi* writers seem to mean by division either the actual partition of a statement from Scripture or else the sermon passage in which the preacher sets out the alternate parts of his division in successive restatements. To say *"In corde prudentis/requiescit/sapientia"* is to divide the scriptural statement; but the statement and restatement in this sentence—theological virtue consists in charity of heart, hope of eternal rest, and faith which in the knowledge of truth leads to wisdom; it is made up of some deeds of goodness, some aspirations for immortality, and some true beliefs about God—*is* the division also. Thus it is not implausible that devices of expression in the restatement are thought of as means of accomplishing the division of the text.

It is in this sense that the scholastic preacher is advised to divide by parts of speech. Robert de Basevorn commends especially division "with nominals, and their two accidents, degree and case."[18] He gives this example for the theme "A wise servant is acceptable to the king" (Prov. 14:35): one part (*"intelligens"*) denotes honored excellence; another part (*"minister"*), meritorious patience; the other part (*"acceptus est regi"*), inexpressible friendship. All are aspects of ecclesiastical virtue—*excellentia honorabilis, patientia praemiabilis, amicitia ineffabilis.*[19] Alan of Lille resorted to such parallelisms phrased with isocolon, parison, and paromoion; and Thomas Waleys seems to think of such devices as merely ornamentation, *"color rhythmicus."*[20] But other *ars praedicandi* writers regard this arraying of words into sets of corresponding termination and grammatical class as actually accomplishing the division of the text. Then division *is* a statement of disjunctive predication as Abelard defined it. And the arraying of corresponding grammatical classes can be a means of phrasing that predication of the alternate parts. However, Aristotle meant to relate not just words but things by predicative statements. And so the terms of these statements, the parts of speech, delimit certain sorts of things. Identical grammatical patterns place things into the same categories.

Although both Aristotle and Boethius consistently denied that language was natural in the sense that the formal nature of words represented what they signified, the way was left open to suppose that classes of words are coextensive with classes of things, that the formal distinctions of grammatical category determined by a word's syntactical function are indicative of the nature of the thing signified. Boethius, drawing out the implications of a passage in Aristotle's *De interpretatione*,[21] comments, "There are three things from which all discourse and reasoning is made up: things [*res*], concepts [*intellectus*], and words [*voces*]. Things are what we perceive by the apprehension of the soul and what we grasp with the intellect. Concepts are the means whereby we come to have in mind things themselves. Words are the means whereby we signify what we have in our intellect. . . . What the particular words and letters are depends on people's locale. But concepts and things are as they are by nature."[22]

The speculative grammarians of the scholastic period drew the further conclusion that the ways things are (*modus essendi*) correspond with the ways things are understood (*modus intelligendi*) and both correspond with the ways things are expressed (*modus significandi*). "The modes of being or properties of things or beings," says Siger of Courtrai, "are prior to the mode of understanding, as cause precedes effect. It is by such properties of things in turn that the parts of speech are distinguished, as

Priscian says, 'Therefore not by any other way can the parts of speech be distinguished from each other except by our taking into consideration for each class the properties of what they signify.'"[23]

The parts of speech match their particular class of things in reality even with respect to their formal, grammatical behavior. The sort of thing that adjectives represent admits of greater or less just as adjectives themselves show degrees of comparison. Thus John of Salisbury observes, "Just as accidents provide raiment and form for substances, so with due proportion, adjectives perform a similar function for nouns."[24]

Then division by parts of speech serves the scholastic preacher as a means of invention. By setting out the disjunctive statement and restatement of alternates in sets of grammatically corresponding phrases, the parts that are to comprise a whole are already members of the same class of things. So, for example, by expressing the constituent ideas of Prov. 14:35 into feminine nouns ending -ia—*excellentia, patientia, amicitia*—Robert de Basevorn would have ordered a set of abstractions drawn from qualities. With this in common, such an array would the more readily suggest how the division might fall into place as parts of a whole—as aspects of ecclesiastical virtue.

Among arts of discourse doctrines there is another source for the *ars praedicandi* methods of division besides the Aristotelian logic of terms. That is the rhetorical procedure of topical invention. "Among those topics," says Cicero, "which entail lines of argument, some are inherent in the very matter which is at issue [*in eo ipso*], others are brought in from without [*extrinsecus*]. The inherent topics are from a whole [*ex toto*], from its parts [*ex partibus*], from the nature of a word, and from things which are in some other way associated with what is being investigated."[25] Arguments "*ex toto*" and "*ex partibus*" turn out to be two ways of pursuing development by definition, whether strictly—by genus and differentiation—or more loosely—by other means of putting together what a thing is.[26] The rhetorician was much less scrupulous about defining than was the logician. Marius Victorinus enumerates fifteen different ways of offering a definition.[27]

Cicero's distinction between *in eo ipso* and *extrinsecus* topics is very like that made by the *ars praedicandi* writers between intrinsic and extrinsic sermon division. However, the scholastic preacher draws his topical development *in eo ipso*, not out of the subject matter at issue, but out of the scriptural statement itself which is to be divided. Boethius's commentary on this passage, apropos of the way kinds of topics are set out, observes that "a division ought to encompass everything all together, and neither include something superfluous nor exclude something necessary."[28] The division in the scholastic sermon was said also to serve the same function as keys.

In the course of his commentary on the *Topics*, Boethius, himself something of an Aristotelian, is embarrassed to find that Cicero's meaning for definition is really rather unscientific.[29] The only true and proper type of definition by strict standards is one that identifies a thing's nature by genus and differentiation; others are only definitions in a manner of speaking.[30] Still, it is granted that all the rhetorician's ways of defining do offer some kind of explanation of what something is. And Boethius disagrees with Cicero on another account in denying that even proper definitions are made *ex toto*; rather, all proceed one way or another through parts. Thus, in proposing his own division of types of topical invention *in eo ipso*, Boethius takes up Cicero's first two sorts, *ex toto* and *ex partibus*, under the one heading of definition, in both its strict and its looser senses.

According to Boethius, there are four ways of developing an argument *in eo ipso* by definition: (1) *definitio*, strictly, by genus and differentiation (e.g., man is a rational, mortal animal); (2) *descriptio*, less strictly, by property (e.g., animal is what is able to move by its own free will); (3) *enumeratio partium*, loosely, by constituent parts (e.g., a house is what is made up of a foundation, walls and a roof); (4) *divisio specierum*, loosely, by constituent species (e.g., animal is substance endowed with sense only or with sense and reason).[31] By each way the speaker would have the occasion to expatiate upon parts of something.

Only the last two, *enumeratio partium* and *divisio specierum*, exhaust a whole in its entirety. They clearly are identical to the first two ways of dividing *secundum se* set out by Boethius in the *De divisione*. In the instance of *enumeratio partium*, even his example—the house made up of foundation, walls and roof—is the same as that for dividing a whole into its constituent members.

In this context the *ars praedicandi* procedures of division emerge as devices of topical invention; but in the scholastic sermon the rhetorician's means of developing arguments by definition, explaining the makeup of the thing at issue, are taken over to partition the meaning of a complete statement from Scripture. This transference of application seems none too appropriate. Such a transference appears to treat something in the order of language, such as a complete statement, as though it were susceptible of procedures proper to something in the order of reality. Boethius himself carefully distinguishes between the signified reality (*significatio*) and the formal character (*figura*) of language. In his commentary on the *Categories*, he identifies some words, such as *noun*, as those that are not names of things but names of names.[32] The *ars praedicandi* writers dealt with a whole in the order of language—called by a name of names, i.e., *statement*—in a way proper to a whole in the order of reality signified by a name of things, i.e., *whatever is at issue*. By trying to combine what is proper to *significatio* and what is proper to *figura*, they made a mistake of the sort that John of Salisbury exemplifies by the absurd phrase, "patronymic horse."[33]

But the doctrines of the medieval arts of discourse were such that this separation of the formal and the significative aspects of language could not be consistently maintained. There persisted the idea that a complete and meaningful statement, if true, correlates with a real, combined whole of a certain nature. The *locus classicus* is in Plato's *Sophist*. There, the combining of subject-expression and verb-expression in a true statement is said to correlate with a "weaving together of forms" ($\tau\grave{\eta}\nu$ $\tau\hat{\omega}\nu$ $\epsilon\grave{\iota}\delta\hat{\omega}\nu$ $\sigma\upsilon\mu\pi\lambda o\kappa\grave{\eta}\nu$) (*Sophist* 260A, 262D) in the order of reality. This correlation between the syntax of language and the interrelationship of things as they actually are would seem to hold most simply in the case of statements of universal validity, such as mathematical propositions. And it is just such statements to which the ancients gave their particular attention.

The authoritative texts for both grammar and dialectic in the medieval arts tradition passed on this ambiguous understanding of the nature of the statement (*oratio*) as a predication of terms but also as signifying the interrelationship of things. Priscian defines *oratio* as "the ordered connection of words in agreement, expressing a complete thought [*sententiam perfectam*]."[34] Here the formal property of the agreement of inflectional endings has a place in the definition, but so too does the idea of the full meaning that is signified by the completed syntax. He goes on, "There are two parts of speech according to the dialecticians, the noun and the verb, for just these alone joined with each other constitute a complete statement [*plenam orationem*]. The other parts of speech are called '*syncategoremata*,' i.e., 'those which signify indirectly' [*consignificantia*]."[35] In his chapters on syntax, Priscian specifically states that an *oratio* lacking a subject or verb is deficient, and his reason is clear from his explanation of why a noun must precede a verb in word order: "for it is proper to something real [*substantia*] to act or be acted upon, and nouns have their place from that. And the property of the verb to express this acting and being acted upon grows out of nouns."[36] Thus, a statement in which a verb is predicated of a noun represents a real interrelationship, i.e., something befalls an essence. So also Peter Helias, commenting on Priscian in the twelfth century, remarks that "not just any joining together of words ought to be called an '*oratio*,' but only such as represent some inherence, i.e., a combination of things."[37]

The ambiguity of Aristotle's *Categories* centers on the dilemma of how to understand what is involved in the combination of noun-expression and verb-expression. Is his analysis primarily in regard to syntax or to the interrelationships of things in reality? He further confuses the matter by calling a definition a statement (λόγος), even if it lacks a verb.[38] After all, he seems to argue, the set of words *rational animal* have about them as much a completeness of meaning as does the statement *Socrates runs*. Boethius translated Aristotle's λόγος in its several uses as "*oratio*,"[39] and in his commentary on the *De interpretatione*, he struggles to sort out the natural and artificial criteria for the unity of a statement.[40] It is not surprising Abelard should remark that in his time there was "great disagreement" (*magna dissensio*) regarding what should be included under the term *oratio*.[41]

The speculative grammarians seem to speak most unambiguously of a real unity in the order of things to which the complete statement corresponds. Martin of Dacia goes so far as to say "syntax [*constructio*] involves other things besides words. For there is a syntax of things and a syntax of concepts, as well as a syntax of words, and that is why it is usual to say that there is a real, a mental and, of course, a verbal syntax, this last subject to logical analysis."[42]

The *ars praedicandi* writers themselves, when they advise the preacher on how to distribute the words of the text into the parts of the division, seem to regard the scriptural statement not as made up of discrete words, in the way the ancient grammatical commentators took it, but rather as a whole predication. And yet the terms of that predication are not analyzed for their formalistic function, but the statement is taken to correlate with a real whole that is divided by partition of the simple sentence that represents it. Thus, Robert de Basevorn warns that some words cannot by themselves serve as members of the division—prepositions, conjunctions, the copulative *est*, and in general any word that does not signify something in its own right but whose meaning involves the statement itself as a whole.[43] Thomas Waleys, too, advises the preacher to discern the meaning of the entire aggregation constituted by the words of the parts and of the whole.[44] In their treatises on the *syncategoremata*, the scholastic logicians gave much attention to just those terms of the statement that perform nonsignificative functions.[45] The *ars praedicandi* writers, however, do not dwell on a precise analysis of the function of terms but use the overall collected meaning as the basis for topical invention.

Given the loose sense of definition—any explanation of what the makeup of a thing is—and given the ambiguity of the term *oratio*—a whole statement but also one that signifies an actual combination in the order of reality—the scholastic preacher's means of division may seem less implausible. In partitioning the scriptural text, he can divide a whole *oratio* into its parts according to the ways the rhetorician might develop by definition his argument about what is at issue, because a complete, meaningful, and true statement signifies some actually existing, coherent entity.

Besides division, the other characteristic feature of the scholastic sermon according to Jean de Galles is the confirmation. Although development of the scriptural text by grammatical means grew out of the very words themselves, the scholastic procedure of invention by division, with its ultimately topical antecedents, involves some measure of extracting the statement's meaning by rational analysis. However, the operations of reason must be scrupulously substantiated by the citation of scriptural authority at each step. As Augustine stated in the *De doctrina Christiana*, the meaning of all the Bible is everywhere consistent within itself, and the truth of one place can be found as the truth of another. The preacher cannot depart from the true sense of the words themselves in the course of his dividing if a biblical text from elsewhere confirms his extraction of a certain idea from a segment of his theme. Thus, the ideas drawn out of the statement by procedures of topical invention and locked into a whole by the keys of division are also securely fastened to the words themselves of Scripture.

In confirming his division, the preacher would adduce, for each member, a text that concords upon a significative word in that section of his theme and that has the same sense, preferably explicitly, as the idea extracted from that section. Thomas Waleys remarks that the citation of confirming authorities was made easier by the compilation of alphabetical concordances of Scripture and of patristic writings.[46] This was primarily the achievement of the new orders of friars in the thirteenth century.[47]

Once the theme has been divided and the division confirmed, meanings can be multiplied in various ways by subdivision and recombination. For example, there is *correspondentia*, a contrivance something like that to which Alan of Lille resorted in shuffling and variously recombining the signification of the words in the phrase *keys of the kingdom of heaven*. For the verse "it is now the time for us to rise from sleep" (Rom. 13:11), the division can be accomplished thus: tasks have been fulfilled on behalf of various conditions of men (*"Hora est jam"*), man's faculties have been redeemed (*"nos surgere"*), evils have been overcome (*"de somno"*). The first member might be confirmed by citing Jth. 13:7 with concordance on *"hora"*: "look on the works of my hands in this hour [*hora*]." Three particular instances for each member could then be presented, Iabc, IIdef, IIIghi. Waleys proposes as the first of each set of three, Ia, a task fulfilled on behalf of some condition of men: the wayfarer is shown the way to God; IId, one of man's faculties redeemed: the intellect is redeemed through the contemplation of heavenly things; IIIg, an evil overcome: wickedness, which dulls the senses, has been conquered. Because the members are connected into an intelligible whole by a completed syntactical structure, corresponding instances of each member can be taken together as a coherent variation of the scriptural statement. Combining a, d, g, we read: Now is the hour for us wayfarers to have our intellects raised out of the stupor of wickedness. "And in this way the whole text is taken up three times,"[48] (i.e., Ia, IId, IIIg; Ib, IIe, IIIh; Ic, IIf, IIIi).

The preacher may also subdivide the confirming text and

proceed from there. For the text of a sermon on the occasion of St. John's day, take Prov. 11:8, "The just man is delivered out of distress." The text is divided by the three forces involved in man's struggle against sin—good, evil, and God's grace: the faithful life of righteousness on the part of John (*"justus"*), the senseless wickedness on the part of his adversary (*"de angustia"*), the infinite goodness on the part of a gracious God (*"liberatus est"*)—*in Joanne sanctitas custodita, in suo adversario malignitas infrunita, in Deo propitio bonitas infinita.* A confirming text, concording on *"justus,"* is then adduced for the first member: the path of the just (*justorum*) like a shining light, leads on (*"justorum semita quasi lux splendens procedit,"* Prov. 4:18). This text is then in turn divided by what Augustine says of Abel's blameless life: he was a virgin, a priestly teacher of doctrine, and a martyr.[49] So too was John, and thus his faithful life of righteousness likewise consists of these parts: chastity, the pure and lovely light (*"lux splendens"*); holy doctrine to show the way to redemption (*"semita"*); and the willingness to go out to suffer obediently (*"procedit"*). This division of the confirming text can in turn be confirmed by another text, and both can be concorded with the *"justus"* of the first member of the theme and with the *"lux"* of the first member of the confirming text.

Thus, to return to the original text, the first section of the theme ("The just man is delivered out of distress") is *"justus."* The extracted idea for this first section is John's faithful life of righteousness. The appropriateness of this idea to the section from which it is drawn is confirmed by another text concording on *"justus."* This text too is divided. The extracted idea from its first section (*"lux splendens"*) is chastity. The appropriateness of this idea to the section from which it is drawn is confirmed by another text concording on *"lux"*: "Light [*lux*] is risen to the just [*justo*]" (Ps. 96:11), i.e., virginity ascends to shine brightly in the life of the righteous.[50] This has traced how only the first members are confirmed, but the pattern is clear. Proceeding this way, a sermon's development by successive division may fittingly be likened to a tree: "As a real tree develops from a root to trunk and the trunk into main branches, and the main branches multiply into other branches, so it is in preaching."[51]

The preacher can then go on to fill out this structure erected upon his theme by any means of amplifying a text or topic that the arts of discourse afford. The less elaborate his divisions and confirmations, the more he would rely on such means. The procedures for dilatation (*dilatatio*) are as numerous as the ways of passing from one idea to another.[52]

The resources of grammar have their usefulness here. For instance, the treatise attributed to William of Auvergne would have the preacher bring out the precise meaning of a word, its force and weight, as *differentiae* do: "'I sat' is the word here, not I stood, I walked, I lay."[53] Thomas Waleys reiterates the commonplace of grammatical doctrine assumed by such differentiations of words: "A difference in the thing has as its consequence a difference in the way of speaking."[54]

Augustine suggested that the reader of Scripture faced with a transferred expression whose meaning was uncertain look to natural science for the attributes of the thing as indications of the direction in which the figure should be taken. The *ars praedicandi* writers commend this as a means of dilatation "by explaining metaphors according to the properties of a thing and by applying them for our edification."[55] There is a thoroughness on the part of scholastic preachers, which Augustine himself may not have expected, in taking *all* the thing's natural properties to be allegorically instructive. Thomas Waleys gives this example for the text Is. 11:1, "'And there shall come forth a rod out of the root of Jesse; and a flower shall rise up out of his root,' to be interpreted of the Blessed Virgin and her Son; now the properties and circumstances in nature of the rod can then be applied to the holy family, and, too, the properties of the root and of the flower, either flowers in general or some particular flower."[56] Richard of Thetford urges the preacher to consult this "Book of the World": "For God made creatures not only for the nourishing but also for the edifying of mankind."[57] It is here that the medieval bestiaries, lapidaries, and herbals, the complete encyclopedias of natural science such as Bartholomaeus Anglicus's *De proprietatibus rerum*, serve the preacher. Full sermon reference works, some arranged as *distinctiones* collections, include much material of this sort.

The scholastic preacher adduced concording verses, preferably connecting *vocaliter et realiter* ("by word and by idea"), to confirm his divisions; but just *realiter* is allowed and that sometimes not with clear places but by interpretation.[58] He might also amplify his sermon by linking texts together with the same word or idea into chains, *catenae*. Each link would ideally include two significant connecting words—the one concording with the preceding, the other with the following text. Because of the interrelation and consistency of all of Scripture, such a progression of texts should provide a coherent development of some topic.

Having set out many intricate procedures for division, confirmation, and dilatation, the *ars praedicandi* writers often warn the preacher against carrying contrivance to the point of *curiositas*.[59] These means of invention may perhaps take ingenuity to put into operation; however, the rules themselves are not whimsical but are quite in keeping with the arts-of-discourse doctrines of the schools. Multiplication of the meaning of the text must have as its basis real, not merely verbal, distinctions. The conclusions of reason must be checked against scriptural authority. The usual views are held regarding the consistency and interrelation of Scripture. There is nothing inherently bizarre in the assumptions about language or in the procedures for developing its meaning to be found in the *ars praedicandi* treatises.

What is new are the predominantly dialectical, i.e., topical, rather than grammatical, methods of invention. The sermon development is pulled slightly away from the very words of Scripture at the point of the division, when the preacher says, "Three things are touched on in this text." The constituent meaning of the statement is gathered and then divided as though susceptible to partition the way a thing might be. Nevertheless, the scholastic preacher goes to great lengths to tie the very words of Scripture into the structure of the discourse itself by concordancing.

SECTION B / A SERMON BY BONAVENTURE

When the many and complex resources of the *ars praedicandi* are turned to account by an accomplished master in the idiom, the sermon gives a remarkable impression of coherence and necessity. The elaborately ordered and intricately related structure seems tied together by the sound determinations of reason and the authoritative words of Scripture. Perhaps none of the scholastics succeeded better than Bonaventure in the practice of this manner of preaching. One of the fullest among his sermons, as they have come down to us,[1] was probably preached to the religious in Germany in 1259 or in the winter of 1270–71.[2]

The text is Ps. 106:8–10: "Let the mercies of the Lord and His wonderful works to the children of men give glory to Him, for [quia] He has satisfied the empty soul [satiavit animam inanem], and has filled the hungry with good things, such as sat in darkness and in the shadow of death, bound in want and in irons." It is an unusually long passage to preach upon, but Bonaventure dispenses with some of the preliminary steps of the prescribed dispositio as he often does in his later sermons.[3]

The verses are first distinguished into (1) an exhortation to thanksgiving and, following "quia," (2) the reasons for gratitude. After the development of each of these reasons, the prophet's words of exhortation are appropriated by the preacher himself, who urges his hearers to give thanks for the prefigurations of the sacrament of the Mass in the Old Testament.[4] At the conclusion all are exhorted to benefit by partaking in the Sacrament. By using a command in the hortatory subjunctive, Bonaventure on this occasion is among those mentioned by Robert de Basevorn who make a point of including in their text affective words to move the congregation to devotion.[5]

Only the text following "quia" is partitioned.[6] The subordinated statement rather than the exhortation is divided for extracting the parts of the meaning. Each member represents an instance of a failing in ourselves remedied by God in His mercy; each taken with the sense of the entire complex sentence is a reason to give thanks for what God through Christ has done for us. The division yields six parts and is extracted altogether five times. The restatements are phrased with parallel alternates that consist of words in the same grammatical classes with the same inflectional ending and thereby extend the members in corresponding ways.

The first two declarations of the division dwell on man's insufficiency. We were (1) in a condition of destitution because (2) we lacked fulfillment of our needs without God's gracious giving of Himself. Thus, the first members in these first two declarations, for the first section of the text, "satiavit animam inanem," are (1) man was empty, (2) man was empty because he did not have within himself the indwelling presence of God.

The next pair of declarations of the division sets out what God has accomplished for us. He (3) overcame for us our failings by (4) providing Himself for our fulfillment. Again, to follow the first member through, God (3) filled the empty soul (4) with His indwelling presence. The fourth restatement includes the previous three: man was empty, and He gave Himself to him as an indwelling presence.

The fifth reiteration of the division concludes from the accumulated meaning of all the other restatements set out together in the fourth that (5) God fulfills our needs, particularly for all six members. He is fulfillment for those who are empty, nourishment for the hungry, light for those sitting in darkness, redemption for those lying in the shadow of death, wealth for those in want, and a softener for hard hearts: *"ipse est repletio inanium, refectio esurientium, lumen in tenebris sedentium, reconciliatio in umbra mortis jacentium, ditatio mendicantium, et ferreorum mollificatio cordium."* The five restatements progress step-by-step toward this conclusion so that each of the six members, arrayed as nouns, can fall into place as a part of a whole. The concluding version is the one carried through the rest of the sermon. Bonaventure adds the accepted formula to indicate that the division has been made: "These are all the matters touched on in the words of the text."[7]

However, the preacher has not yet turned the keys of his division; the necessity and sufficiency of his dealing with the text is not yet clear. For this he resorts, not to parts of a whole in the order of nature, but to parts that constitute all the varied means of expressing a certain idea within one particular field of language, the Old Testament. The six members comprise all the instances of Old Testament signs that represent the eucharistic sacrament. According to Bonaventure the Sacrament serves as an intermediary for God's merciful intervention on man's behalf; grace is made more efficacious in its operation by the mediating power of the Sacrament.[8] Thus, for each section of the divided text after *"quia,"* there is extracted (1) a failing in man, (2) some capacity of God through which that failing has been remedied, (3) an Old Testament prefiguration of the Eucharist, through which God more efficaciously bestows the gift of fulfilling man's insufficiencies.

As species of a genus, the members are shown to exhaust a whole only by the authority of scriptural usage. That the six parts cover all the distinct failings of man is assured by the fact that each goes with a sacramental prefiguration found in the Old

Testament. The conclusions of reason in its interpretation of Scripture and in its own pursuit of the truth must substantiate each other. The realm of language comprised by the Bible itself has a reality of its own that is consistent with the world of things.

Those prefigurations that represent the eucharistic sacrament in the Old Testament are synonymous by interpretation: they are all signs of the same thing. Their appropriateness as signs in each case is explained by some property of the thing that provides an indication of its proper meaning. Oil is something that penetrates, dilates, and pervades; so it appropriately goes with the first section of the text: God is the thing that fills those who are empty. The rest of the six members are similarly associated with a prefiguration.

The first section of the text is "He has satisfied the empty soul" ("*satiavit animam inanem*"); the equivalent first member is the idea that man's emptiness is filled with God's indwelling presence, the more efficaciously so through the sacrament of the Mass, prefigured in the Old Testament most appropriately in this instance by oil. The preacher should proceed now to the confirmation of his division. At this point Bonaventure interposes instead another layer as a further multiplying factor by introducing a *distinctio* on oil, *pinguis*. Both "*animam*" in this first section of the theme and *pinguis* are concorded upon simultaneously three times for the three connotations of the prefiguring sign in the Old Testament. The concording texts are then in turn subdivided and confirmed.

There are three places in the Old Testament where oil prefigures the eucharistic sacrament: Gen. 49:20, Jer. 31:14, and Ps. 62:5–6. Each place signifies particularly one of the species of love with which God's indwelling presence fills the emptiness of man's soul. He imbues us with a love for three different objects: self, neighbor, and God. Because these three objects are just those which we are enjoined to love by the two great commandments (Mark 12:29–31), their sufficiency is assured.

Partaking of the Sacrament helps to sustain the love we feel within ourselves for these three objects. And oil has three properties that make it an appropriate sign for each of the three ways in which the Sacrament provides for love in each of its three species. Oil has the property of making food flavorful; by the willful act of coming to receive the nourishment of the Sacrament, a person is reconciled with himself, the bitterness of his own disappointments is overcome, and he is thus thought to love himself better. Oil also has the property of dilating the skin; by sharing the Sacrament in community, a person relates to others, feels concerned about them, and thus loves his neighbor better. Again, oil has the property of burning; by being present at the Mass and realizing the meaning of Christ's sacrifice, a person feels an ardent sense of gratitude, his soul catches fire with devotion, and he loves God better.

Thus, when Bonaventure adduces the three confirming texts, they all concord on the *"animam"* from the first section of the theme *"satiavit animam inanem,"* but also they will all concord with each other on oil, *pinguis*. They must show the appropriateness of the idea extracted from the first section (God is what fills those who are empty), and they must show the appropriateness of the particular connotation of *pinguis* in each place when seen in context.

The confirming text in which *pinguis* ("oil"), while prefiguring the Sacrament, has the particular connotation of imbuing the empty soul with love of self is Gen. 49:20: "As for Aser, his bread shall be rich with oil [*pinguis*], and he shall yield dainties to kings [*regibus*]." Here oil, as it should, shows the particular property of making food flavorful. The verse relates *per allusionem* with the sermon's theme because the kings (*regibus*) represent right reason in governance of the soul (*"animam"*). The confirming text is subdivided into the four afflictions whose bitterness is removed by the sweet nourishment of the Sacrament: (1) the bread of Aser remedies ill will, *malitia*; (2) the bread sopped in oil remedies ignorance, *ignorantia*; (3) the bread providing dainties remedies carnal appetite, *concupiscentia*; (4) the bread for kings remedies weakness, *impotentia*. The sufficiency of this subdivision is established by adducing another passage that more clearly enumerates these same afflictions: "I am afflicted and humbled exceedingly. . . . My heart is troubled, my strength has left me [i.e., *impotentia*] and the light of my eyes itself is not with me [i.e., *ignorantia*]. My friends and my neighbors have drawn near and stood against me [i.e., *concupiscentia*] and they that were near me stood afar off [i.e., *malitia*]" (Ps. 37:9–12). The subdivision is confirmed (1) by an *onomastica sacra* on Aser, which means blessedness, because man is blessedly delivered from all ill will; (2) by the property oil has to burn, as the Sacrament illuminates ignorance; (3) by a concordance *realiter* with Wisd. of Sol. 16:20, "bread . . . having in it all that is delicious and the sweetness of every taste," which takes away carnal appetite; (4) by a concordance *realiter* and *vocaliter* with Prov. 20:8, "the king [*rex*] that sits on the throne of judgment, scattereth away all evil with his look," as reason strengthened by the Sacrament can rule the soul righteously.

The confirming text in which oil has the particular connotation of imbuing the empty soul with love of neighbor, is Jer. 31:14: "And I will fill the soul [*animam*] of the priests with the fatness of oil [*pinguedine*] and my people shall be filled with my good things, saith the Lord." This text concords *realiter* and *vocaliter* on "*animam*" with the first section of the theme and confirms well the appropriateness of the idea, taken from that first section, that God is what fills those who are empty. Rather than subdividing this confirming text from Jeremiah, Bonaventure develops the aptness of this verse from oil's property of dilating the skin. As oil spreads the skin out in all directions, so the priest and the people are filled with an all-embracing love for those with whom they share the Sacrament; that includes all of those within the church as a timeless and universal institution. The communicant's love of neighbor goes out in all directions to the various classes of the church's people, which, too, extend out in all directions: up, the blessed; down, those in purgatory; to the right, the just; to the left, the unjust; back, those in the past; forward, those in the future. Here there is a division of a whole into its parts, but it is not a text that is divided. Rather, some aspect of the property that relates the prefiguring thing (oil) with its particular connotation (spreading in all directions) has been drawn out in such a way that exhausts all possibilities.

The confirming text in which oil has the particular connotation of imbuing the empty soul with love of God is Ps. 62:5–6: "in thy *name* I will lift up my *hands*. Let my soul [*anima*] be filled as with marrow and *oil* [*pinguedine*], and my mouth shall *praise* thee with joyful lips." This text again concords *realiter* and *vocaliter* on "*anima*" with the first section of the theme and also confirms well the appropriateness of the idea taken from that first section, that God is what fills those who are empty. Oil's property of burning seems to have no place here, but the Psalm verses certainly do express the idea of fervent adoration and worship. The properly worshipful and devout manner of partaking of the Sacrament consists of four actions, into which the confirming text is subdivided: (1) to invoke God's *name* with the proper intention in the first place; (2) to lift one's *hands* in an attitude of prayer; (3) to share in the sacrament of the altar, prefigured here by *oil*; (4) to perform generous deeds of *praise* and thanksgiving. The first two of these members are then confirmed concording *realiter* and *vocaliter* (1) on *name* ("All whatsoever you do in word or in work, do all in the name of the Lord Jesus Christ," Col. 3:17) and (2) on *hand* ("I will therefore that men pray in every place, lifting up pure hands," 1 Tim. 2:8). The remaining two members are not confirmed. Bonaventure then concludes the development of this first of the six members of the sermon's theme by returning to David's exhortation: "'Let the mercies of the Lord give glory to him . . .' because He signified His body in the Sacrament to us, in the first place, under the figure of oil."

Bonaventure's division of the text and his confimation of its first section occupy four of the sermon's seventeen pages as printed in the Quaracchi manual edition. There is almost no dilatation or amplification at all. The sermon consists in elaborating the bare structure itself, following along lines of verbal associations in Scripture, and multiplying out various significations and extracted meanings, which are distinguished and locked in place by necessary reasons. It is as if there were certain ideal sermons laid up in heaven to be preached on each text, so convincingly does the preacher interlock the logical determinations of reason and the sacred words, which seem to have to be just what they are where they are in Scripture.

Augustine proposed a system of invention to which the preacher might have recourse as he moved through the text from word to word. The *moderni* do not move through a scriptural passage but rather through a system of invention that rests on a complete unit of text, the statement. The individual words that represent reality by their formal nature are not analyzed; rather the complete statement, whose formal entirety represents a whole, understood of reality and susceptible of rational analysis into parts, is considered. The procedures of topical invention serve not to open the way to copious amplification but to fasten the logical sufficiency and completeness of this multiplication of the ideas extracted from the text.

The more enthusiastic among the Reformed preachers might reply to Jean de Galles that the Schoolmen with their strictly prescribed rules of division and confirmation never gave the Spirit a chance. Donne, however, would never have said so. The achievement of the scholastics in reasoning about the tenets of faith certainly excited the admiration of one with such an intellectualistic cast of mind himself. The church's learned exponents in all her periods of greatness drew his interest and scrutiny. And to some extent anyway, even the model of the *ars praedicandi* procedures of division deserved, he thought, his imitation.

CHAPTER 3

Rhetoric

SECTION A / *RENAISSANCE TREATISES OF*
ECCLESIASTICAL RHETORIC

> ⟂ *Beholde therefore these common places to the*
> *number of fower and twenty upon a briefe*
> *evangelycall hystory packed and heaped of us*
> *together.*
>
> JOHN LUDHAM,
> 1577

Ludham, whose *Practis of Preaching* is a lively English version of
a Latin treatise by Hyperius, draws attention with this boast[1] to
the success of his procedures for accomplishing that most im-
portant task of the Renaissance preacher, turning up an abun-
dance of appropriate and effective rhetorical commonplaces or
topics from the literal sense of a scriptural passage. At the
beginning of Ludham's work, the familiar distinction is made
between sermons developed *intrinsically*, on the basis of the text
alone, and those developed *extrinsically*, drawing more widely
on related matter. The first is proper when speaking *ad clerum*,
the second when speaking *ad populum*. The first relies particu-
larly on logic; the second, more on rhetoric. The teacher in the
schools takes up his text and "sticketh wholly therein, as one
shut up in a streight prison, pinfolde & enclosure," while "he
that instructeth the people, sercheth and selecteth out of an
argument proposed, some certaine common places."[2] Thus, the
preacher of the new school, scornful of dry classroom exercises,
thought of himself in the role of Christian orator addressing the
people in persuasive and wide-ranging discourse laden with
relevant themes.

Hyperius's distinction between the scholastic and topical ser-
mon is not as neat as he would have it. Bonaventure on Psalm
106 would, of course, fall under the heading of scholastical, but
Hyperius would also include in this category less strictly con-

structed sermons that are developed by means quite different from those prescribed in the *ars praedicandi*. These other procedures, although branded as "dialectical" by a Ciceronian such as himself, have much in common with his own topical practices. None of the humanist methods of invention had about them the same concern with logical necessity and universal validity that the scholastic *divisio* had, but still *dialectical* and *rhetorical* allegiances were distinguished in the topical doctrines of the time.

Thus, Renaissance doctrines of the topics were aligned to a greater or lesser extent around the poles of either dialectic or rhetoric, and the various parties, differentiated accordingly, were given to contentious and extravagant claims. In antiquity the topics were common to both dialectic and rhetoric. The eclecticism resulting from this overlap of the arts and the accumulation of authorities accounts for the confusion and controversy to which Renaissance humanism fell heir. Erasmus looked to the rhetorical tradition derived from Cicero, while Agricola and Ramus, despite the latter's vigorous protestations against Aristotelianism, looked to the dialectical tradition derived from Aristotle. Both traditions gave rise to treatises of ecclesiastical rhetoric that were current in England later in the sixteenth century.

In the opening chapter of his *Rhetoric*, Aristotle complains that rhetoricians devote too much attention to winning favor in the courtroom and not enough to convincing by sound arguments. The orator should persuade by reasoning with enthymemes, syllogisms made up of generally accepted or probable opinions. Dialectic in its narrow sense is properly occupied with such arguments.

The subjects about which the speaker reasons must first be found. In the *Topics*, one of the logical works that together comprise the *Organon*, Aristotle considers the types of predication, the components of logical statements, in order to identify certain formal categories—such as definition, genus, accident, and the like—within which the speaker's subjects or argument would fall. He deals with invention also in the *Rhetoric*, where the topics are less formal, more specific to their subject matter, and appropriate to what an orator might have to say regarding a particular purpose on a particular occasion, whether in the courtroom or in the assembly.

Cicero, at the beginning of his work on the topics, states an intention to explain Aristotle's system for finding arguments. The treatise proceeds as though meant to provide the logical means for working up material in any inquiry. However, it seems to be addressed to a fellow jurist, and the general categories are soon appropriated to forensic subject matter. Cicero defines the topics this way: "'place' [*locus*, τόπος] can be defined as the seat of an argument, and an 'argument,' in turn, is reasoning which brings a person to commit himself to one side or another in a question uncertain by nature."[3] There is scant mention here of the formal composition of such arguments; the configuration of syllogisms is a matter "not necessary to this work."[4] The whole question of logical validity seems relegated to "judgment" rather than to "invention" and has no place in the *Topics*.[5] If Aristotle sought to set out the structure and elements necessary to reason by enthymeme, Cicero seeks to turn up an abundance of relevant information that could shore up a case. The dialectical topics, very general in scope, may prove useful in accumulating material under the various "issues at stake" (*consitutiones* or *status*); but it is these latter, developed particularly for legal pleading, that serve as the rhetorician's principal means of invention.

Boethius in his *De differentiis topicis* tried to compare and contrast the ways in which the two arts put the topics to use. The dialectician looks for the elements with which to reason; he proceeds by steps of question and answer according to logical rules. The rhetorician looks for matter relevant to a certain case with particular circumstances; he pleads to judge or jury in continuous discourse and avails himself of whatever devices prove most effective.[6] Both traditions had currency in the Middle Ages.[7]

The Renaissance humanists found in the topics an alternative to scholastic practices in the arts of discourse—a more readily useful dialectic than the subtle investigations of nominalist logic and a rhetoric more authentically Ciceronian than the medieval adaptations of classical oratory to the particular purposes of chancery, schoolroom, and pulpit. No one more tellingly denounced scholastic preoccupations and procedures than did the eloquent Erasmus. In his *Ratio* (1518) he accuses the Schoolmen of supposing they could pursue the study of theology by attention only to the instrument of logic: "Furthermore, those who rely on dialectic alone think themselves well enough prepared by that to treat of any matter whatsoever"[8] without, in fact, a notion of what they are disputing. Indeed, none of the old logical distinctions have anything to do with the New Testament: "Where, pray tell, in Paul's letters is there anything which concerns Aristotle, however brilliant and learned he may have been, where anything that concerns the profane Averroës? Where is there any mention of 'primary and secondary intention,' of 'figures of the syllogism,' of 'formality,' or 'haecceitas,' terms with which the writings of these others are stuffed full?"[9]

The *ars praedicandi* procedures of division and subdivision seem to come in for their share of ridicule. "This part," says Erasmus, "is divided into three, the first of these, in turn, into four, and each of these, again, have three senses, first, *ibi*, second, *ibi*."[10] Perhaps the repetition of "*ibi*" here is meant to mimic the corresponding phrases with which the scholastic preacher restated his division. Erasmus's most frequent word of reproach to describe the learned and intricate endeavors of the schools is *"frigidus"*—"cold," without warmth of feeling for the good news of Christ. In contrast to the unfeeling sermons of the scholastics, he would commend the example of Jehan Vitrier, whose preparation for delivery from the pulpit was not to work out division and confirmation of a text in accordance with complicated rules, laboriously consulting the concordances, but instead "to take up St. Paul, and to spend the time reading him till he felt his heart grow warm."[11]

Particularly in the early pages of the *Ratio*, where the matter of the relevance of the arts to theology is considered, Erasmus often refers to the *De doctrina Christiana*. He is respectful of Augustine's views in general but seems to regard his procedures as perhaps too susceptible of misuse. Rather, the preaching of Origen among the Fathers especially elicits his admiration. He gives his readers, as an instance, some indication of how powerfully affective Origen's preaching is by quoting from his homily on Gen. 22:2, where Abraham is commanded by God to sacrifice his son Isaac. It is a sermon, he says, "to kindle fervent hearts."

[It is Abraham] in whom an example and an illustration is set before our eyes of the fact that the strength of faith is mightier than all the human emotions. But let the point of the presentation be to realize, by considering the various details, by what and how many means the heart of Abraham, the father, is assailed and assailed again by testing.

God says to him, "Bring your son." What father's feelings would not give way upon hearing the word "son"? But that His assault might be the more forceful, He modifies "son" with "dearest." And still not satisfied with that, He adds, "whom you love." These things might seem sufficient to break the heart of any man. But he adds the boy's name, that most delightful of sounds to fatherly affections, "Isaac." And this recalls to his mind the divine promise, when he was told, "Through Isaac shall thy descendants be traced" (Gen. 21:12), and "In Isaac there will be for you a renewal of promises" (Gen. 17:19). This nation was given to doting on its children like no other nation. This worthy man wished to have offspring, but should Isaac be killed there would be no hope left of that, for by him alone might his issue continue. And yet God does not just order him to be killed, but He commands him to be sacrificed, so that the strength of his obedience might again and again mortify the heart of the old man in order to prepare him. How many and how great are the burdens of this testing![12]

Erasmus refers back to this passage later in the *Ratio*. The preacher can certainly make use of the traditional four senses of Scripture in developing his text, but also he ought to consider the details of each situation in order to bring out what the steps (*gradus*) are, what the differences (*differentiae*) are, and what the reason for the action (*ratio tractandi*) is, for "look at all the ways in which Origen presents God's testing of Abraham, and what the commonplaces are he finds, dealing just on the literal level."[13] *Gradus*, *differentiae*, and *ratio tractandi* seem to be technical terms from Quintilian, where they are among the rhetorician's devices for building up gradually to an emotional climax, varying by comparison, and presenting the motive or meaning of events.[14] The preacher would do well, then, to discern certain themes in the scriptural narrative and to avail himself of rhetorical means for elaborating these generalities.

To this end, Erasmus, albeit with some hesitation, suggests the expedient of compiling a commonplace book of biblical themes to supply abundant material from which the preacher might draw in developing his essential idea. He proposes that it might be useful

either on your own or relying on someone else's work, to have at hand some theological commonplaces under whose headings you could set down in order within some easily comprehended format all that you read about, so that you might the more readily both store away and bring forth what you would want, for example, about faith, fasting, patience, [etc.]. These topics would be arranged by some plan, according to the principle of either opposition or affinity (as I have proposed previously in my *Copia*),[15] and whatever would be worth noting down from anywhere in the Old Testament or the New, whether it seems to agree or not, would be relegated to one or another of these commonplaces.[16]

It is noteworthy that Erasmus mentions the relevance of his *Copia* in this regard. In that work he sets out rhetorical methods and examples for varying the same idea with different words and for turning up abundant matter for the elaboration of some general statement. Clearly, in contrast to Augustine and to the scholastics, Erasmus would have the preacher rely for his invention, not on grammatical or dialectical procedures, but on the topics as they are to be found in forensically oriented rhetorical doctrine. A sermon must move the hearts of its hearers, and for that purpose the resources of ancient rhetoric can be also utilized.

The *Ecclesiastes* (1535), because it is specifically a treatise on preaching as Christian oratory, is even more explicitly Ciceronian in its view of topical invention than is the *Ratio*. Although Erasmus is careful to insist that the lawyer's pleading differs from the churchman's preaching,[17] so compelling is the attraction of his model, Cicero, that he feels it necessary to give some consideration to the jurist's argument from the testimony of torture.[18]

It would, for example, be useful for the preacher to lay out his discourse as does the lawyer his argument for or against the defendant—as the reasoned and persuasive elaboration of a single theme or point to be made, the *status* (Cicero's *Topics*, 25.93). In a sermon this might well be one of the theological commonplaces:

Status is a general heading for an issue or matter in question, under which the speaker arranges everything he has to say and on which the listener focuses his attention. So in legal cases, attention is focused on whether the deed which is alleged has been committed, what kind of deed it is, how it is to be defined, etc. . . . Someone asks, what have these things to do with spreading the Gospel? First, they have this value, that when the argument to be presented is held in mind this way, everything is arranged under a heading, within set limits, and there is no digression from the topic into needless rambling or wandering in foolish ranting or speaking on unrelated or even polemical matters. And this is the chief use of the *status* procedure, that whoever speaks to the people, by way of persuading, exhorting or consoling, sets himself some particular thing that he wishes to accomplish by it.[19]

The preacher should at the outset of the sermon clearly and concisely state in a single sentence the sum and substance of what he has to say. This is the *propositio*, "which right away at the beginning encompasses the gist of the whole argument."[20] While Cicero set out six parts for an oration—*exordium, narratio, partitio, confirmatio, reprehensio, conclusio* (*De inventione* 1. 14. 19) —and Aristotle just two (*propositio, confirmatio*), the sixteenth-century English rhetorician Thomas Wilson adds this *propositio*, as a seventh element, to Cicero's enumeration.[21] However, the rhetoricians do not mean by it the proposal of a logical statement to be strictly proved but rather a general statement of the subject, "as if one should display merchandise first through a lattice-work, or rolled up in carpets, then should unroll the carpets and disclose the merchandise, exposing it completely to sight."[22]

How do these procedures of topical invention involve the biblical text itself? Erasmus insists that the preacher work up his sermon directly from Scripture: "For a preacher to take up the scriptural passage suitably and to the point, it is not sufficient to gather pithy sayings from collections or indices, but he must go to the source itself."[23] And yet his own advice on invention seems remarkably detached from the words of the Bible, and his examples are, for the most part, exhortations to virtue that are not expositions of a text. Still, the subject matter is scriptural in a broad sense, and he offers some advice on how to extract themes out of a biblical passage. Here he seems to follow the procedures Cicero proposes for arguing judicial cases involving a written document. Issues that arise over ambiguity, letter and intent, seemingly contrary laws, validity of reasoning, or defini-tion can all be given consideration.[24] For example, an argument might be developed from a biblical passage by way of definition: "It is generally agreed that Adam's offspring could not have had children except by the marriage of brother and sister. This is a *status definitivus*. There are countless instances of this sort of argument to be found in Scripture."[25]

Only twice in the *Ecclesiastes* does Erasmus show at any length how the preacher might deal with a particular scriptural epi-sode. Supposing a sermon be preached on the paralytic (Matt. 9:1 ff., Luke 5:18 ff.): "First of all if the event is suitably told, that account will convey much pleasure and insight and nothing at all affected. Right away in the exordium an obvious com-monplace concerns the marvelous goodness of our Lord, Jesus

Christ, whose whole life was spent in nothing else than in public acts of generosity towards all men. You might then take up to whom else he had given help."[26] The development moves on to other topics with the remark "there comes in here the matter of."[27]

Although spiritual interpretation is not in itself irresponsible by any means, extracting a sequence of instructive points from the text is preferable to indulging in excessive allegories. "We should take up, for example, how Abraham received so hospitably the three visitors. This story, which is told in Genesis eighteen, serves as a basis for such a subject. If you would adopt it to commend hospitality, many lines of reasoning are open to you."[28]

It is apparent here that scriptural passages subjected to this method of invention, forensic as it is, naturally yield issues oriented to social and moral judgment. Erasmus esteems especially the tropological, or moral, among the four senses of Scripture, because it expresses matters of immediate concern to everyone: "This sense is to be preferred, in my opinion, because acknowledgment of the things it deals with bears an immediate usefulness in promoting men's morals. On this account it moves its hearer greatly, because matters of conduct are recognized by each and every one of us as important and as relevant to ourselves, so that we listen with greater earnestness."[29]

Thus, for Erasmus, the preacher must strive above all "to kindle fervent hearts" with his sermon, to move his hearers to a lively conviction of Christ. He will best succeed in this by focusing on some general idea or commonplace drawn from the overall meaning of a biblical passage and by developing that with all the resources of ancient forensic rhetoric for the copious amplification of a topic. The scholastic *divisio* had its antecedents also in the topical invention of Cicero, but the idea extracted from a part of the divided scriptural text had to be confirmed by reason and authority as the meaning of those very words. Erasmus's procedures of invention involve the text itself much more loosely.

This predominantly Ciceronian ecclesiastical rhetoric is represented in English later in the century by John Ludham's translation and expansion of Andreas Gerardus's (Hyperius) *The Practis of Preaching*. Hyperius himself was a German Protestant humanist of the school of Melanchthon and Sturm. He seems to have taken Erasmus's advice in compiling a compendium of commonplaces suited to the pulpit, his *Theological Topics* (1565), which he commends in his treatise for preachers. Like Erasmus, too, he avails himself of the resources of ancient rhetoric for the purposes of Christian oratory: "To be short, whatsoever is necessarie to the preacher in disposition, elocution and memorye, the rhetoritians have exactlye taught all that in their woorkhouses; wherfore (in my opinion) the preachers may most convenientlye learne those partes out of them."[30] Of Cicero's five parts of the rhetorical art,[31] this omits delivery and invention. Delivery can best be learned by imitating the exemplary preachers of one's own country.[32] The preacher differs from the orator primarily with respect to invention, for he "shall wholly be occupied in handlying and discoursing of these places most chiefly which are conceived under faith, love and hope. Now to faith, belong these places [*loci*]: of the goodness and power of God, of the free mercy of God towarde us [etc.]."[33] Hyperius finds much less of forensic invention relevant to the preacher's task than had Erasmus. The sermon's topics should be drawn out of the scriptural text more according to its own terms.

Still, with Hyperius as with Erasmus, there is the same procedure of reducing a passage down to an issue. "Thou shalt dilligently recount," he advises, "and gather with thy selfe, what the author's meaninge is in the whole, and so far forth as may be, thou shalte in a brief sentence comprise the summe and effect thereof. The sentence shalbe the 'state' [*status*] of the whole Sermon."[34] The statement of this in the sermon is again the "proposition."[35] It is then determined under which type the issue falls, whether it is of doctrine, redargation (i.e., reproof), institution, correction, or consolation, as Paul is thought to have distinguished them in 2 Tim. 3:16.[36] For each type "it is necessarye that [the preacher] have at hande places of invencion congruent and correspondent to this kynd, by the direction whereof he shall excogitate and utter those thinges, that may holsomelye be put foorth to the multytude. . . . Certes this invention of common places is . . . the grounde worke and foundation, whereuppon the whole frame of all Divine Sermons doth consist."[37]

The other pole around which the parties of humanist rhetoricians aligned themselves was that of Aristotelian topical invention, which is more formal than the Ciceronian in its attention to the elements and composition of valid arguments. An early proponent of this school was Rudolph Agricola, whose *De inventione dialectica* (1479) was much admired and very influential in the course of the sixteenth century. Even Erasmus esteemed his fellow countryman—Agricola was Dutch—for his study of Greek and Hebrew[38] and perhaps welcomed his work as a possible alternative to the vagaries of scholastic logic. Furthermore, in the *Ecclesiastes* he remarks that the subject of the topics has been confused by the variety of authors and adds "that man worthy of immortal glory, Rudolph Agricola, has written about these things in our own day with great accuracy."[39]

Erasmus's praise on this account is unwarranted. In fact, Agricola's indiscriminate eclecticism produces an ill assortment of disparate rhetorical doctrines. He makes much of his particular indebtedness to Aristotle[40] but acknowledges also that he has drawn on Cicero, Quintilian, and Boethius.[41] As a result, there is the terminology of formal logic but without the properly demonstrable certainty of an Aristotelian science, since the rhetorician's much wider concern with courtroom effectiveness intrudes. Thus, identifying dialectic in its broadest sense with Cicero's "study of argumentation," Agricola includes in its first division invention, Aristotelian doctrine on the terms of the premises in logical syllogisms for supplying abundant material for making an argument. This muddle of Aristotle and Cicero eventually spawned Ramism.

Formal logic is thus harnessed to the plow of rhetorical invention to turn up copious subject matter. Dialectic has become a system for finding and cataloguing certain very general categories of related things that could be relevant to a given issue. "And so very intelligent men," says Agricola, "have sorted things out from their vast variety under certain common headings, so that when we turn our minds to consider some matter, consulting these headings we find out immediately about its entire nature and its parts and all about what is alike and what diverse from it, and thereby we draw out the argument developed from these things."[42]

The purpose of the argument constructed with the topics is said to be not to convince by logical necessity but to instruct, *"docere."*[43] Of the three objectives enumerated by Cicero for the orator's attention—to teach, to delight, to move—the other two are here subsidiary to the first. Teaching is the common denominator that insinuates dialectic into all the arts of discourse: "In fact all discourse seems to have this as its primary and proper function, viz., to teach something to him who listens."[44]

Agricola thus attributes to dialectic, understood both as a technique for finding and organizing ideas around a given issue and as a process susceptible to presentation in the terms of formal logic, a central place among the trivium. "And so," he says, "dialectic, which leads and guides all the other arts, supposing its widest application is denied, is learned for itself alone; but indeed it is not studied just for itself (if the truth be known), seeing that once it has been studied in that way, still, not just for its own sake, but for the sake of all the arts it is thought necessary to have it."[45] This notion of an all-encompassing dialectical invention will likely lend a certain dull formality of procedure and generality of subject matter to whatever it touches.

Peter Ramus, like Agricola, held that dialectic should inform all discourse. In fact, he makes the most extravagant claims for its applicability by asserting it to have its uses "not only in the schools set apart for learned men, but even in legal proceedings, in government, in preaching, on the stage and finally in all walks of life."[46] Both men accomplish this universalization of the scope of formal logic by appropriating dialectical doctrines for rhetorical purposes and then calling the result dialectic. Ramus is more dauntless even than his predecessor in this respect; at his hands dialectic swallows up almost all the tasks of both rhetoric and grammar without, however, really assimilating them very successfully. Ramist logic consequently takes on several layers, one on top of the other in some confusion.

Cicero distinguishes two parts, invention and judgment,[47] in the "study of argumentation," which both Agricola and Ramus identify with dialectic. As does Agricola, Cicero himself in the *Topics* considers only invention. Judgment seems to consist of assessing the formal validity of syllogisms. Ramus has a place for both invention and judgment in his logic, which is made over to rhetorical purposes. There is a place for invention and judgment in both the theory and the practice of the art.

I. Theory: The theoretical doctrines of dialectic involve the principles of the way a discourse should be composed, the way the lines of reasoning are to be drawn.

A. Invention: This consists of those means, which had long been common to both rhetoric and dialectic, for turning up the subject matter of arguments, the topics. Like Agricola, Ramus formally sets out the topics as very general logical categories, such as subject, effect, relation, etc.

B. Judgment: Ramus meets with some embarrassment here, as one might expect, since the logical doctrine most formal in its nature—the Aristotelian propositional logic and syllogistic as found in the *De interpretatione* and *Prior Analytics*—does not readily lend itself to appropriation by rhetoric. Still, he does expropriate it by subsuming it under rhetorical disposition. The speaker orders his discourse according to a certain plan. Likewise, a syllogism is nothing but "a natural and valid arrangement of a line of *argument* about what is being sought";[48] and a proposition, in turn, "is a disposition in the which one *argumente* is spoken for (of) another,"[49] i.e., in which a predicate (*consequent*) is said of a subject (*antecedent*). The word *"argument"* has here been so twisted to accommodate the expropriation of logical judgment by rhetorical disposition that it seems to have come to mean merely the cognitive force of a verbal expression. Discourse consists of a sequence of arguments rather than words.

II. Practice: Ramus proposes the training and exercise in the art of dialectic to be as broad as is its doctrine; they should certainly exceed the narrow scope of the disputation. "Many uninformed people are mistaken," observes Talon, Ramus's disciple, "in thinking that use of dialectic can or ought to be made just in exercises in scholastic questions. The profitable application of this art is much greater and wider than that."[50] In the Ramist educational program, classroom practice of logic absorbs some of the traditional provinces of grammar and rhetoric.

A. Invention: "The primary and easiest way to learn how to write and speak is by imitation."[51] Accordingly, the student is instructed in how to compose arguments by copying exemplary models of the various genres and techniques of oratory. The *practice* of dialectical invention comes very close, then, to formulary rhetoric as it is represented in English by Richard Rainolde's *The Foundacion of Rhetorike* (1563). This is termed *genesis* by the Ramists.

B. Judgment: Grammar's long-standing responsibility for expounding the poets is denied it. Instead, since the *vitia* of discourse can be regarded as errors in reasoning, the interpretation of meaning—the assessment of an argument's validity and arrangement—is included in the *practice* of dialectical judgment.

This is analysis, which consists of "discovering the faults of invention and disposition by comparison with how it should be done."[52] This allows verses from poets to serve as examples, not of precedents of language use, but of instances of reasoning in Ramus's *Logic*.

The resolution by analysis of discourse into its logical elements should proceed in the following way: "First, analysis will have to pick out what must be explained, then unravel (*retexet*) the whole matter according to its basic principles. The steps are, to discern the issue which is posed in the argument, to consider the reasoning with which it is developed, and then to carry the procedure and substance of the argument back to the fundamentals from which they are derived. The final step of analysis will be to compare the disposition of the argument with certain established rules of arrangement."[53] The dialectician analyzes discourse, then, Ramus explains, as Penelope undid the fabric on her loom, by reducing its web to constituent lines of reasoning. [54]

Peculiarly Ramist is the elimination of any training in memory. "Skill in memorization," says Talon, "is nothing else than the concentration whereby we learn by heart a certain set speech or theme according to the procedure of the syllogism and 'method.' For the art of disposition is proper not only to judgment and exposition, but is also valuable in remembering things."[55] Dialectic absorbs the art of memory too.

In the Ramist scheme of the arts, figures of thought and speech—the only subject besides delivery left to the art of rhetoric—do not enhance expression but only dilute or vary it. Because devices of style and amplification can be employed to cover fallacious reasoning, they are to be regarded with some suspicion. "But when," says Ramus, "with delectation or some other motion thy chief purpose is to deceave the auditor, then thou shall put some thing away which doth appartaine to thy matter, as definitions, divisions and transitions, and set in there places thinges appartaining nothing to the matter, as digressiones from the purpose and long tarying upon the matter."[56]

Thus, Ramus, carrying the tactic of his predecessor Agricola to an extreme, expropriates dialectic to serve rhetorical purposes, calls the result dialectic, and then belittles anything left in the arts of discourse that the new creature cannot devour. This would seem to lead to a drabness of expression, a generality of reference, and a sparseness of development. Discourse becomes reduced to mere reasoned argument, unadorned and severe. It is enough that the reader or hearer be pleased by the methodically ordered disposition of the work, its sheer, lucid distinctness of meaning.

The Ramist procedure for the practice of dialectical judgment, i.e., analysis, proves most useful to the preacher, for it provides a method of invention from the scriptural text. The analyzer can reduce a text to its essential topic, trace the course of reasoning to be discerned through the passage, and identify the fundamental principles at stake; with the line of argument and the general issues thus set out, he can then find his own arguments about these same and related matters. Ramus offers a closer and more methodical procedure for invention from the scriptural passage than had Erasmus, but it is no more occupied with the words themselves than was his.

The first preaching manual by an Englishman to show identifiable influence of Ramist innovations is William Perkins's *The Art of Prophecying* (English translation, 1606). Perkins was under the tutelage of Lawrence Chaderton at Cambridge shortly after that scholar had expounded the new Ramistic arts-of-discourse doctrines in lectures at Christ's College. The two, student and tutor, became lifelong friends.[57]

At the end of his treatise, Perkins acknowledges his sources: "The writers which lent their helpe to the framing of this *Art of Prophecying*, are: Augustine, Heminius, Hyperius, Erasmus, Illyricus, Wigandus, Jacobus Matthias, Theodorus Beza, Franciscus Junius."[58] It is a diverse company, and Ramus is not explicitly mentioned among them, but his mark is unmistakable. Perkins's presentation is "couched in the method,"[59] and he proceeds accordingly by definition and division by twos. Also quite characteristically, he maintains that the art of memory, "which standeth upon places and images . . . is not to be approved."[60] Not only does Ramist "methodical disposition" serve the purpose instead, but "the animation of the image, which is the key of memorie, is impious, because it requireth absurd, insolent and prodigious cogitations, and those especially, which set an edge upon and kindle the most corrupt affections of the flesh."[61]

The preparation of a sermon discourse from a scriptural text consists of two procedures, (1) "interpretation" and (2) "right division or cutting."[62] Both seem to involve Ramist assumptions about discourse.

"Interpretation is the Opening of the words and sentences of the Scripture that one entire and naturall sense may appeare."[63] The text is to be read in keeping with the Scripture as a whole, with the help of "the analogie of faith, the circumstances of the place propounded, and the comparing of places together."[64] But the interpreter, when he comes to difficult or controverted passages, needs some facility in dealing with figurative language— the ways for disposing of possible misunderstanding so that the intended sense emerges. Perkins calls this "a grammaticall, rhetoricall and logicall Analysis";[65] the figurative way of speaking is to be identified by its technical term, its particular effect is to be noted, and its argument determined in the Ramist manner.

Certain of Augustine's precepts from the *De doctrina Christiana*, particularly the "Tychonian Rules,"[66] are of use here, but Perkins's purpose is to reduce the figures to a simple meaning, not to elaborate an interpretation by multiplying possible significations. Transferred expressions have the effect primarily of emphasis;[67] there are not two registers of signs, words and things. Nor is ambiguity a means of multiplication: "When the naturall sense of the place (propounded) is given . . . a signification of a word signifying divers things shall bee given, which is fitting to the place."[68] For an example, Perkins offers thirty-seven possible Latin equivalents for a particular Hebrew adverb-conjunction. There is no place here for things serving as signs of various other things in interrelated and reflecting networks within Scripture. "The sense of Scripture is rather to be judged the word of God than the words and letters thereof,"[69] Perkins says elsewhere, and the preacher will develop his discourse not from the words but from the sense of his scriptural passage.

The second part of sermon preparation is "right cutting of the word . . . whereby the word is made fit to edifie the people of God."[70] It consists of two steps, resolution and application. "Resolution is that whereby the place propounded is as a Weaver's web, resolved (or untwisted and unloosed) into sundrie doctrines."[71] Clearly this is the practice of dialectical judgment (analysis) of Ramus. When the doctrine is not to be explicitly found in the text, it must be gathered or collected: "This is done by the helpe of the nine arguments, that is, of the causes, effects, subjects, adjuncts, dessentanies, comparatives, names, distribution and definition."[72] This list of formal topics is adapted from Ramus's *Logic*.[73] For Augustine the preacher weaves into a sermon (*contexere*) the multiple strands of meaning spun out of the words of the text, but for Perkins he unravels (*retexere*) the logical issues from the scriptural account and lays them out in arguments.

Such a procedure of invention will, then, tend to extract a generalized line of argument from the scriptural text. The order of the reasoning should be followed through the passage; the consequences should be drawn with this in mind: "an example in his owne kinde, that is, an Ethicke, Oeconomicke, Politicke, Ordinarie, and Extraordinarie example hath the vertue of a generall rule in Ethicke, Oeconomicke, Politicke, Ordinarie, and Extraordinarie matters. . . . It is a Principle in Logick that the genus is actually in all the species."[74]

Perkins offers an example of proficiency in this procedure, in which the entire Bible is resolved by dialectical formulation: "The Summe of the Scripture is contained in such a syllogisme (or forme of reasoning) as this is which followeth. '(a) The true Messias shall bee both God and man of the seede of David; he shall be borne of a Virgin [etc.]. But (b) Jesus of Nazareth the Son of Mary is such a one. He (c) therefore is the true Messias.' In this syllogisme the Major is the scope or principall drift in all the writings of the Prophets, and the Minor in the writings of the Evangelists and Apostles."[75]

The second part of "right cutting of the word" is application, "whereby the doctrine rightly collected is diversly fitted according as place, time and person do require."[76] The preacher's essential task becomes then, teaching scriptural truths clearly and appropriately. In sum, this means propounding the Law and the Gospels—first declaring the disease of sin and secondly proclaiming its remedy[77] in various proportion and with suitable emphasis, according to the condition of the hearers.[78]

The kinds of teaching are two, mental and practical. Mental consists of doctrine and redargation; practical, of instruction and correction. Perkins has here adapted Hyperius's five types of sermons to the Ramist scheme of twofold division by including consolation and exhortation under instruction.

Like Erasmus and Hyperius, Perkins recommends that the preacher keep a commonplace book that he might "have in readinesse common place heads of every point of divinity."[79] Still, the sermon is to be rather narrowly contained within the topics extracted by analysis from the text. "The perfect and equall [i.e., adequate or fit, OED, 3] object of preaching is the word of God," he says and adds in the margin, "Or, the word of God is the whole and onely matter about which preaching is exercised; it is the field in which the preacher must containe himself."[80] The commonplaces will not serve as convenient means of working up copious and wide-ranging rhetorical flourishes but as a doctrinally sound method for deriving from the passage "seats" of strict arguments.

Hyperius would probably term Perkins's preaching scholastic, but although the *ars praedicandi* procedures of division also derive ultimately from topical doctrines, the invention of the medieval scholastic sermon was differently related to the words of the biblical text than was the invention of the Ramist sermon. For Perkins all discourse, Scripture included, consisted of arguments; the meaning of a passage was drawn through a general topic as through a die hole and then developed by reasoning, thereby leaving behind the words themselves. The *ars praedicandi* preacher, on the other hand, took up a complete unit of language—the statement—partitioned it, and substantiated the necessity of that division of the whole by logical and verbal confirmation. The sermon is thus a complexly interrelated structure erected on a scriptural statement and held together both by reason and by words, rather than lines of argument that come out of some general idea.

Donne was, of course, educated in the arts-of-discourse doctrines of his time, and he certainly thought of himself as a Christian orator with all the rhetorical resources of the commonplaces at his disposal. If he can be called by some the Reverend Billy Sunday of his day, it is because he, like Erasmus, believed that the preacher should stir the hearts of his listeners to a fervent and active realization of Christ. At the same time, medieval procedures of invention—grammatical and dialectical rather than rhetorical—furnish some of the most characteristic and most effective figurative developments in his sermons.

The preachers of the English Reformation stood in the tradition not only of Latin learning but also of medieval vernacular homiletics. The friars, who carried on much of the preaching in English in the later Middle Ages, were largely responsible for putting into the hands of the clergy the pastoral manuals whose use came to characterize the popular sermon. This material consisted for the most part of scriptural and patristic citations, canon law, and exempla. Middle English homilies urged partaking of the sacraments, with particular attention to penance, and exhorted with homely imagery and anecdote the correction of social misconduct.[1] The sermons of John Fisher at the beginning of the sixteenth century represent the type well.

The means to which the popular preacher resorted to illustrate his point or to hold his listeners' attention were disparaged by both humanists and reformers. Erasmus deplored the tactics of "contrived stories and senseless tricks,"[2] and Calvin, too, muttered his disapproval: "Indeed what one sermon was there from which old wives might not carry off more fantasies than they could devise at their own fireside in a month?"[3] The abuses of penitential practice in the late medieval church seem to have tainted for William Tyndale all of scholasticism: "Yea, they make us believe that the work itself, without the promise, saveth us; which doctrine they learned of Aristotle."[4] Hugh Latimer expressed naive surprise at a certain "doctor Gorrham, Nicholas Gorrham: I knew him to be a school-doctor a great while ago, but I never knew him to be an interpreter of scripture till now of late."[5] In fact, Nicholas de Gorran, O.P. (d. 1295), wrote many postils on Scripture and compiled a *distinctiones* collection.[6]

However unfair the reformers may have been to the medieval past, the zeal that carried them beyond the mark sprang from a fervent preoccupation with new concerns: "For the conscience is a very delicate thing," Luther said.[7] His theology of preaching insists on the efficaciousness of the Word in bringing each person to an openness toward redemption, to a real sense of release from guilt without losing a profound awareness of his own unworthiness. If the Word were available to the people, Tyndale believed, "then . . . [should] the Spirit work with thy preaching, and make them *feel*."[8] God works through the ministry of the Word, and He intervenes manifestly in the daily affairs of people's lives and in the life of the nation. Preaching thus has the task of prophecy, that of calling the elect nation, England, back to obedience. Latimer considers Jonah's warning to a wicked city to be a model discourse: "And yet here in this sermon of Jonas is no great curiousness, no great clerkliness, no great affectation of words, nor of painted eloquence; it was none other but . . . 'yet forty days, . . . and Ninive shall be destroyed': it was no more. This was no great curious sermon, but this was a nipping sermon, a pinching sermon, a biting sermon."[9] Preaching serves a function, then, for both divine grace and judgment by initiating God's work of renewal in the individual and by urging on His subjects demands of both personal and social virtue. The latter has obvious political implications. An incipient Puritan, John Stockewood, told the nation at Paul's Cross in 1579, "The preacher entreth into the very soule and mind of man, and prieth and sercheth every corner and hole of the same, and frameth it unto inward obedience unto God: out of which springeth and issueth the true outwarde obedience unto his civil Magistrate."[10]

Invective against Rome poured out from the pulpit in the cause of both Protestant doctrine and English nationalism. The threat of Catholic Spain aggravated the sometimes scurrilous denunciation of popish errors and abuses. The controversies were waged with exchanges of scriptural and patristic texts in order "to beat the adversaries with their own weapons."[11] John Jewel in his "Challenge Sermon" (1560) recognizes the authority of writings by the Fathers up to about 600.[12] Some impression of the vehemence and, ultimately, of the futility with which these contentions were pursued can be gained from the comparison of two exclamatory passages, one from a sermon by James Brooks to commemorate the restoration of the English church to Rome in 1553 and the other delivered by Jewel at the same place seven years later:

If the Host of the Mass is not, as Rome teaches, "the very bodie and bloud of Christ in dede," then all the Fathers and Martyrs must have held a wrong belief. "Yea, all moste undoubtedly dampned? O what an absurdity, what an inconvenience is this? Was Ignatius that blessed Martyr damned trowe you? . . . Sainct Hilarie damned? Saint Basil dampned? Saincte Hierome damned? Saincte Ambrose damned? Sainct Augustine dampned? . . . Oh Lorde God, what a wonderful matier is this?"[13]

Communion, not private Mass, was the practice of the Early Church. "O Gregory! O Augustine! O Hierome! O Chrysostom! O Leo! O Dionyse! O Anacletus! O Sixtus! O Paul! O Christ! If we be deceived herein, ye are they that have deceived us."[14]

More than once during the English Reformation was there occasion to repeat the dictum of Alan of Lille that "authority has a nose of wax," able to be turned in any direction.[15]

Sermons from the reigns of Henry and Edward provide little explicit indication of a self-conscious endeavor by the preacher to work out procedures of discourse that would follow from the new theological preoccupations. It was enough that the style express forthrightly the speaker's sincere convictions. However, impromptu outpourings by the immediate prompting of the Spirit met with government disapproval. Usually the scriptural passage was taken up topically as an episode, and its meaning was developed as it might bear on personal redemption from sin or on the destiny of the nation. Latimer does apply a term current in the rhetorical doctrines of the time to his manner of exposition when he remarks, "It is not requisite in a parable to expound every word of the same. For every parable hath *certum statum*, 'a certain scope,' to the which we must have a respect, and not go about to set all words together, or to make a gloss for the same: for it is enough for us when we have the meaning of the principal scope, and more needeth not."[16]

For Jewel, who for a term held the post of public orator at Oxford, the arts of discourse form an integral part of the instrument of preaching, necessary to the effective penetration of the Word: "We say eloquence and other liberal arts are to be likened to that part of the carpenter's wimble which turneth about, goeth around, and by little and little draweth in the iron or steel bit. The wooden handle entereth not into the wood, but wreatheth in the piercer: so do these, if they be rightly used, further the understanding of the word of God."[17]

With the broad handle of Ciceronian *copia*, Jewel may have worked the scriptural message ingratiatingly into the hearts and minds of his listeners, but other preachers used the procedures of the arts to extract and present plainly the sense of a biblical text with topical and largely inductive logic. For John Hooper, Scripture is "full sufficient to make a perfect man in all things."[18] The Christian strives for perfection by ascertaining what God teaches in Scripture and by conforming himself to those precepts. Hooper's sermons on Jonah set out the lessons drawn from the text and exhort his hearers to obedience. Generally the account of the prophet's ordeals instructs us that "there is no corner of the world wherein man may hide himself from the knowledge and punishment of God, if we neglect the works of our vocation."[19] On verse 1:17, which reads, "Now the Lord had prepared a great fish to swallow up Jonah," Hooper observes, "If we purge and cleanse our knowledge, religion and manners, the Lord will find means sufficient to save us; which we may not appoint to ourselves, but commend them to the providence of God."[20] The episode is reduced to clear and simple teaching on duty.

The Elizabethan Calvinist Thomas Cartwright, in his preaching series on Colossians, deals with the text methodically. The disposition of the whole letter, "the conveyance of the matter of it," is analyzed;[21] several verses at a time are paraphrased; the "sume" or "scope" or "drift" is extracted; "doctrine" and "use" are explicitly set out; questions are posed and answered. The demands laid upon men by divine pronouncement in the Scriptures can be made by such a procedure very particularized and precise. In the first verse of Colossians, "the apostle sets forth himself by his name Paul. . . . Hence, heathenish names may be used of Christians, so there be no hindrance of the church's edification."[22] From the profitable example of Isaac and Rebecca, it can be concluded with certainty that God intends for husband and wife to pray sometimes together, sometimes separately.[23] To deliver the Christian from this reduction of scriptural teaching to regimentation, Richard Hooker, writing against Cartwright in *Of the Laws of Ecclesiastical Polity*, appealed to natural law and tradition.

That Perkins's preaching had much in common with Cartwright's is evident from his series of sermons on Matthew 5–7 given at Cambridge. Presumably these were sermons that Perkins delivered as lecturer at Great St. Andrew's Church, a position he held from 1584 until his death in 1602. His preaching from that pulpit was of such renown that it attracted large crowds from both the university and the town. John Donne, during his student years at Cambridge, 1588–89, could well have been among those who heard him there.

Perkins's text is the Sermon on the Mount. As a sermon itself, in which Christ instructs his disciples in their ministerial duties, there are occasions to remark on the office and procedures of preaching, and Perkins does so in much the same terms as are in his *Art of Prophecying*. "To prophesie," he says, "here (Matt. 7:22) signifieth to teach the people of God by *expounding* the Scripture and *applying* the same to the consciences for their edification."[24] These would be, again, the two parts of "right division," resolution and application. The preacher should endeavor especially to fit the Law to particulars in a way that would bring his hearers to a keen sense of their sin and stir them to repentance. "Men may take long discourses upon a text of Scripture, but that onely is preaching which gives this light of knowledge [of sins] to the mind and conscience, which leadeth to God."[25] A discourse that fails to do so is stigmatized as "scholastical."[26] This term of disapprobation is thus used by Perkins against those with whom he disagreed in matters homeletical, just as Hyperius used it; and each of them might very well have applied it to the other.

A "scholastical" sermon does not touch the conscience of the hearer but rather leaves him unaware of his sin and makes a show of learning to win his admiration. "There is a carnall and human kinde of preaching," complains Perkins, "which now adaies takes place, wherein nothing is so much regarded as the vaunting of wit, memorie and learning by fine contrived sentences, multiplicitie of quotations, variety of allegations of Fathers, Schoole-men and other learning, but herein is no mercie nor compassion to the poore soul."[27] Still, the preacher can use learning to advantage if instead of parading his erudition he includes in his sermon only the profitable result of his preparation.[28] Of particular usefulness is the art of logic: "Here then observe the necessitie of the study of humane Arts, and among the rest, especially the Art of Logicke, whereby we may discerne between true and false collections."[29] Augustine observed that the Jews fell into idolatry because of a mistake in grammar—they mistook signs of things as merely things. Perkins maintains that the Jews failed to keep the Law properly because of mistakes in logic. "Their . . . fault," he says, "is a false collection and consequent that because a man must love his friend, therefore he must hate his enemy; this is against the rules of Art, for unlesse the contraries be equall, a consequent will not thence follow in this sort."[30]

Here the rule for expounding that has been misapplied by the Jews would seem to be that "where any vice is forbidden, the contrarie vertue is commanded" and vice versa.[31] Clearly the preacher will find the art of dialectic to be of great use in deriving the full Law from the several explicit commands in Scripture and also in inferring from narrative passages what God requires of us so that the faithful might know what "Scripture doth fully and absolutely determine of all things needful of salvation concerning faith and manners."[32] Instances can be classified by topic and the inference drawn for all cases of such a sort, as Cartwright did. The argument of a passage can be the more readily picked out, and the preacher can set out his own reasoning, whether hortatory or controversial, in a convincing order. "The office of the faithful teacher" is thus well served by logic, understood broadly as the "study of argumentation."

And yet Perkins's preaching, despite its formality of procedure, is not as bare as one might expect; it is certainly not as extreme in its plainness as are the expositions of some of the continental Ramistic Calvinists, such as Piscator. Perkins does not give the impression of feeling cold about his subject; and, although his discourse proceeds schematically, he develops his arguments amply, if somewhat repetitively, with examples and the citation of other scriptural passages to bring the doctrine home to his hearers. The preacher begins his series of sermons by stating that the matter of these three chapters from Matthew will be dealt with under twelve topics, "12 heads or places of doctrine. The first whereof concerneth true happinesse or blessednesse, from the 2. verse of this Chapter to the 13. [the Beatitudes], wherein are propounded sundry rules directing men to attaine thereunto. The scope of them all must be considered, which in generall is this . . . that true happinesse before God, is ever joyned, yea covered many times with the crosse in this world."[33] This overall doctrine is *collected* by considering the circumstances in which Christ delivered his Sermon on the Mount to his disciples and taught them about the outward hardships but inward benefits of the life to which he had called them.

As Cartwright had done, Perkins goes on to draw "uses" from this "first generall head": "As this is the scope of the doctrine following, so it stands us in hand to learne the same, and to finde experience hereof in our owne hearts, that true comfort and felicity is accompanied with manifold miseries in this life."[34] So with each of the "branches," once the doctrine is expounded, it is then applied in "uses." Every topic and each of its parts has as its consequence some principle or regulation that the hearer is to take to heart.

In his treatise on preaching, Perkins does not direct that the "right division or cutting" should involve the actual breaking up of the sentences themselves into parts as arguments, but in practice this is usually what he does. Each Beatitude, such as "Blessed are the poor / for theirs is the kingdom of heaven," is *resolved* into "(1) the parties blessed, and (2) wherein this blessedness consists."[35] Other passages that clarify the interpretation are adduced; he is thus "expounding Scripture by Scripture."[36] Sometimes the lines of reasoning implicit in a passage are set out, as when Christ elaborates on the last Beatitude with his own methodical interpretation: "rejoice and be glad [etc.]" (Matt. 5:12). "Here," says Perkins, "Christ drawes a conclusion from the former Rule, for having said in generall, 'that they which suffer for righteousnesse sake are blessed,' ver. 10, and applying it in particular to his Disciples, ver. 11, hereupon he inferres that they must rejoyce in affliction."[37]

Each Beatitude is a "rule." Thus, "blessed are the mercifull" (Matt. 5:7) is reduced by the logical procedures of expounding, to "be ye mercifull"; in the development of each verse Perkins sets out how the true, inward virtue in each case is to be recognized and attained. Mercy is first defined as "an holy compassion of heart, whereby a man is moved to helpe an other in his miserie."[38] Thus, knowing in what this virtue consists, "we may see who is a mercifull man."[39] Perkins goes on, "And because this dutie is so necessarie and excellent, I will propound certaine Rules to be observed for our furtherance herein."[40] The preacher relies rather heavily on his legalistic deductions to touch the heart—the conscience—of his hearers.

Sometimes the passage presents the occasion for Perkins to argue his Calvinistic theological position, particularly against Roman doctrine. Who are the poor in spirit (verse 3)? The popish teachers' "voluntary poverites will not agree with this text."[41] He proceeds to state his case. Or again later, the right interpretation of a phrase must be argued against various other alternative readings. Who hunger and thirst after righteousness (verse 6)? "By righteousnesse wee may well understand in the first place, the righteousnesse of faith, whereby a sinner is justified through grace in Christ. . . . And that this imputed and renued righteousnesse may here bee understood will appeare by these reasons."[42] Like Cartwright, Perkins occasionally interrupts his exposition to answer a question that might occur to the mind of an attentive listener. The preacher had ample opportunity to avail himself of logic's resources in an age in which the expositor of Scripture could hardly avoid theological controversy.

Ramism could clearly have its usefulness in Protestant preaching directed especially at preparing the hearer's receptiveness to sanctification by stirring his heart to a profound conviction of his own sins and the need for Christ's mercy. Latimer's lively exposition of Scripture on the basis of the "meaning of the principal scope" and Hooper's extraction of general principles of duty already anticipate some of the characteristics of Perkins's preaching. The topical procedures and methodical argumentation of Ramism must have seemed opportune to the Reformed preachers' purposes. On the other hand, the extremes of Ramist practice are perhaps somewhat tempered in Perkins by the moderating traditions of English Reformation preaching.

Still, those of the High Church party were already setting themselves apart from the legalistic reductionism and topical procedures of Puritans like Perkins. Donne was among those who ridiculed the "Rhapsoders, and Common placers, and Method-mongers" (1. 6. 167–70). He was to look instead to patristic and medieval means of developing the scriptural text as alternatives to the arts-of-discourse methods of the Puritan textmen.

PART II *Donne's Preaching*

CHAPTER 4

Procedure

SECTION A / THE REACTION OF THE
HIGH CHURCH PARTY

> *Though for no other cause, yet for this; that*
> *posterity may know we have not loosely through*
> *silence permitted things to pass away as in a*
> *dream, there shall be for men's information*
> *extant thus much concerning the present state of*
> *the Church of God established amongst us and*
> *their careful endeavour which would have upheld*
> *the same.*

> RICHARD HOOKER,
> *from Preface to* Of the Laws
> of Ecclesiastical Polity
> 1594

Even if he should fail to achieve the immediate purposes of his undertaking, Hooker here[1] states his belief that, nonetheless, his great work will stand as a monument to vindicate the ancient established church and the earnest, though ineffectual, efforts of some to preserve it. Yet there were other more immediate causes. The Marian exiles who returned to England after Elizabeth's accession were becoming more insistent in pressing their Calvinistic scruples. Besides his own personal confrontation with Walter Travers at the Temple, where both men shared the preaching responsibilities, Hooker set himself to answer the public challenges to the Elizabethan settlement issued in the Puritan manifestos of 1572–73—the first *Admonition to Parliament*, by Field and Wilcox; the second *Admonition*, by Cartwright; and the *Book of Discipline*, by Travers and Cartwright. These tracts constituted a bold attack on ecclesiastical authority and a dangerous precedent in their appeal to the civil power of Parliament against "the Lordly Lordes, Archbishopps, Bishoppes, Suffraganes, Deanes, Doctors, Archdeacons, Chauncelors, and the rest of that proude generation, whose kingdome must downe, holde they never so hard, bicause their tyrrannous Lordshippe can not stande wyth Christes kingdom."[2] There was clearly strong popular support even for these seditious contentions. It was against such spokesmen that Hooker addressed his "words uttered with charity and meekness,"[3] and, despite the forboding implication of the opening sentence that his great undertaking would fail to reconcile his adversaries, elsewhere he expressed the modest hope of seeing the controversies "end with concord and love on all sides."[4]

The "careful endeavour" of defending the established religious forms consists for Hooker, not in mere rebuttals, but in a thoroughgoing reconsideration of the fundamental grounds of ecclesiastical authority and the traditions of church order to determine where the truth of these controverted matters lies. It is an enterprise that requires such qualities of mind as discretion, patience, diligence, and wide learning, qualities that may be summed up in the word *judiciousness*. The forms proper to the true means of attaining salvation cannot be as summarily concluded as some have supposed: "The way for all men to be saved is by the knowledge of that truth which the word hath taught. . . . But as every thing of price, so this doth require travail."[5] The Christian must use the mind's rational discernment, exercised with humility and respect, and he must give careful consideration to the opinions and practices of former ages. Thus, Hooker frequently cites the Fathers, and his First Book, which lays the theoretical basis of ecclesiastical law, owes much to the arguments of St. Thomas.

The Puritans, on the other hand, have no regard for any such careful and respectful means of pursuing the truth in disputed matters but resort instead to peremptory methods of their own. "Now because that judicious learning," says Hooker, "for which we commend most worthily the ancient sages of the world, doth not in this case serve the turn, these trencher-mates (for such most of them be) frame to themselves a way more pleasant; a new method they have of turning things that are serious into mockery, an art of contradiction by way of scorn, a learning wherewith we were long sithence forewarned that the miserable times whereinto we are fallen should abound."[6] The time-honored and sober procedures of argumentation, perhaps difficult to acquire but capable of subtlety and profound insight, are replaced by ridicule and superficiality. This passage might bring to his reader's mind again Hooker's previous remarks about Ramism, even though he does not explicitly associate Ramist method with his Puritan adversaries. "In the poverty of that other new devised aid," said Hooker, drawing a contrast to the achievements of Aristotle, "two things there are notwithstanding singular." One is its "marvellous quick despatch"; the other, the limitations it sets upon our curiosity by restraining it "unto such generalities as every where offering themselves are apparent unto men of the weakest conceit that need be."[7] A too-facile certainty and a small-minded reductionism might all too readily conduce to presumption and mockery of the efforts of others to attain the truth.

Hooker accuses the Puritans of prejudicing the case in their favor also by approaching Scripture in a way that must necessarily substantiate their own claims. Like the Pythagoreans, who "through their misfashioned preconceits" beheld the elements of number in all of nature, so they too fashion "the very notions and conceits of men's minds in such sort, that when they read the Scripture, they may think that every thing soundeth towards the advancement of that discipline, and to the utter disgrace of the contrary."[8] Hooker seems to have in mind here doctrinal prepossessions rather than any particular procedures for dealing with the scriptural text. Yet the point might be as aptly taken in this other respect as well, and in fact elsewhere he does object to their methodical "rules for expounding," which yield the many precise regulations for everyday conduct. "Their common ordinary practice," he says, "is to quote by-speeches in some historical narration or other, and to urge them as if they were written in most exact form of law. What is to add to the law of God if this be not?"[9]

The authors of the first *Admonition* compared the condition of "the old church" with that of the Elizabethan and drew their censorious conclusions, among them that "then the ministers wer preachers; now bare readers."[10] The Puritan spokesmen cited in this regard 2 Tim. 3:16—"all Scripture is profitable to teach, to improve, to correct, to instruct in righteousness"—the text that is given such prominence in the Protestant ecclesiastical rhetorics, including those of Hyperius and Perkins. "They teach us," remarks Hooker, "the meaning of the words to be, that so much the Scripture can do if the minister that way *apply* it in his sermons, otherwise not."[11] It is not enough just to read the word of God. To be efficacious the biblical text must be "applied to the people's use as the speaker in his wisdom thinketh meet."[12] This Hooker denies and maintains instead that "the Church as a witness preacheth His mere revealed truth by *reading* publicly the sacred Scripture."[13]

Hooker seems not to propose any particular procedures for developing the meaning of a scriptural text to replace the methods of the Puritans. However, later preachers who shared Hooker's position on church affairs might well have turned to grammatical procedures of *reading* as an alternative to topical methods of *applying*. There is evidence that Donne knew Hooker's great work; perhaps he was influenced by it to give attention to the means of invention in patristic and medieval preaching.

In the last two decades of the sixteenth century, there is apparent in the actions of the highest ecclesiastical authorities a decided reaction against the Calvinist position in matters both of church order and of theological doctrine. This reaction in theology would later be called Arminianism and in church affairs would be called Laudianism. Since the installation of Whitgift as Archbishop of Canterbury in 1583, the government had proceeded with some severity against those who actively opposed uniformity. Hooker's work came at an opportune moment for it to be regarded as providing the intellectual underpinnings of the new official resolve, and Whitgift encouraged the publication of the book. The intervention of the crown in matters at the universities in the 1590s seems to have favored the Arminian position, which denied absolute predestination and allowed the concurrence of free will and grace. Historians[14] have seen an incident involving Peter Baro at Cambridge as the first clear instance revealing the new official preferences. Baro had preached a Latin sermon in the university church in January 1596, which was thought by some to broach criticism in matters set out in the Calvinistic Lambeth Articles. Proceedings by university officials against him were abruptly terminated by intervention from the court. Among those in the university at the time who sided with Baro over the issue were Thomas Playfere and Lancelot Andrewes.

Playfere was one of the few in the late sixteenth century who went through the complete program of the theology faculty. He received his D.D. at Cambridge in 1596 and soon succeeded Baro as Lady Margaret Professor of Divinity. Later he was to become chaplain to King James; in that capacity he often delivered sermons at Westminster.

Playfere's rejection of Calvinism seems to have extended to a conscious repudiation in his preaching of the reductive procedures of the Puritan textmen and a return instead to patristic and medieval precedents for developing the text, precedents with which he perhaps became familiar during his long theological education. He opens one sermon with the request to his hearers "that you would not prescribe mee any methode or order, how I should handle this Text, but that you would give mee leave to follow mine owne method and order."[15] His own means of development here is to divide the short text by sorting out its few words into several different combinations, a tour de force perhaps for a Renaissance preacher but a procedure for division commended in the medieval *ars praedicandi* treatises.[16] And Playfere uses the writings of the Fathers, not as weapons in the exchange of controversy, but to suggest richly significative scriptural imagery for assimilation into the language of his own preaching. In his sermon "The Difference between the Law and the Gospel," there occurs a succession of figures that represent the agreement of the two testaments: "Wherefore it is manifest, that the Old Testament and the New Testament as Ezechiels wheeles, are one within another (Ezek. 10:10). Yes moreover, as those cherubims, they looke one toward an other (Exod. 25:20); as those seraphims, they sing one to another (Isa. 6:3); as those young roes, they feede both together (Song of Sol. 4:5); as those golden pipes, they flowe forth both together (Zech. 4:12)."[17] All of these images signifying the concord of the testaments have patristic or medieval precedent.[18]

These are synonyms, different signs representing the same meaning, in what Playfere calls "God's dictionarie, which is the holy Scripture."[19] But in that dictionary of the sacred words there are homonyms as well, for which different meanings can be distinguished for the same sign.

The Church militant here on earth is resembled to a turtle. "The voice of the turtle is heard in our land" (Song of Sol. 2:12). Because [*Turtur gemit non canit*] the voice of the turtle is not cheerefull or merry, but groaning or mourning. Now in sacrificing the turtle (Lev. 1:15), among many other ceremonies, the Priest was appointed to wring the heade of it backeward. David also, cleapeth himselfe a turtle when he saies, "O deliver not the soule of thy turtle dove into the hands of the enemies" (Ps. 74:19). And hee is sacrificed by having his heade wrung backeward is it were, when as looking backward to his former sinnes, hee groaneth.[20]

Under the entry for *turtledove* in Garnier de Rochefort's *distinctiones* collection, the meaning of the word in Song of Sol. 2:12 is taken to be that "the longing of the Church is heard in the heavenly country" and in Leviticus, that "the priests sacrifice a hidden remorse of tears."[21] Thus, for these particular occurrences in Scripture, Playfere seems to have taken over traditional medieval significations attributed to the turtledove, the Church here on earth yearning for transcendence (Song of Sol.) and the penitent remorseful for his sins (Lev.).

Lancelot Andrewes, whose preaching style is very different from that of Playfere, nonetheless also relies on patristic formulations of scriptural exposition, for he believes that their consecrated inspiration lies very near to that of the apostles. "This way," he says, "come we to our annointing, now, by bookes: This Booke chiefly; but, in a good part also, by the bookes of the Auncient Fathers, and Lights of the Church, in whom the sent of this ointment was fresh, and the temper true; on whose writings it lieth thick, and we thence strike it off and gather it safely."[22] Although much explicit citation of the Fathers would be obtrusive in Andrewes's distinctively close prose, patristic material is drawn into his development of the text. The pattern of the Christmas sermon on Psalm 85, for instance, is based wholly on a discourse by Bernard on the Annunciation.[23]

Making the assumptions about language that patristic and medieval authors accepted, Andrewes seems to resort particularly to grammatical procedures for developing a text into a sermon. Half of the Christmas sermon on Isaiah 7 consists of the investigation of one word *Immanuel*: "But His name, St. Matthew tells us the Prophet but brought, it was God that sent it. And the names of His imposing, there is no surer place in logic than from them. His nominals be reals."[24] A word's nature—its sound, origin, place in grammatical categories—can be made to correspond meaningfully with what the word signifies. There is something marvelous about these affinities between words and things: "Signes are taken for wonders. . . . And, in this sense, it is a Signe, to wonder at. Indeed, every word (heer) is a wonder: τὸ βρέφος, an infant; *Verbum infans*, the Word without a word; the aeternall Word not hable to speake a word; A wonder sure."[25] The *"Verbum infans"* is the Christ child, but, taken by themselves, the contradictory meanings of the words that make up the expression—*Verbum*, "spoken word" and *infans*, "incapable of speech"—also represent the paradox of the Incarnation.

Andrewes returns to Jerome's notion of the *ordo mysterium* that "every word stands exactly in his place and order."[26] This supposition provides for the effective development of an Ash Wednesday sermon on Joel 2:12–13, which reads, "Therefore also, now (saith the Lord); Turne you unto Me, with all your heart, and with Fasting, and with Weeping, and with Mourning. And rend your heart, and not your clothes, and turne unto the Lord your God." Andrewes observes on this text, "Repentance it selfe is nothing els, but *'redire ad principia,'* a kind of circling; to returne to Him by repentance, from whom, by sinne, we have turned away. And much after a circle is this text: begins with the word 'turne,' and returns about to the same word again."[27]

The divisions of the text in Andrewes's sermons are so elaborate that they might have been done with the *ars praedicandi* precepts for *divisio* in mind. Also, sets are matched with sets in intricate correspondence according to the medieval pattern, so that one is "answerable" to the other[28] or "each is sorted to the other."[29] The Christmas sermon of 1622 on the magi develops Matt. 2:1–2 by such procedures reminiscent of scholastic preaching. "The Text is of a starr," says Andrewes, "and we may make all runn on a starr; that so, the Text and Day may be suitable, and Heaven and Earth hold a correspondence."[30] The wise men's errand and the star in the East are taken up by distinguishing the five works of faith that the magi performed and the five beams of the star risen in their hearts so that the two sets match and divide most of the text. This division is confirmed by scriptural verses that substantiate the appropriateness of these five activities as manifestations of faith. All parts exhaust a whole, or at least all are instances of one species. The impression of the sermon's structure is of elaborate proportionality and logical completeness.

Hooker's "careful endeavour" thus soon had other capable and powerful proponents, and the reaction took on ramifications beyond those immediately involved in efforts to uphold the status quo in church order. For one thing, a theological position that could allow for the rereading of works by the Schoolmen with profit was countenanced. Also, new procedures adopted from patristic and medieval precedents for developing the scriptural text into a sermon discourse seem to have come into vogue. Invention by the grammatical analysis of words as signs and division according to the practice of medieval scholastic preachers were taken up as alternatives to the topical methods of the Puritans. As a result the words of the text are chewed over, meditated upon, and drawn into rich and complexly structured associations of scriptural imagery rather than reduced to general headings and rules. Hooker, Playfere, and Donne must all have had some personal acquaintance with Andrewes.[31] The four of them shared in the High Church reaction against the Calvinist position and, too, against the arts-of-discourse procedures associated with that position.

SECTION B / DONNE ON HOW THE PREACHER
            SHOULD DEAL WITH HIS TEXT

Donne's preaching also shows that his procedures for developing the text were adopted in reaction to the Puritan reduction by topical logic and were drawn instead from the patristic and medieval practice of taking up Scripture grammatically. In an early sermon Donne insisted that "we steale our Learning, if we forsake the Fountaines, and the Fathers, and the Schooles, and deale upon Rhapsoders, and Common placers, and Method-mongers"(1. 6. 167–70).[1] His objection is that such means of extraction as gathering and applying are too simplistic and presume of God that our understanding of His ways is exact enough to regiment even the routines of life: "Every Commonplacer will adventure to teach, and every artificer will pretend to understand the purpose, yea, and the order too, and method of Gods eternall and unrevealed decree" (3. 16. 233–36). The inductive logic of those like Cartwright and Perkins who would conclude very precise precepts from Scripture is too facile: "It is not safe concluding out of single Instances. . . . One instance to the contrary destroys any peremptory Rule" (6. 10. 110, 118–19).

Donne was familiar with such expository methods not only on the part of contemporary English Puritans but also from the scriptural commentaries by continental Lutherans and Calvinists, which he consulted and which he occasionally cites in his sermons. A mention of Philipp Melanchthon seems to allude to his practice of extracting doctrinal commonplaces from the text: "No man denies that which Melancthon hath collected and established to be the summe of this text" (3. 4. 147–48); and Donne may number Ramist procedure among the idiosyncrasies of Piscator, a Calvinist analyzer, "who is of the Reformation, and of the most rigid subdivision in the Reformation, and who hath many . . . singularities" (8. 5. 519–21).

It is instead the interpretations of the Fathers that are to be given preeminent consideration; the preacher should keep to "th'old broad way in applying."[2] Preaching at Lincoln's Inn, Donne depicts himself poring through the Fathers in the preparation of a sermon: "I am at home in my Library considering whether S. Gregory or S. Hierome, have said best of this text, before" (3. 3. 693–95). To such an extent does Donne insist on the authoritative precedence of patristic interpretation that he sometimes speaks of it in terms reminiscent of the Roman Catholic apologists. Taking God's activity on the second day of Creation figuratively, he says:

He hath limited our eyes with a firmament beset with stars, our eyes can see no farther: he hath limited our understanding in matters of religion with a starry . . . firmament too; that is, with the knowledge of those things, *"quae ubique, quae semper,"* which those stars which he hath kindled in his Church, the Fathers and Doctors, have ever from the beginning proposed as things necessary to be explicitely believ'd, for the salvation of our souls . . .; here God raises up men to convey to us the dew of his grace, by waters under the firmament; by visible sacraments, and by the word so preach'd, and so interpreted, as it hath been constantly, and unanimously from the beginning of the Church. [2. 11. 241–54]

The Latin cited here is from Vincent of Lerins's *Commonitorium*, always a convenient text for Roman apologetics, and the word *"unanimously"* seems to recall the Tridentine canon.[3]

However, it is also the Fathers' means of developing the text into a sermon discourse that should be adopted by the preacher: "Old doctrines, old disciplines, old words and formes of speech in his service, God loves best" (2. 14. 664–66). The assumptions about sacred language and the procedures of the arts of discourse that largely determined how the Fathers expounded the Scripture's signification are particularly suited to God's own manner of expression in the divine Word. Observes Donne in the *Devotions*:

The institution of thy whole worship in the old law was a continual allegory; types and figures overspread all, and figures flowed into figures, and poured themselves out into farther figures. . . . This hath occasioned thine ancient servants, whose delight it was to write after thy copy, to proceed the same way in their expositions of the Scriptures, and in their composing both of public liturgies and of private prayers to thee, to make their accesses to thee in such a kind of language as thou wast please to speak to them, in a figurative, in a metaphorical language.[4]

Like Old Testament typologies, the things designated by the sacred words are signs of other things, and the multiple significations spread out in networks of interrelated meanings throughout all of Scripture. The Fathers read and explicated the Bible with this realization of the nature of scriptural language in mind and drew out these figurative associations in their own discourses.

Some ten years earlier Donne had not been sympathetic to Augustine's procedures of scriptural exposition when he encountered them in the Prologue to Nicholas of Lyra's *Glossa ordinaria*: "And as Lyra notes, being perchance too Allegoricall and Typick in this, [the Bible] hath this common with all other books, that the words signifie things; but hath this particular, that all the thinges signifie other things."[5] It is peculiar that Donne does not recognize this doctrine about sacred language to be Augustine's since he refers elsewhere in the *Essays* to the *De doctrina Christiana*.[6] In a later undated sermon he does quote verbatim from this work.[7]

Again at another place in the *Essays*, Donne is critical of the tenuous subtleties of patristic exposition when he complains of "the curious refinings of the Allegoricall Fathers, which have made the Scriptures, which are strong toyles, to catch and destroy the bore and bear which devast our Lords vineyard, fine cobwebs to catch flies."[8] The *Essays in Divinity* were written early, before Donne had read extensively in the Fathers for himself, but even much later he seems to take somewhat lightly their more fanciful turns. "Truely the later Schoole," he remarks, "is . . . a more Poetical part of divinity, then any of the Poems of the Fathers are" (9. 3. 214–17), and most of the Fathers were poets (9. 1. 500). "Poeticall" is at least tinged here with the derogatory sense used by Thomas Wilson in speaking of "misticall wisemen and Poeticall Clerkes."[9] And elsewhere Donne says of patristic and medieval interpretations of the "house" of John 14:2, "A House, in the designe and survay whereof, the Holy Ghost himselfe is figurative, the Fathers wanton, and the School-men wild" (7. 4. 708–9). *"Wanton"* is a word commonly used by the advocates of the plain sense in condemning the excesses of allegorical exegesis.[10]

Donne's views regarding the soundness of patristic scriptural exposition thus run the gamut from high Roman veneration to low Protestant suspicion. Any speaker, of course, must take into account the circumstances of the occasion of his discourse. The spokesman for the established English church had adversaries on both sides and had to say what needed to be said in answer to each of them. Still, Donne's appreciation for the Fathers' procedures and interpretations seems to have grown with his more extensive familiarity with their works. As he became less involved with religious controversies, he could perhaps be more appreciative of the meditative and devotional richness of the Fathers' readings of Scripture.

Donne's interest in the correlations between words and their meanings was perhaps first aroused by his contact with the then fashionable ideas of the Christian Cabalists, Pico della Mirandola and Johann Reuchlin. "The Cabalists," he says in the *Essays,* "which are the Anatomists of words, and have a Theologicall Alchimy to draw soveraigne tinctures and spirits from plain and grosse literall matter, observe in every variety [of names] some great mystick significance."[11] "Theologicall Alchimy" probably alludes to their devices of occultist interpretation—Gematria, Notarikon, and Temurah. Gematria involved matching one word with another by means of mathematical equivalence. The letters of the Hebrew alphabet served also as numerals. Words were somehow considered alike in meaning if the sums of the numerical values of their letters were equal. Notarikon is a way of turning a word into a phrase that expands the word's meaning. Each letter of a given word serves, in turn, as the initial letter of each word of the phrase. In Temurah the letters of a word are substituted anagrammatically according to some formal arrangement of the alphabet in order to form another word. For example, the twenty-two letters of the Hebrew alphabetical series might be set out in two rows of eleven each with the letters of one row over the letters of the other row; the original word would then be turned into another word of the same or relevant meaning by substituting for any or all of the letters of the original word the other letter above or below it. Such were the means of Cabalistic verbal anatomizing.

The Cabala—particularly its mystic exegetical devices—afforded Pico the means of assimilating into his syncretistic Christian Neoplatonism the Old Testament and the accretions of Jewish learning upon it. The *Heptaplus*, the work of Pico to which Donne explicitly refers in the *Essays*,[12] is a multilayered and luxuriant commentary on the verses of Genesis that relate the divine acts of Creation. In it the cosmological doctrines of Plato's *Timaeus* are mingled with the biblical account. Recourse to the Cabalistic resolution and recomposition of words reveals the correspondences between the several worlds of Pico's cosmology, for the letters that comprise the sacred words are traces of the universal emanations and processions of the Godhead. These correspondences, which can be investigated in the names and natures of things, make possible an allegorical sense of Scripture: "All these worlds, bound together with ties of concord, manifest an unstinting reciprocity between each other of natures and names. From this source the discipline of a consistent allegorical sense has arisen. The ancient Fathers could not have represented appropriately some things by other figurative things unless they were knowledgeable concerning the secret relationships and affinities throughout all of nature."[13] It is noteworthy that Pico regards the figurative interpretations of the Fathers as essentially the same sort of endeavor as his own.

Johann Reuchlin met Pico in Florence in 1490 and thereafter pursued Cabalistic studies enthusiastically. He was particularly interested in the various manifestations in Scripture of the divine name, which were revealed by the new exegetical techniques. The tetragrammaton—IHUH, Yahweh—becomes the name of the Messiah—IHSUH, Jesus—by the mere addition of the letter S. Now the letter S in Hebrew is called Sin, which by Notarikon can be expanded into the phrase *the tetragrammatic name uttered*, i.e., brought forth in the Incarnation. Donne refers in the *Essays* to a passage in the *De arte cabalistica* that develops this idea further: "The Cabalists (as one which understood them well, observes) have concluded, that the word *Judgment* applyed to God, hath every where a mixt and participant nature, and intimates both *Justice* and *Mercy*."[14] Even Jewish interpreters, Reuchlin says, maintained that the tetragrammatic name has manifestations in the Messianic titles Mercy and Compassion. David prophesied in the Psalm that God would give to the Messiah the power "to judge thy people in justice and thy poor in judgment" (Ps. 72:2). Yet according to all the Cabalists, justice admits of clemency. As Gikatilia said in the *Portae lucis*, "Judgment is partly rigor and partly clemency," and he went on to cite Hos. 2:19, where God promises to reestablish the covenant with his people by sending the Messiah: "I will marry you to me in justice and judgment, in Mercy and in Compassion." Furthermore, by Gematria, Mercy and Abraham are equivalent, so that Habakkuk is in fact referring to the anointed one, in whom the promises to Abraham will be fulfilled, when he says (3:2), "in wrath, remember Mercy." "This, then," adds Reuchlin, "is the only domain of true contemplation, where just a single word is a mystery and where words, syllables, letters and points are full of secret meanings."[15]

Donne does have misgivings about some of the metamorphic feats of the Cabalistic resolution and recomposition of words. He asks in the *Essays*, "But since our merciful God hath afforded us the whole and intire book, why should wee tear it into rags, or rent the seamless garment?"[16] And yet he is clearly interested in the mystic significance of names; in a sermon as late as 1629, he alludes to the Cabalistic device of Gematria.[17]

In fact, Donne's sermons show his persistent interest in the implications of the way things are signified by names. His speculations in the *Essays* on the various names of God[18] are but the first instance of an investigation that occupied him in his preaching. "As God hath spangled the firmament with starres," he says as Dean of St. Paul's, "so hath he his Scriptures with names, and Metaphors, and denotations of power. Sometimes he shines out in the name of a Sword, and of a Target, and of a Wall, and of a Tower, and of a Rocke, and of a Hill; And sometimes in that glorious and manifold constellation of all together, *Dominus exercituum*, The Lord of Hosts" (7. 1. 510–15).[19] Also Donne sometimes explains how the proper names in the Bible represent something by their designations in the original language. Referring to Exod. 1:1—"Now these are the names of the children of Israel"—he says in the *Essays*, "So that if one consider diligently the sense of the Names register'd here, he will not so soon say, That the Names are in the History, as that the History is in the Names."[20] The course of a man's life is somehow signified by his name. Just as the name *Stephen* means "crown," a martyr's crown for Stephen, so "every man owes the world the signification of his name" (8. 7. 244–45). Though it may be that "every nominal John is not a real John" (1. 9. 361), Donne resorts fairly often in his preaching to such *onomastica sacra*.[21]

In a way all nouns are names and thus designate particular things by convention or according to their natures, just as the classical and medieval grammarians taught: "Names are either to avoid confusion, and distinguish particulars, and so every day begetting inventions (and the names often overliving the things, curious and entangled Wits have vexed themselves to know, whether in the world there were more things or names). . . . Or else, names are to instruct us, and express natures and essences. This Adam was able to do."[22] In the sermons there is mention several times that Adam named the creatures according to their natures;[23] so research into a word is an investigation of what it signifies. "To know the nature of the thing, look we to the derivation, the extraction, the Origination of the word" (3. 7. 21–23). This is again the assumption of the ancient grammatical commentators.

Donne thus shared in the High Church reaction against the Puritan methods of developing Scripture by reductive topical logic and preferred to follow the patristic and medieval example of reading the text with attention to the rich and interrelated significations of the words.[24] To deal with the language of Scripture itself is to utilize the very gift meant by God to help accomplish man's redemption as a resource for the preacher's invention, as an object of his meditation. This the Fathers realized: "That is true which Saint Basil says of all words in the Scriptures, '*Habent minutissimae particulae sua mysteria.*' Every word hath force and use, as in Pearle, every seed Pearle is as medicinall as the greatest, so there is a restorative nature in every word of the Scriptures, and in every word, the soule findes a rise, and a help for her devotion" (5. 8. 106–11). In Donne's preaching, grammatical procedures of invention are an alternative with venerable precedents and rich possibilities of sermon development.

CHAPTER 5

The Sermons

> ℘*And, Beloved, this distribution of the text,*
> *which I have given you, is rather a Paraphrase,*
> *then a Division, and therefore the rest will*
> *rather be a Repetition, then a Dilatation.*
>
> JOHN DONNE,
> from the *divisio* of a sermon
> preached at St. Paul's
> 1627

Before Donne is far into a sermon, he is careful to explain how the scriptural text upon which he is preaching will be divided and taken up in the several parts of his discourse. In the printed version of the sermons, the paragraph in which the text is thus transmuted into a structure to be developed is usually noted in the margin as the *divisio*. The consistency of terminology used regarding the distribution of the words of the text as explained in the *divisio* suggests that Donne was quite deliberate in his procedures and aware of the patristic and medieval precedents for his own practice.

In the above quotation,[1] Donne, having explained how his verse from Psalm 66 is to be taken up, remarks that since he has not *divided* the text into parts but has instead examined each word singly for glossing by *paraphrase*, the rest of his discourse will be to go through again or *repeat* the reading of the verse rather than to amplify or *dilate* members extracted from a division of the scriptural statement. In so distinguishing between "Paraphrase" and "Division," he seems to refer to the essential difference between the ways the Fathers and the scholastics developed a scriptural text into a sermon discourse. Augustine elaborated upon a passage by reading it through with grammatical, paraphrastic glosses and by drawing out the multiple associations of words; so such a sermon would appropriately be called a repetition of an introductory survey of the text. Bonaventure, on the other hand, divided a scriptural statement into parts of a whole and then built upon that a complex structure by adducing confirming texts and by subdividing these. The structure would then be filled out by *dilatation*, a term from the *ars praedicandi* that seems not to have been paired with division in any of the Renaissance ecclesiastical rhetorics. In Donne's own preaching, the words of the text are distributed in the *divisio* by either paraphrase or division, but more often by division.[2]

The assumption that the paraphrastic development of a scriptural passage is the usual procedure of the Fathers and of Augustine in particular is explicitly stated several times.[3] Donne once mentions this in the context of a reply to the more enthusiastic Puritans who insisted on frequent extemporal preaching. "It is true," he says addressing the court during Lent 1618, "that if we consider the Sermons of the Ancient Fathers, we shall finde some impressions, some examples of suddain and unpremeditated Sermons. Saint Augustine some times eases himself upon so long Texts, as needed no great preparation, no great study; for a meer paraphrase upon this Text was enough for all his hour." Yet Augustine's example in this respect will not be admitted as a precedent to allow prophetical extemporizing now: "Bring such preachers as Basil and Augustine were, and let them preach as often as they will" (1. 6. 309–14, 324–26). Donne would agree with the scholastics, then, that although the Fathers were inspired by the same Spirit as that which inspired the sacred writers themselves to write the Scriptures, the latter-day preacher is not so inspired but must depend upon his own "careful endeavor," and rely on the resources of reason and of ancient authority.

When Donne develops his text by "paraphrasticall distribution" (8. 4. 552–53) he does not, then, extemporize, but, anticipating and recapitulating, picking up the thread of coherent meaning again and again as he reads on, he moves continuously through the words of the text. The overall progress of the sermon is set out in the *divisio* near the beginning; so it is apparent that the substance of the discourse has already been deliberated upon and completed. Preaching at court in 1621 upon Prov. 25:16—"Hast thou found honey? Eat so much as is sufficient for thee, lest thou be filled therewith, and vomit it"—Donne offers this preview of his paraphrastic development of the text:

In which words, there being first a particular Compellation, *"Tu,"* hast "thou" found it? it remembers thee, that there be a great many, that have not found it, but lack that which thou aboundest in; And *"Invenisti,"* thou has not inherited it, nor merited it, thou has but "found" it; and for that which thou hast found, it is "Honey," sweetness, but it is but Honey, which easily becomes choler, and gall, and bitternesse. Such as it is, *"Comede,"* thou maist "eat" it, and eat it safely, it is not unwholesome; but *"Comede sufficientiam,"* eat no more then is "sufficient"; And in that, let not the servant measure himselfe by his Master, nor the subject by the King, nor the private man by the Magistrate, but *"Comede sufficientiam tuam,"* eat that which is sufficient "for thee," for more then that will "fill" thee, over-fill thee; perchance not so full as thou wouldst bee, yet certainly so full, as that there will bee no roome in thee for better things; and then thou wilt "vomit," nay perchance thou must vomit, the malice and plots of others shall give thee a vomit, And such a vomit shall bee *Evacuans,* an exinanition, leave thee empty; and *Immundum,* an uncleannesse, leave thee in scorne and contempt; and *Periculosum,* a danger, breake a veine, a veine at the heart, breake thy heart it selfe, that thou shalt never recover it. "Hast thou found honey? eat so much as is sufficient for thee, lest thou be filled therewith, and vomit it." [3. 10. 49–69]

Honey is here a sign of the temporal delights of this world, the objects of man's greed and ambition. Within the limited scope of this single verse, the figurative meaning is sustained without stretching its coherence to any great extent. The overall transferred signification of the text might be stated as: excessive ambition will likely lead not to eventual contentment but rather to a catastrophic fall. The grammarian's procedure of moving through the text word by word, stopping then going on, and accumulating meaning to be repeated and held in mind as more is added serves particularly well here. It is the verbs—"found," "eat," "fill-full," "vomit"—that Donne comes back to over and over again. Thereby he stresses that by his own willful acts man indulges his insatiable appetites and so comes to grief and disappointment.

It is likely that even in Donne's time at least some semblance of the medieval *ars praedicandi* was still taught in the higher faculty of theology at the universities, where the delivery of a Latin sermon *ad clerum* was a requirement for the degree.[4] After all, the formalities of that other scholastic exercise, the disputation, were certainly retained at Oxford and Cambridge during

Elizabeth's reign. Whether Donne became familiar with the *ars praedicandi* during his years at the universities or through his acquaintance with contemporary divines or from his extensive reading in the works of the Schoolmen, he certainly knew the scholastic procedures for developing a text by division, restatement, confirmation, and subdivision. Here, for instance, is how he divided 2 Cor. 4:6—"For God who commanded light to shine out of darkness, hath shined in our hearts to give the light of the knowledge of the glory of God in the fact of Jesus Christ"—in a public sermon preached at the Spittle on Easter Monday 1622:

Our parts therefore in these words, must necessarily be three; three Lights. The first, shows us our Creation; the second, our Vocation; the third, our Glorification. In the first, We, who were but, (but what?) but nothing, were made Creatures: In the second, we, who were but Gentiles, were made Christians: In the third, we, who were but men, shall be made saints. In the first, God took us, when there was no world: In the second, God sustains us, in an ill world: In the third, God shall crown us in a glorious and joyful world. In the first, God made us; in the second, God mends us; in the third, God shall perfect us. First, "God commanded light out of darkness," that man might see the Creature; then "he shin'd in our hearts," that man might see himself; at last, he shall shine so "in the face of Christ Jesus," that man may see God and live, and live so long, as that God of light and life shall live himself. [4. 3. 126–39]

Donne's successive restatement of his division here is formally very like that of Bonaventure's in the sermon on Ps. 106:8–10. There is, of course, the same parallel phrasing, whereby the parts are set out with isocolon, parison, and paromoion ("our Creation, . . . our Vocation, . . . our Glorification") so that the members are extended in corresponding ways in terms of the same parts of speech. Also, both preachers restate their division a total of five times in the pattern of two pairs followed by a final restatement, which seems to conclude from the accumulated meaning. Thus, in his first pair Donne sets out (1) what events the Lights reveal and (2) wherein these events consist. So the first members drawn from the first section of the text ("God commanded light out of darkness") in the first two declarations of the division are (1) the Light shows our Creation and (2) in our Creation we who were nothing became something. The next pair brings out what God's part is in these events. Again, to follow the first member through, He (3) took us out of nowhere and (4) gave us being. Then in the final reiteration Donne concludes what the divine intention must be: that by the light of all that God has accomplished for man, he might see objects in such a way that would lead him to a recognition of Christ.

The keys of necessity and sufficiency are here provided by the correspondence of the three species of time—past, present, and future—with the parts of the division, "God made us, . . . mends us, . . . shall perfect us." It is a means of establishing the logical completeness of the division that the *ars praedicandi* treatises commended to the preacher and one of which Donne seems to have been particularly fond.[5] Thus, setting out the parts of another text (Ps. 63:7) some years later, he says, "So that we have here the whole compasse of Time, Past, Present, and Future; and these three parts of Time, shall be at this time, the three parts of this Exercise" (7. 1. 35–37). This division is confirmed by adducing a single text, "He is yesterday, and to day, and the same for ever" (Heb. 13:8). Later in this sermon at a transition between sections, the division is restated with paromoion as "retrospect, . . . aspect, . . . prospect" (7. 1. 490–94). Not infrequently does Donne take care to establish the logical validity of his divisions of the scriptural statement into parts by showing the members to be parts of some whole, whether universal or constituent.

Donne was also versed in the rhetorical procedures of his own time, and like Erasmus and Tyndale he endeavored as a speaker to bring his hearers to a fervent and heartfelt realization of the meaning of Christ for themselves and to move them to act in accordance with their faith. To this end he employed all the resources of the art of persuasive eloquence, including those of topical logic. A topic or commonplace[6] drawn extrinsically from the circumstances of the scriptural account or from an overall survey of the entire text might serve as one of the parts of the division. However, his procedures for developing the topic were different from the reductionist procedures of the Puritans.

It is often explained in the course of the *divisio* that the partition of the text is meant to assist the *understanding* and the *memory* in their grasp of the Word.[7] These two faculties, together with the will, represent in the human mind an image of the Trinity. "As the three Persons of the Trinity created us," says Donne, "so we have, in our soul, a threefold impression of that image, and, as Saint Bernard calls it, 'a trinity from that Trinity,' in those three faculties of the soul, the Understanding, the Will, and the Memory" (2. 2. 21–24).[8] Thus, he who hears Scripture read and preached upon can, if he is willing, respond to God's revelation by understanding and remembering, for it is these activities of the mind that bear the impression of the divine nature.

By the understanding Donne seems to mean the capacity to discern what is true and morally right. It is the ability to arrive at the "evident and necessary conclusions" of natural theology (9. 16. 187–88); and it is "the receptacle of faith" (9. 17. 567), because it apprehends and holds the contents of belief. Presumably, the preacher's *divisio* can best assist the understanding by distinguishing rationally the issues into clear-cut topics.

St. Paul addressed himself particularly to the understanding; so Donne fittingly speaks of him as proceeding by topics. "S. Paul continues here," he says in a sermon on Acts 20:25, "that way, and method, which he alwayes uses; That is, to proceed by the understanding, to the affections, and so to the conscience of those that hear him" (8. 6. 93–95). Less than two years previously he remarked, "That a resurrection there is, the Apostle opens severall Topiques, to prove it" (7. 3. 132–33).[9] Donne, like Paul, tends to employ topical division for developing by argument a predominantly doctrinal discourse.

The statement summing up the gist of what is to be said under a certain topic is fairly often referred to as the "proposition."[10] Donne seems usually to mean what Erasmus or Wilson meant by this term, but occasionally he suggests a more formal sense by associating it with argumentation (8. 3) or particularly with the reductionist procedures of Calvin and the Calvinists.[11] "Calvin," he says, "collects this proposition from this story (Acts 28:1–6). . . . In all ages, and in all places this hath ever been acknowledged by all men, That when God strikes, God is angry, And when God is angry, God strikes" (8. 14. 91–95). The Puritans, however, were more relentlessly methodical in their collection of "rules" and their application to particular cases than Calvin himself had been. Donne would not carry topical logic so far: "And as there is a curse laid upon them, that take away any part, any proposition out of this Booke, so may there be a curse, or an ill affection, and countenance and suspicion from God, that presses any of his general propositions to a narrower, and lesse gracious sense then God meant it" (7. 9. 397–401).

In the division mention is sometimes made of explication and application of the scriptural text: "The parts are, first, the Literall, the Historicall sense of the words; And then an emergent, a collaterall, an occasional sense of them. The *explication* of the wordes, and the *Application*, *Quid tunc*, *Quid nunc*, How the words were spoken then, How they may be applied now, will be our two parts" (4. 7. 76–81). These procedures seem not too different from Perkins's "resolution" and "application," the two parts of "right division or cutting." Donne once speaks of *thesis* and *hypothesis*, other technical expressions associated with topical methods.[12] "For," he says, "in that action, first, *in Thesi*, for the Rule, thou art a Preacher to thy selfe, and thou hast thy Text in St. Paul, 'He that eateth and drinketh unworthily, eateth and drinketh damnation to himselfe' (1 Cor. 11:29); And then *in Hypothesi*, for the application to the particular case, thou art a Prophet to thy selfe" (7. 11. 398–402). These terms were used in this sense in the *Ecclesiastical Rhetoric* of Bartholomew Keckermann, a German systematic and semi-Ramist whose work seems to have circulated in England during the early seventeenth century.[13] Thus, Donne was certainly aware of how the procedures of topical logic could organize the issues that the preacher would then develop, and he availed himself of such means when he endeavored particularly to address his hearers' understanding by presenting to them the doctrines of Christianity and the relevance of that faith to their lives.

And yet perhaps it is the more important function of explication and application to engage the memory than to reach the understanding. "And here," says Donne in a sermon to the king in 1627, "is the Latitude, the Totality, the Integrality of the means of salvation; you shall have Scriptures delivered to you, by them the Holy Ghost shall teach you all things; and then you shall be *remembered* of all, by the explication and application of those Scriptures" (7. 16. 290–94). The preacher's task is especially to involve the Word of God in the memory of his hearers, where it can remain present and work. He says elsewhere, "And truly the Memory is oftener the Holy Ghosts Pulpit that he preaches in, then the Understanding"; "this [the memory] is the faculty that God desires to work upon" (8. 11. 303–5, 2. 11. 85–86). The text of Scripture must be divided and developed in such a way that will engage particularly this faculty.

When Donne mounted the pulpit, he would have had, if

notes at all, only an outline from which the entire sermon, worked out in his mind, would be recollected.[14] The *divisio* would provide headings, then, under which the preacher could recall the substance of what he had to say and which also would establish the scheme for the sermon's development in his hearers' memories. So he introduces the distribution of Acts 20:25, "In the words chosen for this day, wee shall reduce to your memories, first" (8. 6. 55–57).[15] Sometimes Donne speaks of the *divisio* as laying out "places" in terms of *loci et imagines*, the mnemonic device of classical rhetoric whereby the subject matter to be committed to memory is associated with certain artifacts or images variously situated in some familiar place through which the speaker makes his way as he develops his discourse.[16] Thus, the *divisio*, as it were, provides the overall construction that houses the sermon or the itinerary that guides it. "These words (Luke 23:24)," says Donne, "shall be fitliest considered, like a goodly palace, if we rest a little, as in an outward Court, upon consideration of prayer in generall; and then draw neare the view of the Palace, in a second Court, considering this speciall prayer in generall as the face of the whole palace. Thirdly, we will passe thorow the chiefest rooms of the palace itself" (5. 12. 20–25).[17] Or as he moves into the sermon's development, so "we proceede now to the furnishing of the particular roomes" (4. 10. 83–84).[18]

Yet Donne conceives of the memory's function in the preacher's ministry of the Word to be more crucial than that of simply recalling the points covered in the discourse. St. Bernard is credited with calling the memory "the stomach of the soul" (2. 11. 45–47, 88–89), but it is, of course, an image of Augustine's, who extended it to speak of meditation on Scripture as "rumination." Words drawn from the memory are tumbled over in the mind; their various meanings, implications, and associations are chewed over; and thereby the reader experiences Scripture delightfully renewed for him. In the *Essays* Donne speaks in terms of this same image about his meditations upon the first verses of Exodus. "Only to paraphrase," he says, "the History of this Delivery, without amplifying, were furniture and food enough for a meditation of the best perseverence, and appetite, and digestion; yea, the least word in the History would serve a long rumination. If this be in the bark, what is in the tree? If in the superficiall grass, the letter; what treasure is there in the hearty and inward Mine, and Mistick and retired sense? Dig a little deeper, O my poor lazy soul, and thou shalt see that thou, and all mankind are delivered from an Egypt."[19]

For Donne, the preacher reaches his congregation and stirs them to a lively sense of their faith by engaging in their memories the meanings of the words of the text with their own personal history, tumbling it together, and drawing out the implications and associations. The past events that the hearer himself or the nation has experienced become involved in the meditative remembering of the words of Scripture; so the awareness of God's activity in the world and of His revelation in His Word touches the hearer's experience and makes it all "his own case" (6. 2. 190–91). "Nay, he that hears no Sermons," says Donne preaching at Lincoln's Inn, "he that reads no Scriptures, hath the Bible without book; He hath a Genesis in his memory; he cannot forget his Creation; he hath an Exodus in his memory; he cannot forget that God hath delivered him, from some kind of Egypt, from some oppression; he hath a Leviticus in his memory; He cannot forget that God hath proposed to him some Law, some rules to be observed. He hath all in his memory, even to the Revelation; God hath revealed to him, even at midnight alone, what shall be his portion, in the next world" (2. 2. 72–80).[20] Each person's own course of life manifests the same divine presence, the same meaning, as does the whole compass of sacred history; so the reader of Scripture reads there about his own past. This experience in the memory of the full meaning of God's words and actions is Donne's alternative to the topical reduction and legalistic regimentation of the Puritans.

Thus, to explication and application Donne adds *complication*. By this term he seems to mean particularly the correlation of the scriptural text to the ritual observance at which it is expounded. Having explained the appropriateness of his verse, John 10:10 ("I am come that they might have life, and that they might have it more abundantly"), to the occasion, Christmas Day, of his preaching upon it, he goes on, "And so much being not impertinently said, for the connexion of the words, and their *complication* with the day, passe we now to the more particular distribution and explication thereof" (9. 5. 74–76).[21] Complication thus associates the preacher's meditations on his text with a sacred event in scriptural history; so the sermon is thereby a *commemoration*, in which the congregation reexperiences the event through the ritual observance and recalls by listening to the discourse the meaning of God's revelations in the words of Scripture and in their own lives. Complication thus serves especially well to engage the hearers' memories.

Yet complication seems to have another, broader sense as well. It is the combination or folding together of "the differences among similar things . . . and the similarities among different things" into a complex structure upon which the sermon discourse takes shape, in the manner of the *distinctiones* procedures of medieval preachers such as Alan of Lille. When Donne preaches upon a certain text that is to be found substantially the same in three different places in Scripture ("Lord, who hath beleeved our report?" Is. 53:1, John 12:38, Rom. 10:16), he calls his development of the various meanings for the various places "Complication."[22] In the division or subdivision of a good many of Donne's sermons, the sense of a single scriptural expression is variously taken in such a way and then perhaps further multiplied by other factors to build up a complicated, static structure that the preacher subsequently fills out in his development. Complication in this sense, too, involves the memory, for the mind draws out these implications and associations by ruminating upon the words of the text, recalling similar but different instances of them elsewhere in Scripture, and distinguishing multiple significations.

By consulting the various commentators on a passage and comparing "Translation with Translation, and Exposition with Exposition" (9. 11. 451–52), Donne makes available for his own use a rich accumulation of different readings and interpretations. He accepts such diversity, unless a matter essential to right belief is at stake: "Here we accept willingly, and entertain usefully their doubt, that will not resolve, whether our *'Gnoshehu'* in the Text, be *Factorem Ejus*, or *Factorem Suum* . . . Be it either; Be it both" (8. 12. 497–501). It is the attitude, as he recognized, held also by St. Augustine:

But yet though he [Augustine] found, that divers senses offered themselves, he did not doubt of finding the Truth. For . . . O my God (sayes he), the light of mine eyes, in this dark inquisition, since divers senses, arise out of these words, and all true . . . , What hurt followes, though I follow another sense, then some other man takes to be Moses sense? for his may be a true sense, and so may mine, and neither be Moses his. . . . So far I will goe, saies he, so far will we, in

his modesty and humility accompany him, as still to propose . . .
such a sense as agrees with other Truths, that are evident in other
places of Scripture, and such a sense as may conduce most to
edification. For to those two, does that heavenly Father reduce the
foure Elements, that make up a right exposition of Scripture; which
are, first, the glory of God . . . ; secondly, the analogie of faith . . . ;
and thirdly, exaltation of devotion . . . ; and last, extension of charity.
[9. 3. 87–129][23]

Whether from the *Confessiones* or from the *De doctrina Christiana*
itself, Donne shows here his familiarity with Augustine's as-
sumptions in multiplying the sense of the scriptural text. He
even follows Augustine's example in allowing the possible use-
fulness of mistranslations, a remarkable admission in that philo-
logically contentious age.[24]

In the division itself Donne sometimes complicates the struc-
ture of his sermon by distinguishing several senses for a single
expression, each sense to serve as a part of the overall develop-
ment. The multiplicity of meaning can derive from the ambigu-
ity of a word or phrase, from the homonymy of a thing in
Scripture that is a sign of other things, or from just taking the
import of what is said from several different points of view. A
sermon given before the Virginia Company in 1622 plays upon
the ambiguity of *"But,"* the first word of the verse, with an
ingenuity worthy of the poet. The text was Acts 1:8, "But yee
shall receive power, after that the Holy Ghost is come upon you
[etc.]."

The first word of the Text is the Cardinall word, the word, the hinge
upon which the whole Text turnes; the first word, "But," is the But,
that all the rest shoots at. First it is an exclusive word; something the
Apostles had required, which might not bee had; not that; And it is an
inclusive word; something Christ was pleased to affoord to the
Apostles, which they thought not of; not that, not that which you
beat upon, "But," but yet, something else, something better then
that, you shall have. [4. 10. 45–52][25]

The different acceptations that divide the discourse are the two
senses of *but* the conjunction, meaning here both 'the preceding
is excluded' (worldly power you shall not have) and 'neverthe-
less the following obtains' (spiritual power shall be yours).
Several plays on words are worked in with making this distinc-
tion. *Cardinal* comes from the Latin for 'door hinge,' that on
which all else turns but also that which distinguishes the inside

from the outside, the exclusive from the inclusive. *"But,"* the first word of the text, is thus the *butt* 'base end or pivot' on which the meaning of the sentence turns as upon a hinge by excluding one thing while including another. The sense of *butt* as 'shooting target' is also played upon.

The ambiguity of an expression may lie, not in the word itself, but in the thing, which takes on various significations or connotations in different places in Scripture. This is the *distinctiones* procedure of medieval preachers.

We have a great deale of comfort presented to us, in that Christ is presented to us as a stone [in this text, Matt. 21:44], for there we shall finde him, first, to be the foundation stone (Isa. 28:16), nothing can stand which is not built upon Christ; Secondly, to be *lapis angularis*, a corner stone (Ps. 118:22), that unites things most dis-united; and then to be *lapis Jacob*, the stone that Jacob slept upon (Gen. 28:11); fourthly, to be *lapis Davidis*, the stone that David slew Goliah withall (1 Sam. 17–49); And lastly, to be *lapis petra* (Matt. 7:25), such a stone as is a Rock, and such a Rock as no Waters nor Stormes can move or shake. [2. 8. 38–45]

Here, the thing *stone* has a consistent transferred sense, 'Christ,' which carries through all the adduced scriptural instances. Yet each context brings out a certain different respect in which Christ is a stone and so extends our understanding of the various ways Christ benefits us. These beneficial senses are then contrasted with the meaning of this same sign in the text upon which the sermon is preached, Matt. 21:44, "Whosoever shall fall on this *stone* shall be broken, but on whomsoever it shall fall, it will grinde him to powder." The sermon is thus divided by these various and contrasting connotations of *stone* meaning 'Christ.'

The import of the text can also be seen from different viewpoints, particularly as a scriptural event is conceived as recurring at different moments in time. The principle here is that of the liturgy and of typology, the commemoration or prefiguration of a happening that holds an important place in sacred history, participates in that event, and is the same as that event yet different. Donne seems to have accepted the traditional typologies, which related the Old and New Testaments into one coherent account of God's activity in time. Fairly often the final acceptation in the division of a text is eschatological and looks forward to final judgment and glory. It is the course of many of Donne's sermons, proceeding by "blessed and glorious gradations" (4. 2. 80), to conclude in the hopeful anticipation of eternity. Such is his division of Mic. 2:10, "Arise and depart, for this is not your rest": "These words have a three-fold acceptation, and admit a three-fold exposition, for, first, they are a Commination, the Prophet threatens the Jews; Secondly, they are a Commonition, the Prophet instructs all future ages; Thirdly, they are a Consolation, which hath reference to the Consummation of all, to the rising at the general judgment" (5. 9. 8–13).[26] Thus, the same statement takes on various meanings according to the context of time within which the event is regarded.

Once various senses have been derived from a single scriptural expression in any of these ways, the preacher can multiply these several acceptations by some other factor to add another story or another wing to the structure of his discourse. Preaching at St. Paul's on Easter 1628, on 1 Cor. 13:12 ("For now we see through a glasse darkly, but then face to face; now I know in part but then I shall know, even as also I am knowne"), Donne sets out a scheme for his development that is reminiscent of that of Alan of Lille on the keys of the kingdom of heaven. He first distinguishes *seeing* from *hearing*. Then, there is a sight and a knowledge in this life and a sight and a knowledge in the life to come. For each of these differentiations, he considers (1) the place or "theatre," (2) the medium, and (3) the light. Two times two times three gives twelve parts in all.[27]

Thus, Donne's terminology in setting out his division and his ways of putting together the structure whereby the text is developed into a discourse show his conscious assimilation of means of invention from patristic, scholastic, and Renaissance sources. But because of the function he attributes to the memory, he gives particular importance to those procedures that best serve to engage that faculty, and those are essentially grammatical procedures. By this division he endeavors to teach the understanding, to move the will, but above all, to plant the words of the text in the memory where their meaning can be present, branch out, and remain alive. "For to remember," he says, "to recollect our former understanding, and our former assenting, so far as to *doe* them, to Crowne them with action, that's true goodnesse" (9. 2. 606–8). By remembering the true doctrine we have been taught and the right course of action we have been shown and have resolved upon, we act. To experience the meaning of Scripture complicated with our lives is one with doing good.

SECTION B / MULTIPLYING THE WORDS OF SCRIPTURE

The multiple senses of an ambiguous verbal expression in Donne's text can complicate the structure of the sermon discourse as he sets it out in the *divisio*. The multivalence of the expression can be brought out by adducing, in the manner of patristic and medieval preachers, various other scriptural contexts in which it occurs. This procedure of drawing out various significations and consignifications of the words of the text also develops and fills out the body of the discourse; it dilates the division.

Donne speaks of the network of associations enclosed within Scripture in various terms. It is a garden set with plants; the words of the text are "fecund," the parts of the division are "branches" (6. 6. 265–66); "the word growes to signifie" (9. 15. 276).[1] A figurative expression is a packet in which meaning is enwrapped,[2] much is folded up or "implied" in it;[3] so the preacher must explicate and complicate these compact bundles of language. A recurring and careful representation of the precious resources of meaning in Scripture is the pearl:

When our Saviour forbids us to cast pearl before swine, we understand ordinarily in that place (Matt. 7:6), that by pearl, are understood the Scriptures; and when we consider the naturall generation and production of Pearl, that they grow bigger and bigger, by a continuall succession, and devolution of dew, and other glutinous moysture that falls upon them, and there condenses and hardens, so that a pearl is but a body of many shels, many crusts, many films, many coats enwrapped upon one another, To this Scripture which we have in hand, doth the Metaphor of pearl very properly appertain. [2. 15. 1–8][4]

He cites Jerome's observation that "'*Margarita est, et undique perforari potest*'; the Scripture is a Pearl, and might be bored through every where" (4. 8. 369–70).[5] The reader penetrates to the center of the text's significance by passing through a configuration of correspondences: "The Scriptures are made to agree with one another" (5. 1. 165). It is a sphere consistent in itself with its various elements aligned in patterns like a mosaic,[6] a kaleidoscope reflecting the light in a kind of ricochet: "The Scriptures are as a room wainscotted with looking-glass, we see all at once" (3. 1. 353–54).

One set of mirrors is that whereby things themselves are reflected in the verbal signs of scriptural language. Donne can be impatient with the fine points of philology, the "meere Grammaticall curiosity" of the textmen (10. 2. 185–86),[7] but he shows consistent interest in the sort of grammatical research that reveals the true natures and affinities of things by investigating the words that signify them. Although he does not often elaborate the text by working out the significative implications of its grammatical forms, the instances of such development reveal something about Donne's fundamental assumptions regarding sacred language.

As was apparent in the *Essays*, Donne early in his career was interested in the correlations between things and their names; this interest seems to have persisted through his years of preaching. He evidently shared the assumptions of the ancient grammatical commentators that the formal character of a word assigned to a thing represents the nature of the thing signified and that the network of words corresponds with real relationships among things. Adam gave creatures their names according to a knowledge of their natures, but he did not name himself because he did not understand himself.[8] Preaching at St. Paul's, Donne remarks, "Language must waite upon matter, and words upon things" (10. 4. 326–27). If words are alike, so are the things signified by those words. "The Book is Praise," he says of the Psalms, "the parts are Prayer. The name changes not the nature; Prayer and Praise is the same thing: The name scarce changes the name; Prayer and Praise is almost the same word; As the duties agree in the heart and mouth of a man, so the names agree in our ears" (5. 14. 78–82).

Conversely, if the words are different, so are the things signified by those words. This is the problem posed by the Hebrew parallelisms of the Old Testament that so puzzled the Fathers —whether or not pairs of synonyms designate different things. In dealing with such expressions, Donne is inclined rather to suppose that the difference in name does change the nature:

"The Holy Ghost is an eloquent Author, a vehement, and an abundant Author, but yet not luxuriant; he is far from a penurious, but as far from a superfluous style too. And therefore we doe not take these two words in the Text, 'To rejoyce,' and 'to be glad' (Ps. 90:14), to signifie meerely one and the same thing, but to be two beames, two branches, two effects, two expressings of this joy. We take them therefore, as they offer themselves in their roots, and first naturall propriety of the words" (5. 14. 720–27).[9] The grammarian would recognize the ensuing discussion, which distinguishes the two similar phrases, as a *differentia*. Donne occasionally resorts to the procedure of the grammatical commentators for bringing out the exact meaning of a word by adducing what it is not.[10]

Thus, the grammatical study of a word's formal character and of its associations in the network of language can prove informative about its meaning. So too can the study of the various significations of a scriptural word in its other contexts within the reflecting sphere of sacred language. "We proposed at first," says Donne on Prov. 14:31, "to consider our two parts, the fault, and the duty, in the elegancy of the words chosen by the holy Ghost here, (1) according to their origination, and extraction, in the nature of the words, and (2) in their latitude and extension, in their use, in other places of Scripture" (8. 12. 208–12).[11] Although it is the latter—adducing other places that elaborate an expression's meaning in Scripture—that is Donne's principal means of enlarging upon the words of the text, he does sometimes propose etymologies to further our understanding of the thing signified. This is not so much the scientific philology of the textmen as the grammatical commentators' amplification, for several times two derivations are accepted for a single word.[12]

Donne's consideration of a word's usage is usually confined to Scripture; only seldom does he cite classical instances.[13] Even the pattern of a word's occurrences in the Bible, data readily at hand in a concordance, can be meaningful. Donne considers as significant such patterns as the recurrent combination of a particular word with another, e.g., the collocation "day of visitation,"[14] or the frequency of the many general expressions for God's mercy and beneficence toward men.[15]

The "latitude and extension" of a word in the verse preached upon is drawn out by accumulating its significations and connotations in other scriptural contexts. Donne notes repeatedly that it is "the same word" or "the very word" of the text that occurs elsewhere,[16] as though the identical verbal representation always designates meanings that would reflect with some relevance on each other. Alternative significations are sometimes contrasted; so the preacher distinguishes the sense in his text from what it is elsewhere. To make careful distinctions in what is meant by a word can, as the scholastics recognized, sort out many a theological problem; and often when touching on a controversial matter, Donne contrasts the meanings of a scriptural expression in its various contexts. Preaching on Romans 8:16 ("The spirit it selfe beareth witnesse with our spirit [etc.]"), he says, "A slacknesse, a supineness, in consideration of the divers significations of this word 'Spirit,' hath occasioned divers errors, when the word hath been intended in one sense, and taken in another"(5. 2. 45–47). By adducing some dozen scriptural texts in which the word *spirit* occurs, he draws four distinctions in its attribution: "It is spoken of God, or of Angels, or of men, or of inferiour creatures." And a further differentiation is made: "Of God, it is spoken sometimes Essentially, sometimes Personally." Donne can thus go on to specify the exact sense of the word as it occurs in his text: "Now in this first Branch of this first Part of our Text, it is not of Angels, nor of men, nor of other creatures, but of God, and not of God Essentially, but Personally, that is, of the Holy Ghost."[17]

Here the consideration of a word's "latitude and extension" has served to sort out its several alternative significances. By thus adducing the various uses in other scriptural contexts, the preacher can also enrich and enhance a given meaning. By this means the ways in which a scriptural expression can be understood are multiplied; this procedure, like a "multiplying glass,"[18] makes more discernible the full abundance of a word's meaning when it is replaced in the text upon which the sermon is preached. The meaning is compounded as the significations in various places are elaborated (*multiplication*) and is then contracted back into the instance of the text as a pearl enwrapped with implications (*condensation*).[19] This linking of concording verses Donne once explicitly refers to as a "chain" *catena*:

So David uses this word (*"dixi,"* Ps. 32:5) in the person of another, *"Dixit insipiens,"* "The foole hath said," that is, *"In corde"* "said in his heart" that is, thought, "that there is no God" (Ps. 14:1). There speaking is thinking; and speaking is resolving too. So Davids son

Solomon uses the word, "Behold I purpose to build a house unto the Lord" (1 Kings 5:5) where the word is, "I say," I will doe it, Speaking is determining; and speaking is executing too, *"Dixit custodiam,"* "I said I will take heed to my wayes" (Ps. 39:1), that is, I will proceed and goe forward in the paths of God. . . . And all those linkes of this religious *Chaine,* Consideration, Resolution, Execution, Thought, Word, and Practise, are made out of this golden word, *"Amar, Dixi,"* I said I will doe it. And then *"Dixi confitebor"* (Ps. 32:5), I considered, that my best way was to confesse, and I resolved to doe so, and I did it; *"Dixi confitebor."* [9. 13. 242–306][20]

The same word takes on various senses from the different places in which it is understood, but when replaced in the sermon text, it seems then to transfer this richness of meaning to its context there.

The reading may be multiplied by adducing other translations of the passage. Donne often turns to the Hebrew, the Latin of the Vulgate, and the several English versions. The meaning rendered by one word in one language may have as its equivalent several words in the Bible of some other language. The preacher would thus be using a concordance in the one language to refer to places in a Bible of another language so distinguishing various meanings of the word. Donne differentiates several meanings for the Hebrew *Shamang,* translated in his text as "weeping," in such a way.

A word of that largenesse in the Scriptures, that sometimes in the Translation of the Septuagint, it signifies hearing, *Shamang,* is *audit,* God gives eare to our teares; sometimes it is beleeving, *Shamang,* is *Credit,* God gives faith, and credit to our teares; sometimes it is Affecting, *Shamang,* is *Miseretur,* God hath mercy upon us for our teares; sometimes it is Effecting, *Shamang,* is *Respondet,* God answers the petition of our teares; and sometimes it is Publication, *Shamang,* is *Divulgat,* God declares and manifests to others, by his blessings upon us, the pleasure that he takes in our holy and repentant teares. [6. 1. 315–24]

This cross-concordancing seems to assume, with Augustine, that translation into other languages provides room within which a word's meaning might grow.

Donne certainly came upon Augustine's doctrine of figurative signification in Nicholas of Lyra or in *De doctrina Christiana* early in his preaching career.[21] He remarks, with a marginal reference to Augustine, that "Christ is not so called Light, as he is called a Rock or a Cornerstone; not by a metaphore, but truly, and properly" (3. 17. 195–97).[22] Clearly here he is distinguishing between the proper and transferred senses. This distinction is expressed in other terms of his own: "Ordinarily in Scriptures, where this word 'lips' (Prov. 22:11) is not taken naturally, literally, narrowly, for that part of the body, but transferred to a figurative and larger sense, either it signifies speaking onely . . . or else it is enlarged to all manner of expressing mans ability to do service to that State in which God hath made his station" (1. 3. 855–62). The proper is the "primary" or "radical" meaning;[23] the transferred[24] is a "metaphor"[25] or an "emblem" or "hieroglyphic,"[26] and once is the sense "metaphysically" taken.[27]

Augustine proposed in *De doctrina Christiana* that a knowledge of natural history would provide the preacher with some indication of how a figurative expression in Scripture is to be understood.[28] What is meant by the thing as a sign can be ascertained by considering what is relevant to the thing in the world—its nature, qualities, circumstances, etc. Donne met with this procedure of exegetical invention in patristic writings:

The Fathers taking the words as they found them, and fastning with a spirituall delight, as their devout custome was, their Meditations upon the figurative and Metaphoricall phrase of purging by Hyssop (Ps. 51:7), have found purgative vertues in that plant, and made usefull and spirituall applications thereof, for the purging of our soules from sin. In this does S. Ambrose, and Augustine, and Hierome agree, that Hyssop hath vertue in it proper for the lungs, in which part, as it is the furnace of breath, they place the seat of pride and opposition against the Truth, making their use of that which was said of Saul, "That he breathed out threatnings and slaughter against the Disciples of the Lord" (Acts 9:1). And by this interpretation, Davids disease that he must be purged of, should be pride. [5. 15. 454–65][29]

Donne speaks of turning to "the Book of the World" or "the Book of Creatures,"[30] of coming to understand what God conveys about Himself in the language of nature;[31] so he does, as might be expected, consult Pliny on the natural history of salamanders.[32] But for him as for the medieval expositors, it was the Fathers, who, as another Adam, had made conventional the meaning of those figurative signs taken from nature in Scripture.

Donne diversified the signification of transferred expressions much as he had extended the sense of words that signify properly, i.e., by investigating what meaning the figure acquires in its use elsewhere in Scripture. But there is this difference: although the attribution of meaning that gives significance to proper expressions is shared by all readers of the language, the conventions by which the meaning of transferred expressions is interpreted are shared only by those who are familiar with how the Fathers read Scripture. Thus, when the preacher concords words that are signs of things that are also signs of other things, he concords them along with their patristic glosses. Since such signs take on transferred senses in addition to their proper senses, the possible ways of multiplying the words of the text are now doubled but are still confined within the sphere of the Word and its authoritative interpreters.

A thing may be appropriated as a sign in more diverse ways than may a word because any of its many characteristics may be taken up to express meaning by analogy. Augustine said that the figurative significations of a single expression could be so different as to be contrary, *in malo* and *in bono*.[33] Donne illustrates this with a familiar example, that of the lion as both Christ and Satan: "And of 'light' (2 Cor. 4:6), we say no more in this place, but this; that in all the Scriptures, in which the word 'Light' is very often metaphorically applyed, it is never applyed in an ill sence. Christ is called a 'Lyon' (Rev. 5:5): but there is an ill Lyon too, that 'seeks whom he may devour' (1 Pet. 5:8). . . . But Christ is the light of the world, and no ill thing is call'd light" (4. 3. 503–9). Water is one of the metaphors most often read by Donne in a variety of ways. "Baptisme, and Sin, and Tribulation, and Death are all called in the Scripture by that name, 'Waters'" (9. 3. 439–40). This is a medieval *distinctio*. These several transferred senses for the thing *water* are distinguished by adducing several scriptural texts and the Fathers' interpretations upon them. Sometimes only one signification is allowed for a particular place, but even so the review of other uses is considered enlightening.[34]

The concordance of a transferred expression may yield but a single signification, which has, however, been elaborated in the course of explaining its appropriateness in several contexts. In the following passage referring to Rev. 7:1, the patristic attribution of meaning is again explicit:

Now as all the parts, and the style and phrase of this Book is figurative and Metaphoricall, so is it no unusual Metaphor, even in other Bookes of the Scripture too, to call the Ministers, and Preachers of Gods Word, by the name of winds. "Arise O North, and come O South, and blow on my Garden, that the spices thereof may flow out" (Song of Sol. 4:16), hath alwayes been understood to be an invitation, a compellation from Christ to his Ministers, to dispense and convey salvation, by his Gospel, to all Nations. And upon those words, *"Producit ventos,"* "He bringeth winds out of his treasuries," and *"Educit nubes,"* "He bringeth clouds from the ends of the earth" (Ps. 135:7), *"Puto Praedicatores et nubes et ventos,"* says S. Augustine, I think that the Holy Ghost means both by his clouds and by his winds, the Preachers of his Word, the Ministers of the Gospel; . . . Clouds because their bodies are seen, winds because their working is felt. [10. 1. 679–93][35]

Scriptural use here creates its own sphere of interconnected signs consistent among themselves.

However, Augustine's translated ambiguous signs, transferred expressions with several diverse senses in Scripture, afford the occasion for the most elaborate development by multiplying the words of the text. Thus, Donne says of Jacob's staff in a sermon on Gen. 32:10, "He came away then, and he came away poor: *'in baculo'* with a staff; God expresses sometimes abundance, and strength, in *'baculo,'* in that word. Oftentimes he calls plenty, by that name, the staff of bread (Lev. 26:26). But Jacob's is no Metaphoricall staff, it is a real staff, the companion, the support of a poor travelling man" (1. 7. 412–16). However, a synoptic problem makes necessary some distinction among the uses of this actual staff. Matthew (10:10) has Christ forbidding the Apostles to carry a staff, while in Mark (6:8–9) he explicitly instructs them to have one. Two other texts (1 Cor. 4:21; Ps. 23:4) help to account for this apparent discrepancy: "Christ spoke this but once, but in his language, the Syriack, he spoke it in a word that hath two significations. *Shebat*, is both *Baculus defensorius* and *Baculus sustentatorius*; A staff of sustentation, and a staff of defence. God that spoke in Christs Syriack, spoke in the Evangelists Greek too; and both belong to us; and both the Evangelists intending the use of the staff, and not the staff itself, S. Matthew allows a staff of sustentation, and support; and such a staff, and no more had Jacob, a staff to sustain him upon his way" (1. 7. 428–36).

Further concording on the word yields figurative senses for both the staff of defense and the staff of support. A staff for support is composed of a man's natural faculties upon which he relies on his way in the world; misused it can become the instrument of unscrupulous ambition, a weapon to the detriment of himself and others, although, Donne adds, to some it is granted to wield beneficially this token of power. Having alluded to 2 Kings 18:21 ("Now, behold, thou trustest upon the staff of this bruised reed, even upon Egypt, on which if a man lean, it will go into his hand, and pierce it"), he continues:

When God hath given thee a staff of thine own, a leading staff, a competency, a conveniency to lead thee through the difficulties, and encombrances of this world, if thou put a pike in thy staff, murmuring at thine own, envying superiours, oppressing inferiours, then his piked staff is not thy staff, nor Gods staff, but it is *"Baculus inimici hominis"*; and the envious man in the Gospel, is the devil (Num. 17:1–8; Mark 15:10). If God have made thy staff to blossom, and bear ripe fruit in a night, enriched thee, preferred thee a pace, this is not thy staff; it is a Mace, and a mark of thy office, that he hath made thee his Steward of those blessings. [1. 7. 458–67]

Thus, the figurative sense of "the staff of support,"—the abilities and accomplishments upon which a man depends—is extended, multiplied, further by adducing two other scriptural contexts in which the word *staff* or *rod* occurs. The text from Kings gives the opportunity to consider how relying carelessly upon one's own resources and achievements can prove injurious even to oneself; and the passage from Numbers, in which the rod of Levi blossoms overnight as a sign of the Lord's favor on the priestly tribe, affords the additional consideration that legitimized authority is God given.

Precisely in the manner of the medieval *distinctio*, three or four transferred significations have been distinguished. All are then condensed, replaced in the Genesis text—"for with my staff I passed over this Jordan"—and their relevance in the original context is worked out:

Hath this then been thy state with Jacob, that thou hast not onely been without the staff of bread, plenty, and abundance of temporal blessings, but without the staff of defence, that when the world hath snarl'd and barked at thee, and that thou wouldst justly have beaten a dog (1 Sam. 17:43), yet thou couldst not finde a staff, thou hadst no means to right thy self? yet he hath not left thee without a staff of support, a staff to try how deep the waters be, that thou art to wade through, that is thy Christian constancy, and thy Christian discretion. [1. 7. 436–44]

To end this, a mans own staff, truly, properly, is nothing but his own natural faculties: nature is ours, but grace is not ours; and he that is left to this staff of his own, for heaven, is as ill provided, as Jacob was, for this world, when he was left to his own staff at Jordan, when he was banished; and banished in poverty, and banished alone. [1. 7. 467–72][36]

Alan read back into Matt. 16:19, in his sermon on that verse, the several senses for "kingdom of heaven" that he had distinguished by adducing other instances of that expression in Scripture. Donne proceeds in just this way here with *staff* but does not set out such a rigid scheme of corresponding patterns. In his hands it seems the figure has been developed according to its protean adaptability rather than by working through a set of possible acceptations. Nonetheless, behind his fluid prose stands a careful procedure for exegetical invention.

Thus, the text's words, proper and transferred, signify simply or diversely as scriptural use and patristic reading establish their meanings. According to Donne's own practice, then, it should enhance his reader's appreciation of his exposition if the instances of his development of a particular figure would themselves be concorded. The implications that each use has for every other in his preaching would thereby be more fully realized. The sermons are, of course, not Scripture; but as Donne develops a text he is reading Scripture to us, so that our reading of him must involve reading what he is reading according to the procedures by which he reads. We must endeavor to draw out to its limit the extent of his own appreciation of that Author whose eloquence knows no bounds, the Holy Spirit.

Those scriptural figures that receive the most elaborate multiplication and condensation are usually associated somewhere in Donne's preaching with the sacramental elements—blood: wine, flesh:bread, and water. Such a metaphor is to be concorded here; it is of vessels, pots, and bottles. The core around which the significations and consignifications are wrapped consists of a cluster of scriptural verses:

And it came to pass, as they were eating of the pottage, that they cried out, and said, O thou man of God, there is death in the pot. [2 Kings 4:40; see 5. 15. 74–75]

And he shall break it as the breaking of the potters' vessel, that is broken in pieces; he shall not spare: so that there shall not be found in the bursting of it a sherd to take fire from the hearth, or to take water withal out of the pit. [Is. 30:14; see 2. 8. 521–26; 2. 11. 169–71; 5. 4. 294–97]

Thus saith the Lord of hosts; Even so will I break this people and this city, as one breaketh a potter's vessel, that cannot be made whole again. [Jer. 19:11; see 2. 8. 530–32; 10. 9. 418]

Neither do men put new wine into old bottles: else the bottles break, and the wine runneth out, and the bottles perish: but they put new wine into new bottles, and both are preserved. [Matt. 9:17; see 5. 4. 289–94]

Nay but, O man, who art thou that repliest against God? Shall the thing formed say to him that formed it, Why hast thou made me thus? Hath not the potter power over the clay; of the same lump to make one vessel unto honour, and another unto dishonour? [Rom. 9:20–21; see 6. 9. 197–201]

In each instance Donne takes the vessel, pot, or bottle to represent man; it is a translated but not an ambiguous expression. The sign and the thing designated by it must share some property that makes the similitude appropriate. Here it is the substance, the dust of the earth, out of which both are made. The name *Adam* given to the first man refers to the matter out of which he was created, for in Hebrew it means "red clay."

In Romans Paul, who may have had the passages from the prophets in mind, makes it clear that he means the earthen vessel to stand for man. Donne develops the comparison to suggest the use proper to the artifact: "as I am Adam, a man of earth, (wrought upon that wheele), and as I am a Christian, a vessel in his house, a member of his Church (wrought upon that wheele)" (4. 6. 466–68).[37] Man is fashioned as a utensil of service to be used for God's purposes. The primeval mud out of which God formed Adam may fittingly be thought of as red in color—red from the blood of his own self-destruction and from the shame of his original sin but red also from our partaking of Christ's blood, the Red Sea of His sacrifice.[38] Yet we are remade vessels of innocence and righteousness[39] by His redemptive cleansing of us; Adam's clay is whitened. "We have dyed our selves in sinnes, as red as Scarlet: we have drowned our selves in such a red Sea. But as a garment, that were washed in the Red Sea, would come out white, ('so wonderfull works hath God done at the Red Sea,' says David [Ps. 106:22]) so doth his whitenesse worke through our red, and makes this Adam, this red earth, '*Calculum candidum,*' that white stone" ("To him that overcometh will I give . . . a white stone," Rev. 2:17) (9. 1. 721–26).[40]

Men and pottery have in common also the property of being fragile. Because of this the prophets find it appropriate to express the threat of God's judgment on a disobedient people utterly dependent on His will by speaking of pots shattered to bits. In a sermon on a Gospel text that warns those who reject the Word of their punishment ("Whosoever shall fall on this stone, shall be broken; but on whomsoever it shall fall, it will grind him to powder," Matt. 21:44), Donne takes up these prophetic texts on pots: "'*Comminuam eos in pulverem*,' sayeth he, 'I will beate them as small as dust before the winds' (Ps. 18:42), and tread them as flat as clay in the streets, the breaking thereof shall be like the breaking of a Potters vessell, which is broken without any pity" (2. 8. 519–23). Several scriptural stones, even hailstones, that could shatter the fragile vessel are concorded in this sermon: "'*Sicut pluit laqueos*,' says David (Ps. 11:6), As God rained springs and snares upon them in this world (abundance of temporall blessings to be occasions of sinne unto them:) So '*pluet grandinem*' (Ps. 105:32), he shall raine such haile-stones upon them, as shall grinde them to powder" (2. 8. 568–72). With another verse from the Psalms, the texts quoted here constitute a chain of texts that recur in Donne's preaching:[41] (1) Ps. 69:22, "Let their table become a *snare* before them"; (2) Ps. 11:6, "Upon the wicked he shall *rain snares*, fire and brimstone, and an horrible tempest"; (3) Ps. 105:32, "He gave them *hail* for *rain*, and flaming fire in their land." The verses are interlinked this way: (1) snare; (2) rain, snares; (3) rain, hail. Other instances for hail, such as Exod. 9:25 or Rev. 16:21, might be adduced.

In a later sermon this same series of associations is again attached to a vessel text:

As in Gods Temporall blessings that he raines downe upon us, it is much in our gathering, and inning, and spending them, whether it shall be *"frumenti"* or *"laqueorum,"* whether this shall prove such a shoure, as shall nourish our soule spiritually, in thankfulnesse to God, and in charitable workes towards his needy Servants, or whether it shall prove "a shoure of snares," to minister occasions of tentations; so when he raines afflictions upon us, it is much in our gathering, whether it shall be *"roris"* or *"grandinis,"* whether it shall be a "shoure of fatning dew" upon us (Ps. 65:12), or a shoure of "Egyptian haile-stones" (Exod. 9:25), to batter us in pieces, "as a Potters Vessell, that cannot be renewed." [10. 9. 409–18]

Thus in this passage, too, progressing from snares to rain to hailstones to battered vessels, Donne leads into the figure of men broken by God's judgment as shattered pots with the same chain of Psalm texts.

For the reprobate sinner there can be no pardon at the final judgment; he shall be broken irredeemably: "And briefly this grinding to powder, is to be brought to that desperate and irrecoverable estate in sinne, as that no medicinall correction from God, no breaking, no bowing, no melting, no moulding can bring him to any good fashion" (2. 8. 501–4). Up to this final desperate predicament the tribulations we suffer are sent for our restoration and recasting. "As long as I have God by the hand," says Donne, "and feele his loving care of me, I can admit any waight of his hand; any fornace of his heating. Let God mould me, and then melt me againe, let God make mee, and then breake me againe, as long as he establishes and maintaines a rectified assurance in my soul, that at last he meanes to make me a Vessell of honour, to his Glory" (5. 16. 624–29). We are tried in that furnace by encountering affliction that both hurts and heals, fires and melts, perfects and destroys.[42] And death is the ultimate suffering that completes our remaking: "God did not induce death, death was not in his purpose; but *veluti medium opportunum, quo vas confractum rursus fingeretur,* As a means, whereby a broken vessell might be made up againe, God took death, and made it to serve that purpose, That men by the grave might be translated to heaven" (6. 2. 366–70).

Men and pots are alike too in that they both can receive and hold things. Unbroken vessels can contain the grace poured out for redemption, but for the sinner uttterly shattered by the irretrievable decree of God, there is no means to catch and hold the submission or mercy that might save him: "And in the breaking thereof, saith the Prophet, there 'is not found a sheard to take fire at the hearth, nor to take water at the pit': that is, they shall be incapable of any beam of grace in themselves from heaven, or any spark of zeale in themselves, (not a sheard to fetch fire at the hearth) and incapable of any drop of Christs blood from heaven or of any teare of contrition in themselves, not a sheard to fetch water at the pit" (2. 8. 524–30).[43] The development of the figure here touches again on the sacramental elements of water and blood, which cannot be received by vessels smashed by divine judgment but can be held by vessels made and remade into utensils in the service of God's church.

Although the sacrament may wash redness from the pot, if lightly received it may be the cause of its breaking:

And into old vessells, (our sin-worne bodies) we put in once a year, some drops, of new wine, of the bloud of our Saviour Christ Jesus, in the Sacrament, (when we come to his table, as to a vintage, because of the season, and we receive by the Almanack, because it is Easter) and this new wine so taken in, "breakes the vessells," (as Christ speakes in that similitude) And his breaking shall be, as the "breaking of a Potters pot. . . . " No way in the Church of God, to repaire that Man, because he hath made either a Mockery, or at best, but a Civill action of Gods institution in the Church. [5. 4. 289–99]

Even if the sacramental wine—given as a means of redemption—can be received, it may thus prove instead to be the occasion of the vessel's breaking, i.e., of God's judgment.

Our reading of a passage in Donne's sermons where this transferred expression *vessels* appears without explicit scriptural reference and without full development can be multiplied out and condensed back again by remembering the biblical verses that underlie the figure and the significations and associations wrapped around them in Donne's development of vessels, pots, and bottles elsewhere in his preaching. Thus, we apply his procedures of reading Scripture in our reading of that reading of his.

In a sermon preached on Rom. 8:16 ("The Spirit it selfe beareth witnesse with our spirit, that we are the children of God"), Donne considers the "we" of the text first in its most inclusive sense to be all mankind:

In the great field of clay, of red earth, that man was made of, and mankind, I am a clod; I am a man, I have my part in the Humanity; But man was worse than annihilated again. When Satan in that serpent was come, as Hercules with his club into a potters shop, and had broke all the vessels, destroyed all mankind, And the gracious promise of a Messias to redeeme all mankind, was shed and spread upon all, I had my drop of that dew of Heaven, my sparke of that fire of heaven, in the universall promise, in which I was involved. [5. 2. 449–57]

Again man is a pot that, as it is broken and dispersed in fragments or as it is intact and receives and holds God's grace, represents our condition, whether irretrievably destroyed or graciously redeemed. "The field of clay" suggests the indistinguishable commonness of that substance from which we are all made. Man, like pots, is composed out of the dust of the earth and fashioned for service. But we are shattered to bits because of our sin. The implicit etymology of Adam, "red earth," here serves to offset the possible inference from what follows, that our Fall is due only to Satan ("When Satan in that serpent was come"); for we are thereby reminded that we are red from the blood of our own self-murder and red from the shame of it. Our fall has been as violent and as utterly annihilating as the destruction of the chinaware displayed in a potter's shop that is smashed to pieces by the flailing of Hercules's club. In another sermon Donne seems to distinguish Hercules's club as a force of senseless destruction from the sword of God's righteous judgment.[44] There is thus here the suggestion particularly of the brutal and indiscriminate devastation that we brought on ourselves by our first disobedience. But Christ's coming has made it possible for us to be remade entire again ("the gracious promise of a Messias to redeeme all mankind, was shed and spread upon all") so that we may all catch and hold the "dew" of His grace (Ps. 65:12), the "fire" from His hearth (Isa. 30:14). The images from the prophets, however, remind us that if we repeatedly spurn God's attempts to turn us to Him, He will not withhold His judgment but will rain down hail upon us and so break us again into pieces.

As the reader's mind meditates upon the words of Scripture and follows out the networks of association, his line of thought seems to bounce back into the center and out again in another direction, like light reflected in a never-ending ricochet. The meaning is multiplied—radiated in different directions by concordancing—and is bounced back and forth by the mirrors of reality, language, and emblematic signification. Grammatical procedures of invention develop the words of a text by such diversification and reflection. Memory here has room in which to play, a room "wainscotted with looking-glass."

SECTION C / DONNE'S SERMON ON PS. 32:1-2

Donne sets out the *divisio* of this text as the framework upon which the sermon takes shape. Multiplying the words of Scripture is one means of filling out that structure. The study of a single sermon can exemplify how these two procedures come together in a discourse. The sermon taken here (9. 11), of uncertain date, is the first of a series on Psalm 32, one of David's penitential songs. It is a representative instance of Donne's preaching, although he does not always pursue controversial theological matters to the extent that he does here.

The wording of the verses is that of the Authorized Version of 1611, but the latinized title[1] is included as part of the text:

Davidis erudiens
Psalm 32:1 Blessed is he whose transgression is forgiven, whose sin is covered;
32:2 Blessed is the man, unto whom the Lord imputeth not iniquitie, and in whose spirit there is no guile.

Already in citing his text Donne has touched on a disputed point, for the authenticity of the titles to the Psalms was affirmed by Rome and challenged by Geneva. Thus, the Calvinist commentator Wolfgang Musculus (1497–1563) dismisses the titles as not being "established by certain reasons, so that they cannot be admitted with undoubted truth."[2] The Jesuit Johannes Lorinus (1559–1634) accepts them on the authority of the church: "Whatever the origin of this title and the others, because they are in our received edition, they have authority and ought to be retained."[3] Donne, with Rome, consistently assumes their canonicity,[4] although for different reasons. "We make it justly an argument," he says on this occasion, "for the receiving the Titles of the Psalms into the Body of Canonicall Scriptures, that they are as ancient as the Psalmes themselves" (9. 11. 13–15). It is not because of their occurrence in the Vulgate but because of their supposed antiquity that he accepts them.

In his *divisio* Donne sets out four parts for the sermon: (1) David's teaching; (2) the believer's understanding of blessedness; (3) God's merciful acts of reconciliation; (4) the sinner's obligation to show good faith. The division is so made that each part receives some of the words of the text.

The title ("*Davidis erudiens*") is distributed in part one: "That so great a Master as David, proceedeth by way . . . of instruction in fundamentall things" (9. 11. 27–29). The independent clauses of the two verses ("Blessed is he . . . Blessed is the man") are taken together as part two, since the second clause but repeats the first: "the first lesson . . . is Blessednesse" (9.

11. 30–31). The first three relative clauses ("he whose transgression is forgiven, whose sin is covered, . . . unto whom the Lord imputeth not iniquitie"), all of which involve actions on God's part in overcoming our separation from Him, are considered together as part three: "this Blessednesse [consists] in our Reconciliation to God, (for we were created in a state of friendship with God, our rebellion put us into a state of hostility, and now we need a Reconciliation . . .)" (9. 11. 50–53). The fourth relative clause ("he in whose spirit there is no guile"), which completes the verses, involves action on our part in reestablishing a favorable relationship with God and constitutes part four: "But then . . . when God hath presented himselfe, and offered his peace, in all these, there is also something to be done on our part; for though the Forgiving of Transgression, The Covering of sinne, The not Imputing of Iniquity, proceed onely from God, yet God affords these to none but him, *In whose spirit there is no guile*" (9. 11. 59–64).

Such are the members extracted by division from the scriptural text: (1) even so learned a master as David taught basic doctrine (*"Davidis erudiens"*); (2) an understanding of blessedness as reconciliation to God is fundamental to Christian belief ("Blessed is he . . . Blessed is the man"); (3) reconciliation consists in overcoming the separation from God that we have caused by our sin ("he whose transgression is forgiven, whose sin is covered, . . . unto whom the Lord imputeth not iniquitie"); (4) we on our part must meet a condition for that reconciliation ("he in whose spirit there is no guile"). Only small liberty has been taken with the order of the text in part two by including the opening independent clauses of both verses (32:1, "Blessed is he . . ."; 32:2, "Blessed is the man") together, for the two phrases are virtually identical in wording.

In the restatement parts two and three coalesce; so the whole division can be encompassed by those factors that together comprise a teaching situation—teacher, subject matter, and student: "And so you have all that belongs to the Master, and his manner of teaching, David Catechising; And all that belongs to the Doctrine and the Catechisme, *Blessednesse*, That is Reconciliation to God, notified in those three acts of his mercy; And all that belongs to the Disciple, that is to be Catechized, A docile, an humble, a sincere heart, *'In whose spirit there is no guile'*" (9. 11. 65–70). This turns the keys of necessity and sufficiency for

Donne's division. The logical completeness of the text's partition is thus assured by correlating its parts with the constituent parts of a virtual whole, the factors necessary and sufficient for instruction.

For the most part, the first, second, and fourth sections of the text are developed with commonplaces, but the third is treated grammatically. The three relative clauses that constitute part three are taken up again in part four, where the preacher considers the conditions we ourselves must meet in order to receive God's acts of reconciliation toward us. "And therefore," says Donne, having completed topical exposition of the fourth section of the text, "suffer your consideration to turn back a little upon this object, that there may be *Dolus in spiritu*, 'Guile in the spirit,' in our pretence to all those parts of Blessednesse, which David recommends to us in this Catechisme, In the 'Forgivenesse of transgressions,' In the 'Covering of sin,' In the 'Not imputing of iniquity'" (9. 11. 632–37). He thus reviews the grammatical development of the words of section three from the point of view of what man should do to accept and cooperate with God's grace. In this analysis of the sermon, the parts developed topically (1, 2, and part of 4) will be examined first, and then both readings of the three relative clauses (3 and the other part of 4) will be considered. The grammatical development in the reading and rereading of the third section of the text comprises about a third of the sermon.

Augustine is cited explicitly more often than any other non-scriptural author—some ten times in all. In passages of topical development, the allusions are to various works, insofar as remarks so Augustinian can be traced to particular sources;[5] but where the language of the text is itself multiplied, the allusions are to that Father's *Enarratio* on this Psalm.[6] Donne was clearly working with Augustine's exposition before him.

In the first part, Donne *collects* from the title of the Psalm (*"Davidis erudiens"*) the notion that since even the learned and accomplished David stooped to teach the elementary tenets of doctrine, there is no reason why any other of God's spokesmen should presume that the divine Word must be proclaimed with a show of erudition and eloquence. "Not the spirit of Rhetorique," says Donne, "nor the spirit of Mathematiques, and Demonstration, But, 'The spirit of the Lord, the Rock of Israel spake by me,' sayes he [David, 2 Sam. 23:2–3]; He boasts not that he had delivered himselfe in strong, or deepe, or mysterious Arts, that was not his Rock; but his Rock was the Rock of Israel, His way was to establish the Church of God upon fundamentall Doctrines" (9. 11. 89–95). He mentions other great authors of the Bible—Moses, Daniel, and Paul—who, although enormously learned in the liberal arts and sciences, did not make apparent display of their vast knowledge in their writings. In another sermon in a similar passage, Donne includes the prophet Isaiah along with the others (4. 6. 145). It was the tradition of scriptural expositors, as it had been the habit of grammatical commentators, to attribute great learning to the authors they were glossing.

However, Donne adds, "Not that a Divine should be ignorant of either; either ornaments of humane, or mysteries of divine knowledge" (9. 11. 122–23), and he cites the opinions and examples of the Fathers in support of the point. He quotes from the passage in Augustine's *De doctrina Christiana* that interprets the spoiling of the Egyptians to mean that the Christian may avail himself of the achievements of pagan culture to serve the new purposes of the church. Donne may have had in mind as well Gregory the Great's exposition of 1 Sam. 13:19–20 ("Now there was no smith found throughout all the land of Israel, for the Philistines said, Lest the Hebrews make them swords or spears. But all the Israelites went down to the Philistines, to sharpen every man his share, and his coulter, and his ax and his mattock"). The teacher of merely secular letters is not to be found among God's people, but in order to acquire instruction in such arts, they must descend to the Philistines and then reascend to the study of sacred Scripture. "Thus Moses," says Gregory, "who set forth for us the initial portion of the divine utterances, did not first learn sacred things; but, so that he might be able to grasp and express such things, he applied his as yet unformed mind to all the Egyptian arts and sciences. Isaiah exceeded all the other prophets in eloquence because . . . he was so accomplished and so splendidly trained. Paul, another who was chosen to bear God's Word, was instructed at the feet of Gamaliel before he was snatched up into paradise and raised to the third heaven."[7] Thus, Gregory mentions several of the same biblical authors that Donne names in the same context. Although Donne returns to the notion collected from the title and seems overall to stress the importance of plain doctrinal teaching, he is certainly not in disagreement with the Fathers about the usefulness of an education in the liberal arts as preparation for the proclaiming of God's Word.

In the second part Donne observes that the philosophers, reasoning only from nature, have been unable to say wherein true blessedness consists. Their uncertainty is reflected in the grammatical form of the first word of the verses: "And as these Philosophers could never tell us, what this blessedness was, so Divines themselves, and those who are best exercised in the language of the Holy Ghost, the Originall tongue of this Text, cannot give us a cleare Grammatical understanding of this first word, in which David expresses this Blessednesse, *'Ashrei,'* which is here Translated 'Blessed.' They cannot tell, whether it be an Adverb . . . Or whether it be a Plurall Noun" (9. 11. 172–81). Thus, the formal character of the Hebrew word for "Blessed" corresponds with the nature of the thing signified; the ambivalence of the word's grammatical category matches the ambivalence of the idea.

Still, the philosophers recognized that man strives for happiness above all, and David, "who is elder then they" (9. 11. 193), also places happiness foremost. Lorinus, to whom Donne refers elsewhere as "a learned and a laborious Jesuit" (8. 4. 18) and whose exhaustive commentary on the Psalter fills three folio volumes, noted that this Psalm begins with blessedness as does the first Psalm.[8] Donne too draws significance from this configuration: "Davids Alpha is *'Beatus vir'* (Ps. 1:1), O the Blessednesse of righteous men! And Davids Omega is *'Laudate Dominum'* (Ps. 150:6), O that men would therefore blesse the Lord! And therefore, as he begins this Book with Gods blessing for man, so he ends it with mans praising of God" (9. 11. 198–202). So the psalmist comprehends and encompasses all that pertains to man's foremost concern, his happiness, in accepting God's reconciliations and approaches toward him and in praising God for them. David puts first what is foremost and finishes with what completes. Thus, even the formal arrangement of the Psalter is taken to be meaningful. Donne, with Andrewes, seems to accept Jerome's notion of the *ordo mysterium.* "The words," he says elsewhere, "are the Parts, and we invert not, we trouble not the Order; the Holy Ghost hath laid them fitliest for our use, in the Text it selfe, and so we take them" (5. 14. 669–71).

Donne then distinguishes two senses of blessedness—blessedness in this life and blessedness in the hereafter, "inchoation" and "consummation" (9. 11. 217, 215)—according to the "gradation" by which the *divisio* is sometimes made.[9] He does not elaborate on the bliss of heaven, since it exceeds man's powers of comprehension; but happiness here on earth is said to consist in knowing how we may be reconciled to God and ordering our wills in accord with that understanding. "And the end of knowing our selves," he says, "is to know how we are disposed for that which is our end, that is this Blessednesse; which . . . [is] well collected and summed by S. Augustine, '*Beatus qui habet quicquid vult, et nihil mali vult,*' He onely is blessed, that desires nothing but that which is good for him and hath all that" (9. 11. 257–62). This quotation seems to be from the *De Trinitate,* a work in which Augustine investigates the faculties of the mind and the vestiges there of the image of God in which we were made. This, then, is how blessedness and self-knowledge are associated. Man's created nature bears in the composition of its mental faculties—the memory, the understanding, and the will— the vestiges of the Triune God Who made it. If man uses his understanding to recognize himself as the creature that he is—if he uses his faculties in a way consistent with their formation— he will come to know how he may be reconciled with his Creator. Man can thus direct the will to its proper object and can desire what will fulfill his nature. Only in this way is it possible for him to be happy in this life. David in this Psalm is giving instruction in religious doctrine so that man might better understand his relationship to God and attain the blessedness for which he longs.

The preacher, like David, is endeavoring to bring his hearers to God. We have seen that in his *divisiones* Donne often explains that the sermon is meant to engage these three faculties of the mind—the trinity of the understanding, the will, and the memory—two of which figured importantly in the Augustinian conception of blessedness. The faculty of the understanding is taught doctrinal truths primarily by topical procedures. Donne will, then, appropriately rely on development by topic when he teaches the understanding the necessary concepts for disposing the will to reconciliation with God.

This he does in a portion of the fourth part of the sermon (9. 11. 538–637, skipping over the third part in our analysis), where the last section of the text, "he in whose spirit there is no guile," is taken up. These words make the point that we on our part must cooperate with God's reconciliatory mercies toward us. We show our good faith by repudiating sin, seeking forgiveness, and making restitution. This raises, of course, the issue of faith and works around which so much theological controversy raged during the Reformation period. Here, where the understanding must be taught fundamental tenets of doctrine about which there is much disagreement, Donne relies on procedures of topical logic. Seemingly contradictory propositions on the issue are extracted from other biblical passages given as "proof texts." St. Paul adduces these same two verses from Psalm 32 in the course of expounding the doctrine of justification, and Donne cites this first: "The Comment and interpretation of S. Paul, hath made the sense and meaning of this place cleare: 'To him that worketh, the reward is of debt, but to him that beleeveth, and worketh not, his faith is counted for righteousnesse, Even as David describeth the blessednesse of Man,' sayes the Apostle there (Rom. 4:4–6) and so proceeds with the very words of this Text" (9. 11. 540–45). The cross-reference was certainly in the margin of his Authorized Version,[10] but Donne's attention could as well have been drawn to the Pauline interpretation by glancing at Augustine's second *Enarratio* on this Psalm.[11]

Donne, however, will not allow an exclusively Calvinist reading to stand without qualification; he cites other texts to the contrary. "Doth the Apostle then, in this Text," asks Donne, "exclude the Cooperation of Man? Differs this proposition, That the man in whom God imprints these beames of Blessednesse, must be without guile in his spirit, from those other propositions, '*Si vis ingredi*, If thou wilt enter into life, keepe the Commandements' (Matt. 19:17); And, '*Maledictus qui non*, Cursed is he that performes not all' (Deut. 27:26)? " (9. 11. 545–51). The propositions are not formally set out, but an attempt is made to reconcile these seeming contradictions by the logical principle that the prior cause includes the intermediate cause: "And these propositions are truly all one, '*Tantum credideris*, Onely beleeve, and you shall be saved' (Luke 8:50); And, '*Fac hoc et vives*, Doe this, and you shall be saved' (Luke 10:28); As it is truly all one purpose, to say, If you live you may walke, and to say, If you stretch out your legges, you may walk. . . . To attribute an action to the next Cause, or to the Cause of that Cause, is, to this purpose, all one" (9. 11. 557–64). Donne has thus extracted propositions from various texts in which the doctrinal point is fairly explicitly made and has then used these general statements in a logical line of argument. The development may thus be said to be *methodical*, but not rigorously so. In fact, the course of his reasoning is left to be inferred rather than being explicitly enunciated. Still, here, where the understanding is to be taught what man must know and what he must do to be reconciled with God, Donne has used what we would term procedures of topical logic.

Donne delimits for the English church a middle position between faith and works, between the hard-line Protestant doctrine of justification and the Roman Catholic teachings on penance. Thus, he accepts the value of contrition, confession, and satisfaction for repentance but understands them "with more exactnesse and severity then they [the Romanists] doe" (9. 11. 581–82).

Luther, in his exposition of the Psalm, condemns the self-deception of a man who "is pious out of fear of hell or hope of heaven, not because of God."[12] The Council of Trent was obliged to reply: "That imperfect contrition which is called 'attrition' and which arises usually from thoughts of sin's infamy or from the fear of hell and its torments, if it replaces the will to sin with the hope of forgiveness, this synod declares that it then does not make a man a hypocrite and a worse sinner, but is even a gift of God sent by the Holy Spirit."[13] Donne likely has in mind this canon when he mentions the opinions of "some of them" regarding attrition (9. 11. 583, 607). On this point he inclines rather to the Lutheran position. Thus, by distinguishing the last relative clause of the Psalm verses ("in whose spirit there is no guile") from the preceding three, Donne provides the occasion to distinguish the doctrine of the English church from that of continental Protestantism while explaining also Canterbury's differences with Rome.

When thus addressing the understanding on controversial points of doctrine, Donne uses topical procedures; but when he speaks of the ways God reaches out to overcome the separation between Himself and ourselves, the preacher turns instead to the resources of the art of grammar. By means of drawing distinctions and associations among words, he involves the memories of his hearers in ruminating upon God's promises and acts of reconciliation recorded throughout Scripture and also engages the meanings of the words with each person's own experience of God's reconciliatory mercies. This Donne does in the third part of the sermon and in a portion of the fourth, where the first three relative clauses of the text—"he whose transgression is forgiven, whose sin is covered, . . . unto whom the Lord imputeth not iniquitie"—are taken up together. We here return to an analysis of Donne's development of this third section of the text.

Calvin observed on these words of the Psalm, "Despite the fact that David emphasizes the point by repeating the same thing three times, it is not a useless repetition."[14] Donne does not agree that there is a repetition here at all: "this Blessednesse David doth not deliver us all at once, in three expressings of the same thing, but he gives us one light thereof, in the knowledge that there is a Forgiving of Transgressions, another, in the Covering of sinnes, and a third, in the not Imputing of iniquity" (9. 11. 55–59). If the verbal expressions are three, then what is signified by them is three as well.

Donne draws a complexly interrelated subdivision in which the divine act of reconciliation expressed by each clause is associated with one of the Persons of the Trinity and with one of the successively more particular realms of each Person's reconciliatory activity.

In the first Act [the forgiving of transgressions], we consider God the Father to have wrought; He proposed, he decreed, he accepted too a sacrifice for all mankind in the death of Christ. In the second, The Covering of sinnes, we consider God the Sonne to worke, *Incubare Ecclesiae*, He sits upon his Church as a Hen upon her Eggs, He covers all our sinnes, whom he hath gathered into that body, with spreading himselfe and his merits upon us all there. In this third, The not Imputing of Iniquity, we consider God the Holy Ghost to worke, and, as the Spirit of Consolation, to blow away all scruples, all diffidences, and to establish an assurance in the Conscience. [9. 11. 470–79]

The Father accomplishes the forgiveness of sins for all mankind, the Son applies that forgiveness to the church, the Spirit gives confidence of that forgiveness to the individual. Thus, these three parts into which the third section of the text is subdivided correspond with the three Persons of the One God and so comprise a whole.

Donne proceeds by considering for the words of these three clauses their "roote and Originall signification" (9. 11. 437), or their etymologies, and their "latitude and extension" (8. 12. 208–12), or their use in other scriptural contexts. Care is taken to differentiate the wording of each clause from that of the others—each noun from the other nouns and each verb from the other verbs. In these verses the gloss tradition found three different kinds of sin—original sin ("transgression"), actual venial sin ("sin"), and actual mortal sin ("iniquity").[15] Donne does not adopt this exposition, but sometimes it seems to be in his mind. Thus in differentiating the noun *transgression* of the first clause ("he whose transgression is forgiven") according to his own distinctions, he excludes the interpretation of the gloss tradition: "The Originall word is *'Pashang,'* and that signifies sin in all extensions. . . . So then, we consider sin here, not as a staine, such as Originall sin may be, nor as a wound, such as every actuall sin may be, but as a *burden*, a complication, a packing up of many sins, in an habituall practice thereof" (9. 11. 270–91).

Donne then elaborates this transferred signification of "burden" as sin. He had preached some time earlier a series of sermons on Ps. 38:4, "For mine iniquities are gone over mine head, as an heavy burden they are too heavy for me." The appropriateness of speaking of sin as an encumbering load is there explained: "And the nature, and inconvenience of a Burden is, first to Crooken, and bend us downward from our naturall posture, which is erect, for this incurvation implies a declination in the inordinate love of the Creature, *'Incurvat.'* And then the nature of a burden is, to Tyre us; our very sinne becomes fulsome, and wearisome to us, *'fatigat'*; and it hath this inconvenience of a burden too, *'ut praecipitet,'* it makes us still apt and ready to stumble, and to fall under it" (2. 3. 79–88). Thus Donne considers this figure of the burden, which occurs with its meaning clearly given in Ps. 38:4, a synonym for his understanding of "transgression" in the text here, i.e., sin as it impedes our way to happiness by extending to cumbersome and onerous proportions.

Donne offers also a sense *in bono* to counter the sense *in malo* of a burden as a load of transgressions. "Our first errors," he says, "are out of Levity, and S. Augustin hath taught us a proper ballast and waight for that, *Amor Dei pondus animae*, The love of God would carry us evenly, and steadily, if we would embarke that" (9. 11. 297–300).[16] Thus, if our souls be beneficially weighted or rightly disposed, then the course of our thought and action is steadied and kept in control, but a burden of sin unbalances or disorders us and oppresses us with its weight. "But as in great tradings," he goes on to say, "they come to ballast with Merchandise, ballast and fraight is al one; so in this habituall sinner, all is sin, plots and preparations before the act, gladnesse and glory in the act, sometimes disguises, sometimes justifications after the act, make up one body, one fraight of sin" (9. 11. 300–5). Burden in a beneficial sense seems to suggest the idea of ballast, weight that gives stability to a ship; that sense is then inverted to signify burden *in malo*, the freight of sin.[17]

Donne then adduces an etymology for the verb *to be forgiven* that extends the figure of sin as a burden: "the word does not onely signifie '*Auferre*,' but '*ferre*'; not onely [for God] to take away sin, by way of pardon, but to take the sin upon himselfe, and so to beare the sin, and the punishment of the sin in his owne person" (9. 11. 325–28). He shows that the word was used elsewhere in Scripture for Christ's act of assuming the load of our sins. In a passage from another of the sermons on Ps. 38:4, this figure is developed more fully: "They [weighty and insupportable sins] were heavy, they weighed him down from his Fathers bosome, they made God Man. That one sin could make an Angel a Devill, is a strange consideration; but that all the sins of the world, could make God Man, is stranger" (2. 5. 351–55). Thus the word *to be forgiven* in its root signification of 'to be taken away, to be taken upon' is predicated very appropriately of "transgression" represented as a burden. The science of grammar, by its etymology of the verb, seems to bear out the figurative development of the subject's meaning.

Part four, as has been seen, provides the preacher with the occasion to distinguish his church's position on the doctrine of justification from that of the extreme Protestants. When the third section of the text is taken up again in the fourth part, the rereading of the clauses in the context of the theological distinctions drawn further extends the interpreted meaning of the figures. Donne thus complicates his reading. The analysis of reason in part four affords the dimension within which further significance and figurative associations can be enfolded into his meditation on the words of the third section of the text.

Donne only suggests the directions in which the figure of sin as a burden might be extended in the context of the theological ideas of part four; yet the ramifications may be discerned by adducing his readings from elsewhere. Preaching on Ps. 38:4, he said that every instance of another's sin, even though we may not bear any direct or indirect responsibility for that sin, still adds its weight to our own burden of transgressions: "But if I have no interest in the sins of other men, by any occasion ministered by me, yet I cannot chuse but feel a weight, a burthen of a holy anguish, and compassion and indignation, because every one of these sins inflict a new wound upon my Saviour . . . and the sins of every man concern every man" (2. 4. 103–15). In the sermon considered here, Donne draws the implication that likewise the grace God shows to others by assuming the burden of their sins on Himself in Christ is an alleviation of all sins: "this forgiving of transgressions, is Christs taking away the sins of all the world, by taking all the sins of all men upon himselfe" (9. 11. 672–74). However if we begrudge God's forgiveness to others, we will suppose our own weight of transgressions less likely to be alleviated by God's mercies, and we will fall into despair. In Christ we share with all other men both the burden and the possible alleviation of sin, and we must not presume that Christ's expiation applies as exclusively as the Puritans maintained.

Taking up the second relative clause ("he whose sin is covered"), Donne is careful to differentiate its terms from those of the preceding clause. "'Sin' in this place," he says, "is not so heavy a word, as 'transgression' was in the former" (9. 11. 343–44). There it was an offense so weighty and extensive that it utterly corrupted our faculties and could be expiated only by Christ's death; here it represents sins of infirmity. In support of this distinction, the etymology in the Hebrew of *sin* is offered, and another instance of its use in Scripture that illustrates its root meaning of 'a near miss' is adduced: "For so this word, 'Catah,' hath that signification (as in many other places) there, where it is said, 'That there were seven hundred left-handed Benjamits, which would sling stones at a haires breadth, and not *fail* [*Catah*]'; that is, not misse the marke a haires breadth" (9. 11. 358–62). Concording the word thus bears out the particular sense of *sin* distinguished here, that of sin as merely a slight falling short. The verbs, too, are carefully differentiated: "As 'Sin' in this notion, is not so deepe a wound upon God, as

'Transgression' in the other, so 'Covering' here extends not so far, as 'Forgiving' did there" (9. 11. 370–72). Thus each predicate exactly corresponds to its respective subject.

Donne extends the figure *covering* by speaking of Christ as a garment, a transferred sign that recalls Is. 61:10, "he hath clothed me with garments of righteousness." "Here it is a part of Gods mercy," says Donne, "in spreading, and applying the merits and satisfaction of Christ, upon all them, whom God by the Holy Ghost hath gathered in the profession of Christ, and so called to the apprehending and embracing of this mantle, this garment, this covering, the righteousnesse of Christ in the Christian Church" (9. 11. 375–80). As two senses were distinguished for the verb *to be forgiven* ('to be taken away' and 'to be taken upon') in the preceding clause, so here too, two senses are distinguished for the verb *to cover*; it can mean either 'to overshadow' or 'to touch.' The distinction is made by cross-concordancing with the Hebrew: where the English translation has the one word *cover*, Hebrew has two, both *sacac* and *casah*, both *tegere obumbrando* and *tegere attingendo*. The sense of *to cover* as 'to overshadow' refers to the overall effect of Christ's sacrifice in shielding us from God's just punishments; the sense of *to cover* as 'to touch' refers to the specific application of Christ's power in ministering to us in the church.

Christ, in his Ordinances in his Church, offers me an application of all that for my selfe, and covers my sin, from the eye of his Father, not onely *obumbrando*, as hee hath spread himselfe as a Cloud refreshing the whole World, in the value of the satisfaction, but *Attingendo*, by coming to me, by spreading himself upon me, as the Prophet did upon the dead Child, Mouth to mouth, Hand to hand; In the mouth of his Minister, he speaks to me; In the hand of the Minister, he delivers himselfe to me; and so by these visible acts, and seales of my Reconciliation, *Tegit attingendo*, He covers me by touching me; He touches my conscience, with a sense and remorse of my sins, in his Word; and he touches my soule, with a faith of having received him, and all the benefit of his Death, in the Sacrament. [9. 11. 412–24]

Christ shields our sins from being exposed to the glaring sunlight of divine justice; but He also covers us like a garment, touches us in the ordinances of the church, and, as Elisha laid himself out on the corpse of the boy (2 Kings 4:34), so He revives us by the efficacy of His Crucifixion.[18]

When Donne rereads this clause in the fourth part of the sermon, he extends the meaning of the figure Christ as a garment in the course of again rejecting some aspect of a too-rigorous Reformation. Here particularly he urges the necessity of retaining the practice of confession in the church. By adducing a series of scriptural texts that concord on *cover*, *hid*, or *nakedness*, the preacher reiterates the warning that if we do not confess our sins, they will be exposed by punishment. It is futile and but aggravates our condition if we endeavor to cover up our sin with excuses and with further sins, as Adam tried to do: "Sin hath that pride, that it is not content with one garment; Adam covered first with fig-leaves, then with whole trees, 'He hid himselfe amongst the trees': Then hee covered his sin, with the woman; 'she provoked him': And then with Gods action, *Quam tu dedisti*, 'The Woman whom thou gavest me' (Gen. 3:8–12); And this was Adams wardrobe" (9. 11. 746–50). Thus, Adam's apron of leaves, his excuses, is a garment *in malo* as opposed to the sense of the garment *in bono* as Christ.

Elsewhere in his preaching Donne develops this figure of Christ as a garment with which the sinner might clothe himself. The occasion was a christening and the text was Gal. 3:27, "For all yee that are baptized into Christ, have put on Christ."[19] Here, too, the sense *in malo*, Adam's covering of fig leaves, is introduced: "And we provide nothing but short Aprons, as that word signified; and those but of figleaves; That which comes first to hand, and that which is withered before it is made, that doe we take for an excuse" (5. 7. 123–26). In the context of a baptism, putting on Christ entails covering the deformity brought on by Adam's disobedience, original sin. "And so perfect effects," says Donne, "this garment, Christ Jesus, works upon us, if we put him on; He doth not onely cover Originall sinne . . . but he covers all our actuall sinnes, which we multiply every day" (5. 7. 136–41). This, however, is not consistent with the sense for the covering sin that the preacher is at pains to distinguish in the Psalm text. There *sin* is 'a near miss,' a falling short, not an offense so grievous as original sin. And yet the Galatians text referring to the washing away of original sin may well have been in Donne's mind, for he remarks, "Howsoever thou wert covered with the Covenant, and taken into the Visible Church, howsoever thou wert clothed, by having put on Christ in Baptisme, yet [etc.]" (9. 11. 710–12). Still, he is careful here not to refer to that aspect of the baptismal rite that would conflict with the distinction he has drawn but mentions instead that aspect that suits perfectly the framework of his subdivision. He speaks of baptism, not as a washing away of original sin, but as an initiation of the believer into the body of the church.

Calvin, in considering this Psalm text, thought David had repeated the same thing three times in the first three clauses, but their effect, he thought, might be either threatening or comforting. Certainly those who would dwell on the doctrine that salvation is utterly dependent on God's free election of them might understandably become fearful and anxious by meditating on these verses. As Calvin comments, "A continual disquietude unsettles those whom God has so effectively stirred that they are touched by a lively sense of their unhappy condition and it is difficult to put their minds at ease."[20] A superficial reading of the third clause of this third section ("he unto whom the Lord imputeth not iniquitie") perhaps seems to Donne too readily conducive to just such a state of mind, for he is careful from the first to take it instead as an assurance that would relieve a too-tender and disheartened scrupulosity. Because Calvinist theology particularly induced some in this period to scrutinize anxiously the condition of their souls for indications of election or condemnation, the entire development of this clause of the text in both the third and fourth parts seems to be directed against the excesses of Puritan doctrine.

Donne reads the clause in the light of other uses of its words elsewhere in Scripture. "We finde the word [*Cashab*, "to impute"], where Hannah was praying, and Eli the Priest, who saw her lips move, and heard no prayer come from her, thought she had been drunke, *Imputed* drunkennesse unto her, and said, 'How long wilt thou be drunk? put away thy wine' (1 Sam. 1:14): So that this *Imputing*, is such an Imputing of ours as may be erronious, that is, an Imputing from our selves, in a diffidence, and jealousie, and suspition of Gods goodnesse towards us" (9. 11. 442–48). The King James Version translated *Cashab* in that passage as "thought": "Eli thought she had been drunk" (1 Sam. 1:13). Such cross-concordancing with the Hebrew also reveals another sense for *iniquity*: at Gen. 4:13 the word *Gnavah* is translated as "punishment." If one substitutes these senses for the original words of the text, the sentence will read: Blessed is he whom the Lord keeps from *thinking* his misfortunes to be *punishments* sent by an angry God Who has chosen not to favor him. Here again cross-concordancing with the Hebrew has provided further opportunity for expanding the meanings of the words.

The hopeful conscience, confident of God's graciousness, is described in meteorological terms. "We justly conceive," says Donne, "that this not imputing of Iniquity, is that *Serenitas Conscientiae*, That brightnesse, that clearnesse, that peace, and tranquillity, that calme and serenity, that acquiescence, and security of the Conscience, in which I am delivered from all scruples, and all timorousness, that my Transgressions are not forgiven, or my sins are not covered. . . . This is that *Serenitas Conscientiae*, The Meridionall brightnesse of the Conscience, when there is not one Cloud in our sky" (9. 11. 465–70, 493–95). The figure may derive from Ps. 37:6—"He shall bring forth thy righteousnesse as the light, and thy judgement as the noone day" (9. 11. 781–83)—which Donne cites later in the sermon. Elsewhere in Donne's preaching "meridionall" signifies properly noontide, the time of the sun's zenith, and figuratively, man's highest glory as a creature made in God's image and destined for resurrection.[21] "For this Image of God," said Donne preaching to the king in 1629, "shall never depart from our soule; no, not when that soule departs from our body. And that's our South, our Meridionall height and glory" (9. 1. 108–10). It is thus appropriate in this sermon on the Psalm text to suggest by this figure that the state of hope is an anticipation of the blessedness of resurrection.

When this third clause is reconsidered in part four, it cannot be taken up as a qualification of an ultra-Protestant doctrine, since in part three it has already been considered as a criticism of a theology that tends to lead to an overly scrupulous and disheartened conscience. However, in rereading the clause, Donne stresses particularly the importance of the Christian's availing himself of the promises of grace by trusting in the sacraments. He speaks several times of this ritual conferment as "the seals of Reconciliation" (9. 11. 487, 810, 820). It seems to have been important for Donne that preaching commend to the congregation the benefits of the sacraments, that it "chaffe the wax" (7. 3. 36–37) so that the seal's imprint might take. Thus, Donne concludes this sermon by bringing together the moment of the ritual conferment of divine forgiveness, baptism, with the moment in whose anticipation our confidence is most shaken, the point of death. "And exalt thy joy," he says, "in the 'not imputing of iniquity,' in that serenity, that tranquillity, that God shall receive thee, at thy last houre, in thy last Bath, the sweat of death, as lovingly, as acceptably, as innocently, as he received thee, from thy first Bath, the laver of Regeneration, the font of Baptisme" (9. 11. 845–50). God's promise and our fear here meet in the sacramental element.

As the restatement of the division in the *divisio* presents it, the part that considers the last section of the text and pertains to the student being catechized is developed by topical procedures. The pupil is taught what he must do to cooperate with God's gracious acts of reconciliation; where there is disagreement about the proper understanding of doctrine, he must be able to define his position. However, in parts two and three, where the message of God's mercies of blessedness, forgiveness, atonement, and comfort are actually presented, the text is developed by grammatical means. The elaboration of the words of the third section of the text as they are read and reread presents the message to the memory of the hearer; there the Word works upon him. He is thereby engaged in the activity of remembering God's revelations to him, both in his own life and in the Scriptures.

The sermon consists, then, of a complex interaction of two basic procedures, making distinctions and making associations. The theological issues about which distinctions are made provide, as it were, a matrix where lines of differentiation can be located in relationship to each other. Thus, parts three and four of the sermon are distinguished by sorting out our reconciliation to God both by His graciously overcoming the alienation caused by our sin and by our acting in good faith with Him. Further division particularizes the meaning. The sermon's structure is made more detailed and its space is further broken up by further separations. Thus, the subdivision of part three relegates the more particular aspects of the divine activity of reconciliation to the three Persons. The matter so divided determines the proportions of its own patterning by its very nature: the division itself is exhaustive.

The associations drawn out of the words by remembering other texts "furnishes the rooms"—diffuses the meaning to fill out the space that opens between distinctions. The scriptural word has an expanse of significance of its own, extended by its nature as a word and its occurrences elsewhere in Scripture.

And if the thing signified by the word in turn signifies something else by way of transference, then the latter also has its own expanse of figurative significance, extended by its nature as a thing and its occurrences elsewhere in Scripture. In such a way does the figure of a burden elaborate the idea of sin.

These procedures—dividing and associating, particularizing and diffusing—can go on at the same time because the sectioning of the verbal statement from Scripture *is* the division of a whole entity of meaning conceived by the mind. Thus the sermon can come together in a discourse both as a structure of ideas and as a grammatical commentary on the words of the text.

I have tried to read Donne's sermon on Ps. 32:1–2 with an idea of the way his discourse comes together. I have filled out the matrix within which his theological ideas take shape by citing both from the Fathers and from writers of the Reformation period. I have traced out the structure of his division and subdivision and seen how it extends and sustains the development of his ideas. I have followed the associations of words by which he dilates the signification of the text, and I have elaborated the figures that he introduces here by concording his development of the same figures elsewhere. Thus I have read this sermon by reading the scriptural text according to the procedures by which he read.

CHAPTER 6 *Conclusion*

Arts-of-discourse doctrines current at a particular period do contribute to the ways in which the preacher goes about taking up the scriptural text and developing it into a sermon. Those procedures are better apppreciated—the sermons are better read—when considered in the broad context of the doctrines of secular learning that helped to shape them. The Bible is still a book to be read and made meaningful, even though, as God's Word, it is what no other book is; and the preacher cannot but avail himself of the commonly taught discipline of humane letters in his fundamental dealings with the text.

The grammatical commentator in particular provided Augustine with the assumptions about language and the procedures for reading that characterize his exegetical preaching. As the natures of things and the words that signify them conform to each other, so do the meanings recognized by faith and the things that signify them by transferred expression in Scripture. As words can be homonymous, so can things that serve as signs of other things. These associations and reflecting registers of meaning are the networks of the memory along which Augustine improvises his sermons. In the Middle Ages this grammatical means of invention hardened into a system, the *distinctiones*, for composing a complexly structured discourse.

The scholastic sermon is also such a structure, but built up of real distinctions drawn by reason and of connections made with the words of other texts adduced as confirming authorities. In the *ars praedicandi* an assumption that a combined unity in the order of reality corresponds to the syntactical completeness of the scriptural statement seems to be implied in the rules by which a preacher is to divide his theme. Thus, the statement is susceptible to division of a whole into parts and to development of its meaning by procedures taken over from ways of arguing a definition. Characteristically dialectical is the scholastic preacher's concern for the statement, his differentiation of parts according to distinctions that hold in reality, and his care to establish the validity by both reason and authority for each step of the construction of his discourse.

As an alternative to the vagaries of scholastic logic, the topical doctrines of the art of rhetoric assumed importance in the humanist learning of the Renaissance. The Christian orator of the sixteenth century developed the scriptural text into a discourse by drawing out from the sense of the passage a topic that he then argued and urged on his hearers with all the resources of the art of persuasion. Those indebted primarily to the Aristotelian tradition, particularly the Ramists, tended to a formalistic reduction of the text's meaning to generalities that were then applied to the conduct of daily life. Such methods are to be found especially in Puritan preaching.

Donne seems to have employed quite deliberately something of all these various arts-of-discourse procedures for developing a scriptural text into a sermon. Thus, the division of the text and its restatement can be accomplished by the paraphrastic distribution of the Fathers or by the exact prescriptions of the *ars praedicandi* or by the methods of topical rhetoric. And the structure thus set out can then be filled in by consideration of the "origination of the words" and " their latitude and extension" in other scriptural contexts or by subdivision or by the amplification of commonplaces. As a preacher of the high party in the English church, he may have felt it fitting to appropriate procedures from all the traditions of Christian culture in the past as his own.

However, Donne's preference for patristic and scholastic arts-of-discourse procedures over the methods of the Puritans is not merely a partisan loyalty; it can be taken as indicative of his assumptions about language in general and about scriptural language in particular. For the Ramists, discourse consists of a series of arguments, which are the cognitive force of verbal expression considered apart from the words. To read a text is to reduce it to its lines of logical reasoning, to unravel its threads; reading the biblical text is in this respect no exception. "The sense of Scripture is rather to be judged the word of God than the words and letters thereof," Perkins said. Language is an expediency for conveying the import of ideas on a topic, and the "method" is a means of interpreting and using language regarded in such a way.

For Donne, the "method-mongers" are "peremptory" in their procedures of reading. They treat the text irreverently by disposing of its words rather than leaving them to stand in their unique richness and mystery. All language is a gift; the ability to name things rightly was bestowed on man by a gracious act of God. That naming revealed to man all the rest of Creation, and Scripture was given as another revelation in words. To subject to reductionist procedures the means by which God makes Himself and His work known to us is a profanation.

The assumptions of the ancient grammarians, on the other hand, seem quite in keeping with the belief that language is a gift. A work has a nature of its own, which in its formality and behavior in grammatical relationships, corresponds by properness of signification with what it means. Language is not a creation of man's ingenuity, subject to the purposes for which he invents it and determined at his convenience like an algebraic cipher. Rather it is something from which man can learn about the reality outside himself. As Servius said, "'noun' [*nomen*] is so called because it renders things known [*notas*] to us."

What is true of language in general is true also of Scripture. Indeed, a belief in the sacredness and inerrancy of revelation would tend to lead to the notion that the words of Scripture conform more immediately to reality than does the rest of language. And as a given corpus, ordered and interrelated to itself, the Bible has about it a completeness and perfection that neither the canon of the classical authors nor the flux of language use possesses. It is, as Donne says, "a room wainscotted with looking glass." The meaning of the scriptural words is born out by this reflection of different instances on each other and by consideration of the place of each word in the whole, but that meaning is first established by God's revelation of Himself and His world in language.

The preacher who conceives of scriptural language in such a way does not unravel his text but rather complicates it by his reading. He does not reduce the sense from the verbal medium but lets the meaning of the sacred words realize itself. By the grammatical procedures of concording, distinguishing, and correlating, the signification of the text spreads out, extends, and ramifies through networks of association. The reader's recognition of meaning is thus drawn out and renewed by the elaboration of the words' own revelatory fullness. In reading the text by such procedures, the preacher allows the gracious gift of revelation in language its full play in the minds and hearts of his hearers.

*Notes
Bibliography
Index*

ABBREVIATIONS USED IN NOTES AND BIBLIOGRAPHY

CCSL	*Corpus Christianorum, series Latina.* Turnholt: Brepols, 1953–.
CR	*Corpus reformatorum.* Brunswick. 87 vols. C. A. Schwelschke, 1834–1900.
CSEL	*Corpus scriptorum ecclesiasticorum Latinorum.* Vienna: Hoelder-Pichler-Tempsky, 1866–.
EETS	Early English Text Society. Oxford: University Press, 1864–.
ELH	*English Literary History.*
JEGP	*Journal of English and Germanic Philology.*
OCT	[*Oxford Classical Texts*] Scriptorum classicorum bibliotheca Oxoniensis. Oxford: Clarendon Press, n.d.—(in progress).
PL	*Patrologiae cursus completus, series Latina.* Edited by Abbé Migne. Paris: Garnier Fratres, 1878–90.
PMLA	*Publications of the Modern Language Association.*
SPCK	Society for the Promotion of Christian Knowledge.
STC	*A Short-title Catalogue of Books, 1475–1640.* Edited by Pollard and Redgrave. London: Bibliographical Society, 1926.

NOTES

INTRODUCTION
1. John Donne, *The Sermons of John Donne*, vol. 5, sermon 1, lines 766–67. Subsequent references to this work will appear in the text. See also, 7. 13. 73: "So that we shall make it a part apart, to consider the Sermon from which this text is taken, before we dilate the Text itself into a Sermon."
2. Martianus Capella *De nuptiis Philologiae et Mercurii* 9. 891.
3. M. P. Ramsay, *Les doctrines médiévales chez Donne*, p. 208.
4. W. F. Mitchell, *English Pulpit Oratory from Andrewes to Tillotson*, pp. 137, 148, 184.
5. Ruth Wallerstein, *Studies in Seventeenth-Century Poetic*, pp. 27–30.
6. Barbara H. Davis, "Ruth Wallerstein's *Studies in Donne*," p. 272.
7. Dennis Quinn, "Donne's Christian Eloquence," *ELH* 27 (1960): 276–97; "Donne's Principles of Biblical Exegesis," *JEGP* 41 (1962): 313–29; "John Donne's Sermons on the Psalms and the Traditions of Biblical Exegesis."
8. Joan Webber, *Contrary Music: The Prose Style of John Donne*.
9. However, Robert J. Bauer includes several authors of Renaissance ecclesiastical rhetorics as "Schoolmen" in "John Donne and the Schoolmen."
10. Winfried Schleiner, *The Imagery of John Donne's Sermons*.
11. Janel M. Mueller, *Donne's Prebend Sermons*.
12. Gale Carrithers, *Donne at Sermons*, pp. 79–82.

CHAPTER 1

Section A / Grammar and Grammatical Commentaries
1. Augustine *De utilitate credendi* 7. 17.
2. Dionysius Thrax *Ars grammatica* (ed. Uhlig), 1i: 5, ll. 2–3.
3. Donatus *Ars grammatica* (ed. Keil), 4:399, ll. 13–14.
4. Ibid., p. 395, ll. 20–25.
5. Servius *Commentarius in artem Donati* (ed. Keil), 4:429, ll. 35–37 (hereafter cited as Servius on Donatus).
6. Ibid., p. 405, ll. 3–4.
7. Marius Victorinus *Explanationum in rhetoricam M. Tulii Ciceronis libri duo* (ed. Halm), p. 182.
8. Servius on Donatus (ed. Keil), p. 405, l. 12.
9. Melampodos *Commentarius in artis Dionysianae* (ed. Uhlig), 1iii: 14, ll. 23–24.
10. Cicero *Topica* 8. 35.
11. See, besides Uhlfelder's collection cited below, the "Appendix Probi" in *Grammatici Latini* (ed. Keil), 4:199–203.
12. Myra L. Uhlfelder, ed., *De proprietate sermonum vel rerum*, 47 and 48.
13. Donatus *Grammatica* (ed. Keil), p. 373, ll. 7–8.
14. Servius on Donatus (ed. Keil), p. 406, l. 29; p. 407, l. 8.
15. Macrobius *Saturnalia* 6. 7. 9.
16. Donatus *Commentum Andriae* (ed. Wessner), 1:80, comm. on l. 142.
17. Ibid., pp. 76–77, comm. on l. 128.
18. Servius *In Vergilii Aeneidos libros XII commentarius* (ed. Thilo and Hagen), 1:197, comm. on bk. 1, l. 703 (hereafter cited as Servius on Vergil).
19. Ibid., 1:33, comm. on bk. 1, l. 51.
20. Macrobius *Saturnalia* 1. 24. 13.

21. Servius on Vergil (ed. Thilo and Hagen), 1:112, comm. on bk. 1, l. 305. I have, however, adopted the reading of the Harvard edition here: ed. Rand et al. (Lancaster: American Philological Association, 1946), 2:161.

CHAPTER 1

Section B | Augustine on Grammar and on How the Mind
Comes to Know through Discourse
1. See Giuseppina Bellissima, "Sant' Agostino grammatico" in *Augustinus magister*, 1:35–42.
2. Augustine *De musica* 2. 1. 1.
3. Augustine *Soliloquia* 2. 11. 19.
4. Augustine *De ordine* 2. 11. 30.
5. Augustine *Soliloquia* 2. 11. 20.
6. Augustine *De ordine* 2. 12. 35.
7. Augustine *De doctrina Christiana* 2. 24. 37 (hereafter cited as *Doctrina*).
8. Augustine *De ordine* 2. 18. 47.
9. Ibid., 2. 5. 14.
10. Ibid., 2. 17. 45. Later Augustine would regret "quod multum tribui liberalibus disciplinis, quas multi sancti multum nesciunt, quidam etiam sciunt et sancti non sunt." Augustine *Retractationes* 1. 3. 2.
11. Augustine *De ordine* 2. 11. 32. This division may owe something to Varro's *Nine Disciplines*. See Prosper Alfaric, *L'évolution intellectuelle de saint Augustin*, p. 443, n. 2.
12. Augustine *De Genesi ad litteram imperfectus liber* (*CSEL* 28. 476).
13. Ibid., pp. 476–77.
14. Augustine *De civitate Dei* 13. 11.
15. Adjectives had not yet been distinguished from nouns. See Donatus *Grammatica* (ed. Keil), p. 374, ll. 2–4.
16. Augustine *De civitate Dei* 13. 11.
17. Augustine *De magistro* 2. 3.
18. Ibid., 1. 2.
19. Ibid., 10. 34.
20. Ibid., 11. 38.
21. Augustine *De Trinitate* 11. 8. 14.
22. Augustine *Confessiones* 10. 14. 21–22.

CHAPTER 1

Section C | Augustine's Exegesis and Preaching
1. Augustine *Doctrina* 1. 1. 1.
2. See Marie Comeau, *Saint Augustin: exégète du quatrième évangile*, pp. 80 ff.; H. I. Marrou, *Saint Augustin et la fin de la culture antique*, pp. 422 ff.
3. Augustine *De ordine* 2. 9. 26.
4. Augustine *De utilitate credendi* 5. 11.
5. Ibid., 6. 13. See also *Doctrina* 2. 7. 9; 2. 9. 14; and 3. 1. 1 for the importance of "pietas" in reading Scripture.
6. Augustine *Doctrina* 3. 2. 2.
7. Ibid., 2. 6. 8: "Nihil enim fere de illis obscuritatibus eruitur, quod non planissime dictum alibi reperiatur."
8. Ibid., 3. 28. 39.
9. Ibid., Proem 9.
10. Ibid., 1. 36. 40: "Quisquis igitur scripturas divinas vel quamlibet carum partem intellexisse sibi videtur, ita ut eo intellectu non aedificet istam geminam caritatem dei et proximi, nondum intellexit. Quisquis vero talem inde

sententiam duxerit, ut huic aedificandae caritat; sit utilis, nec tamen hoc dixerit, quod ille quem legit eo loco sensisse probabitur, non perniciose fallitur nec omnino mentitur." This notion is recalled again later: 2. 7. 10; 3. 10. 14.

11. Ibid., 2. 10. 15. See also 2. 14. 21; 2. 42. 63; 3. 1. 1.

12. See ibid., 2. 1. 1–5.

13. Ibid., 2. 10. 15.

14. Ibid., 2. 11. 16.

15. Ibid., 2. 12. 17.

16. Augustine *Enarrationes in Psalmos* on Ps. 87. 10 (hereafter cited as *In Psalmos*).

17. "*Distinctio*" and "*pronuntiatio*," Augustine *Doctrina* 3. 3. 6. For *distinctio*, see Donatus *Grammatica* (ed. Keil), p. 395, ll. 23–24. For *pronuntiatio*, see Marrou, *Saint Augustin et la fin*, p. 21.

18. See Cicero *De inventione* 2. 40. 117.

19. Augustine *Doctrina* 3. 2. 5.

20. Ibid., 2. 10. 15.

21. See ibid., 3. 6. 10.

22. Ibid., 2. 16. 23.

23. Jerome *Liber interpretationis Hebraicorum nominum* (*CCSL*) 72:59: "Philo, vir disertissimus Judaeorum, Origenis quoque testimonio conprobatur edidisse librum hebraicorum nominum eorumque etymologias."

24. Augustine *Doctrina* 2. 16. 23. In his own commentary on this verse, Augustine says no more about what exactly the "secretum" is than "Haec quia manifesta sunt, transeamus." *In Johannis evangelium tractatus* (*CCSL*) 36:385. Surely Robertson is right in supplying "baptism" in Augustine, *On Christian Doctrine*, trans. D. W. Robertson, Jr., The Library of Liberal Arts (Indianapolis: Bobbs-Merrill, 1958), p. 50.

25. Augustine *Doctrina* 2. 16. 24.

26. See ibid., 2. 16. 24.

27. See ibid., 2. 16. 25; 2. 16. 26; 2. 28. 42; 2. 31. 48.

28. See ibid., 2. 40. 60.

29. Ibid., 2. 39. 59.

30. See Etienne Gilson, *The Christian Philosophy of St. Augustine*, pp. 305–6, n. 26.

31. Augustine *Doctrina* 3. 25. 35.

32. Ibid., 3. 25. 36.

33. Augustine *Sermones* 73. 2. See *In Psalmos* on Ps. 90. 1. 6.

34. Augustine *In Psalmos* on Ps. 103. 3. 22.

35. Augustine *Sermones* 73. 2.

36. Augustine *Confessiones* 13. 24. 37.

37. Augustine *Doctrina* 2. 9. 14.

38. Ps. 28:9 as cited by Augustine, *In Psalmos* on Ps. 28. 9.

39. Augustine *Confessiones* 11. 2. 3.

40. Augustine *In Psalmos* on Ps. 46. 1. Clean animals' chewing of the cud is taken as signifying remembrance also in R. H. Charles, ed., "The Letter of Aristeas," in *The Apocrypha and Pseudepigrapha of the Old Testament in English* (Oxford: Clarendon Press, 1913) 2:109. I am indebted to Lee Whitney of Trinity College, University of Toronto, for this reference.

41. Augustine *Contra Mendacium* 10. 24.

42. Augustine *In Psalmos* on Ps. 103. 3. 3.

43. Augustine *Doctrina* 2. 6. 7–8. See Jean Pépin, "Saint Augustin et la protreptique de l'allégorie," in *Recherches Augustiniennes*, 1:243–86.

44. Cicero *De oratore* 3. 39. 159.

45. See Augustine *Doctrina* 3. 29. 40.

46. Ibid., 2. 6. 7.

47. See R. J. Deferrari, "St. Augustine's Method of Composing and Delivering Sermons," pp. 97–127; 193–219.

48. For Augustine's use of Cicero's three styles in Book 4 of *Doctrina*, see Sister Therese Sullivan, *Augustine's "De doctrina Christiana," Bk. 4, A Commentary, with a Revised Text, Introduction and Translation* (Washington, D.C.: Press of Catholic University of America, 1930).

49. Augustine *Doctrina* 4. 20. 42.

50. See ibid., 4. 13. 29.

51. See Deferrari, "St. Augustine's Method," p. 107.

52. See ibid., p. 101; Christine Mohrmann, "Saint Augustin prédicateur" in *Etudes sur le latin des chrétiens*, 1:391; M. Pontet, *L'exégèse de saint Augustin prédicateur*, p. 4; F. Van der Meer, *Augustine the Bishop*, p. 416.

53. See Augustine *In Psalmos* on Ps. 118. Proem.

54. Ibid., on Ps. 103. 1. 1.

55. See D. de Bruyne, "Enarrationes in Psalmos prêchées à Carthage" in *Miscellanea Agostiniana*, 2:324; Pontet, *L'exégèse*, p. 6; *CCSL* editors say 412 A.D. (*CCSL* 38. xvi).

56. See Pontet, *L'exégèse*, p. 89.

57. Augustine *In Psalmos* on Ps. 103. 3. 1.

58. Ibid., 3. 2.

59. Ibid., 4. 19.

60. See Pontet, *L'exégèse*, p. 388.

61. My translations of the lemmata render Augustine's version of the Ps. 103:16–18:

"Satiabuntur ligna campi
    Et cedri Libani plantavit;
Illic passeres nidificabunt.
    Fulicae domus dux est eorum.
Montes altissimi cervis
    Petra refugium ericiis et leporibus." [*CCSL* 40:1513–15]

62. Augustine *In Psalmos* on Ps. 103. 3. 16.

63. Ibid., 3. 17.

64. Ibid., 3. 1, 5.

65. Ibid., 3. 21.

CHAPTER 1

Section D / The Medieval Distinctiones *Compilations and Their Use*

1. See Jacques Fontaine, *Isidore de Seville et la culture classique dans l'Espagne Wisigothique*, 1:27 ff.

2. Isidore of Seville *Etymologiarum sive originum libri XX* 1. 29. 2.

3. Ibid., 1. 31. 1.

4. See Isidore of Seville *Differentiarum, sive de proprietate sermonum* 1. 5.; 3. 3.

5. Cassiodorus *Expositio Psalmorum* Praefatio 15.

6. Cassiodorus *Institutiones* (ed. Mynors), p. 4.

7. Augustine *De civitate Dei* 11. 1.

8. Smaragdus of St. Mihiel, *Liber in partibus Donati* (ed. Mabillon), p. 358.

9. Smaragdus, quoted by M. Charles Thurot, "Notices et extraits de divers manuscrits latins pour servir à l'histoire des doctrines grammaticales au moyen âge," in *Notices et extraits des manuscrits de la bibliothèque nationale et autres bibliothèques*, vol. 22, pt. 2, p. 85.

10. See Jean Leclerq, "Smaragde et la grammaire chrétienne," p. 17.

11. Smaragdus *Liber in partibus Donati* (ed. Hagen), p. ccxli.

12. Smaragdus, quoted by Leclerq, "Smaragde," p. 16.

13. Smaragdus *Liber in partibus Donati* (ed. E. Kalinka), pp. 113–14.

14. Ibid., p. 114.
15. Agroecius, *Ars de orthographia* (ed. Keil), 7:113.
16. Eucherius *Formulae spiritualis intelligentiae (CSEL)*, 31:42.
17. Ibid., pp. 4–5.
18. Ibid., p. 20.
19. See Cassiodorus *Insitutiones* 1. 10. 1.
20. See s.v. "Eucher de Lyon," in *Dictionnaire d'histoire et de geographie ecclésiastique*, vol. 15., col. 1317.
21. See Beryl Smalley, *The Study of the Bible in the Middle Ages*, p. 246, n. 5.
22. "Melitos of Sardis" (ed. Pitra), *Clavis* 2:147.
23. See Dom André Wilmart, "Un répertoire d'exégèse" in *Memorial Lagrange*, p. 339, no. 3. The text is printed by Migne and attributed to Raban Maur (*PL* 112. 851–1088).
24. See Wilmart, "Un répertoire," p. 339, no. 3. The text of the prologue also is printed in Migne (*PL* 112. 849–51) but more recently by Georges Lacombe, *La vie et les oeuvres de Prevostin*, p. 118, n. 1.
25. See M. D. Chenu, *La théologie au douzième siècle*, p. 201.
26. Augustine's words were "contraria aut diversa." *Doctrina* 3. 24. 36. However, Abelard opens the *Sic et non* saying "Cum in tanta verborum multitudine nonnulla etiam sanctorum dicta non solum ab invicem *diversa*, verum etiam invicem *adversa* videantur" (*PL* 178. 1339A).
27. Adam the Premonstratensian, "Quisquis ad sacre scripture," in Lacombe, *Prevostin*, p. 118, n. 1.
28. Alan of Lille *Distinctiones dictionum theologicalium* (*PL* 210. 704B).
29. Peter the Cantor, *Summa 'Abel'* (a *distinctiones* collection), quoted by Wilmart, "Un répertoire," pp. 336–37, n. 7.
30. Guibert de Nogent, *Liber quo ordine sermo fieri debeat* (*PL* 156. 29B–C). This treatise is referred to by title in others of Guibert's own works (*PL* 156. 21–22A, 875C). For help with Guibert's difficult Latin, I have made use of the translation by George E. McCracken in *Early Medieval Theology*, Library of Christian Classics series (Philadelphia: Westminster Press, 1957), p. 295.
31. "Melitos of Sardis," *Clavis* (ed. Pitra), 2:275.
32. Peter the Cantor *Verbum abbreviatum* 1.
33. See Beryl Smalley, *The Study of the Bible*, p. 209.
34. Ibid., pp. 254, 256.
35. See Lacombe, *Prevostin*, p. 121.
36. Peter of Cornwall, Prologue to the *Pantheologus*, appended to R. W. Hunt, "English Learning in the Late Twelfth Century," p. 40.
37. Clm. 4616 fol. 78^r–78^v, in Ludwig Hödl, "Eine Predigtsammlung des Alanus von Lille," p. 524.
38. For these distinctions in Alan's theology of penance, see Paul Anciaux, *La théologie du sacrament de Pénitence au XIIe siècle* (Louvain, Belgium: E. Nauwelaerts, 1949), pp. 511–12.
39. Isocolon: use of the same number of member clauses.
Parison: use of parallel structure.
Paromoion: use of words with like endings.

CHAPTER 2

Section A | The Scholastic Ars praedicandi
1. Jean de Galles, quoted by Etienne Gilson in "Michel Menot et la technique du sermon médiéval," p. 108, n. 1.
2. See for example, W. O. Ross, ed., *Middle English Sermons.*
3. Thomas Waleys, "De modo componendi sermones," p. 343.
4. Robert de Basevorn, "Forma praedicandi," p. 250.

5. Ibid., p. 275.
6. Thomas Waleys, "De modo," pp. 371–72.
7. Bonaventure, "Ars concionandi," in *Opera omnia*, 9:9A. Attributed to Bonaventure by the Quaracchi editors.
8. Ibid.
9. Richard of Thetford, "Octo modi praedicandi," printed as part three of the "Ars concionandi" attributed to Bonaventure (ed. Quaracchi), 36, p. 17B. For attribution, see Charland, ed., *Artes praedicandi*, p. 77.
10. John of Salisbury, *Metalogicon*, pp. 151–52. Translated by Daniel D. McGarry (Berkeley: University of California Press, 1955), p. 187.
11. Boethius *De divisione* (*PL* 64. 877).
12. Richard of Thetford, "Octo modi," 36:17B. For Robert de Basevorn's borrowing of this passage from Richard, see "Forma," p. 292.
13. Boethius *De divisione* (*PL* 64. 878D–79A).
14. Boethius *Commentaria in Porphyrium a se translatum* (*PL* 64. 80).
15. Boethius *In categorias Aristotelis* (*PL* 64. 162B).
16. Peter Abelard, *Dialectica*, p. 535.
17. Ibid., p. 536.
18. Robert de Basevorn, "Forma," p. 276.
19. Ibid.
20. See Thomas Waleys, "De modo," p. 372.
21. Aristotle *De interpretatione* 16ᵃ 3–9.
22. Boethius *Commentarius I in De interpretatione* (*PL* 64. 297B–C).
23. Siger of Courtrai, "Summa modorum significandi" in *Les oeuvres de Siger de Courtrai*, p. 93. For Priscian see *Institutiones* 2. 4. 17.
24. John of Salisbury, *Metalogicon*, p. 34; (trans. McGarry), p. 40.
25. Cicero *Topica* 2. 8.
26. See ibid., 5. 28.
27. Marius Victorinus *De definitionibus* (ed. Th. Stangl), pp. 17–48. Also in Migne (*PL* 64. 891–910).
28. Boethius *In topica Ciceronis commentaria* (*PL* 64. 1054C).
29. Ibid., 1096A.
30. Ibid., 1096B.
31. Ibid., 1096C–97B. See also Aristotle *Topica* 101ᵇ11–37.
32. Boethius *In categorias Aristotelis* (*PL* 64. 159B–C): "Et est prima positio, ut nomina rebus imponerentur, secunda vero ut al is nominibus ipsa nomina designarentur."
33. John of Salisbury *Metalogicon*, p. 35; (trans. McGarry), p. 42.
34. Priscian *Institutiones* (ed. Keil), 2:53.
35. Ibid., 2:54. The term προσσημαῖνον (Latin, "quod consignificat") appears in Aristotle *De interpretatione* 16ᵇ6.
36. Priscian *Institutiones* 18. 2. 13–14.
37. Peter Helias, *Summa super Priscianum*, p. 103: "Illud quoque addixerunt, quod non quaelibet dictionum conjunctio dici debet oratio, sed illa tantum quae aliquam inhaerentiam, i.e., rerum conjunctionem significat."
38. Aristotle *Poetics* 1457ᵃ24–31.
39. See Boethius, *Aristoteles Latinus*, ed. L. Minio-Paluello (Leiden, Netherlands: Brill, 1969), p. 149, l. 17; Boethius, *Aristoteles Latinus*, ed. Minio-Paluello (Bruges, Belgium: Desclée, 1965), p. 7, l. 20.
40. Boethius *Commentarius II in De interpretatione* (*PL* 64. 442–51).
41. Abelard, *Dialectica*, p. 65.
42. Martin of Dacia "De modis significandi" 2. 56. 198.
43. Robert de Basevorn, "Forma," p. 254.
44. Thomas Waleys, "De modo," p. 377.

45. For example, Peter of Spain, *Tractatus syncategorematum*, trans. Joseph P. Mullally (Milwaukee: Marquette University Press, 1964); William of Sherwood, *Syncategoremata*, ed. J. Reginald O'Donnell, *Medieval Studies* 3 (1941): 48 ff., trans. Norman Kretzmann as *Treatise on Syncategorematic Words* (Minneapolis: University of Minnesota Press, 1968).

46. Thomas Waleys, "De modo," p. 390.

47. Table of medieval concordances and their compilers:

Vocaliter	of Scripture:	Hugh of St. Cher, the three English Dominicans, Conrad of Halberstadt;
	of the Fathers:	Kilwardby;
Realiter	of Scripture:	Grosseteste, Thomas Gallus, Pseudo-Antonio, the anonymous compiler of the *Promptuarium*, John Pecham;
	of the Fathers:	Grosseteste, Kilwardby

See the following articles: D. A. Callus, "The 'Tabulae super Originalia Patrum' of Robert Kilwardby, O.P." in *Studia Mediaevalia in Honorem admodum Reverendi Patris Raymundi Josephi Martin* (Bruges, Belgium: De Tempel, 1948), pp. 243–70; P. Kleinhaus, "De concordanciis biblicis S. Antonio Patavino," *Antonianum* 6 (1931): 273–326; P. G. Théry, "Thomas Gallus et les concordances bibliques," *Beiträge zur Geschichte der Philosophie des Mittelalters*, Supp. 3 i, pp. 427–46; S. Harrison Thompson, "Grosseteste's Topical Concordance of the Bible and the Fathers," *Speculum* 9 (1934): 139–44.

48. Thomas Waleys, "De modo," p. 380. See also Robert de Basevorn, "Forma," p. 299.

49. Pseudo-Augustine (in fact, Augustine of Ireland, says the *Clavis Patrum Latinorum*, no. 1123), *De mirabilibus sacrae scripturae* (PL 35. 2154).

50. See Robert de Basevorn, "Forma," pp. 280–82.

51. *Tractatulus solemnis de arte et vero modo praedicandi*, mistakenly attributed to Thomas Aquinas, translated by Harry Caplan as "A Late Medieval Tractate on Preaching" in *Studies in Rhetoric and Public Speaking in Honor of James Albert Winans* (New York: Russell and Russell, 1962), p. 88.

52. Charland's remark, *Artes*, p. 198.

53. William of Auvergne, "De arte praedicandi," p. 207.

54. Thomas Waleys, "De modo," p. 395.

55. Richard of Thetford, "Octo modi," 43:19A. For Robert de Basevorn's borrowing of this passage from Richard, see his "Forma," p. 294.

56. Thomas Waleys, "De modo," p. 396.

57. Richard of Thetford, "Octo modi," 44:19A.

58. See Thomas Waleys, "De modo," p. 345–46.

59. *Curiositas* is an Augustinian word. See H. I. Marrou, *Saint Augustin et la fin de la culture antique*, pp. 148 ff. For use in *Ars praedicandi*, see William of Auvergne, "De arte praedicandi," p. 197; Robert de Basevorn, "Forma," p. 244, against the "modus Anglicus"; Thomas Waleys, "De modo," p. 336.

CHAPTER 2

Section B / A Sermon by Bonaventure

1. The Quaracchi editors remark that this sermon and another "adeo doctrinae copia abundant et ingenium auctoris manifestant." Bonaventure, *Opera omnia*, 5:xlvA.

2. See Praefatio of Quaracchi editors in Bonaventure, *Opera theologica selecta*, 5:18*.

3. See J. Guy Bougerol, *Introduction à l'étude de S. Bonaventure*, p. 206.

4. See Bonaventure "De sanctissimo corpore Christi" 7, 16, 25, 29, 35, 41, in *Opera theologica selecta*, vol. 5.

5. Robert de Basevorn, "Forma," p. 250.

6. The Section of the sermon analyzed below is in *Opera theologica selecta*, 5:307–11. This sermon is in *Opera omnia*, 5:553–66.

7. Bonaventure, "De sanctissimo corpore Christi," in *Opera theologica selecta*, 5:308. See Th. M. Charland, ed., *Artes praedicandi*, p. 150.

8. "Gratia fit efficacior in sua operatione mediante virtute Sacramenti." Bonaventure, "Commentaria in quatuor libros sententiarum," in *Opera omnia*, 4:21B.

CHAPTER 3

Section A / Renaissance Treatises of Ecclesiastical Rhetoric

1. John Ludham, *The Practis of Preaching*, fol. 71^v. Ludham's treatise is a translation and expansion of Andreas Gerardus [Hyperius], *De formandis concionibus sacris, seu de interpretatione Scripturarum populari* (Basil, 1579).

2. Ludham, *Practis*, fol. 1^{rv}.

3. Cicero *Topica* 2. 8.

4. Ibid., 14. 57.

5. Ibid., 2. 6.

6. See Boethius *De differentiis topicis* (*PL* 64. 1205–6CD).

7. See Richard McKeon, "Rhetoric in the Middle Ages," pp. 1–32.

8. Desiderius Erasmus, "Ratio," in *Opera omnia*, vol. 5, col. 80A.

9. Ibid., col. 82E.

10. Ibid.

11. Erasmus to Jodocus Jonas, June 1521, in *Opus epistolarum Erasmi*, 4:509. This letter translated in John C. Olin, ed., *Christian Humanism and the Reformation: Selected Writings of Erasmus*, trans. Lupton (New York: Harper Torchbooks, 1965), p. 167.

12. Erasmus, "Ratio," col. 81B–D.

13. Ibid., col. 127C.

14. For "gradus," see Desiderius Erasmus, "Copia," in *Opera omnia*, vol. 1, col. 84B; and Quintilian *Institutio oratio* 8. 4. 3. For "ratio," see Quintilian *Institutio oratio* 3. 11. 4.

15. See Erasmus, "Copia," vol. 1, col. 100D.

16. Erasmus, "Ratio," vol. 5, cols. 130F–31B.

17. Desiderius Erasmus, "Ecclesiastes," in *Opera omnia*, vol. 5, col. 858A.

18. See ibid., col. 902A.

19. Ibid., cols. 892F–93B.

20. Ibid., col. 896B.

21. See Thomas Wilson, *The Arte of Rhetorique*, p. 7.

22. Erasmus, "Copia," vol. 1, col. 75A; trans. by Donald King and David Rix (Milwaukee: Marquette University Press, 1963), p. 43.

23. Erasmus, "Ecclesiastes," vol. 5, col. 1026A.

24. See ibid., col. 858C–E; cols. 893F–94A. See also Cicero *De inventione* 2. 42. 121 ff.

25. Erasmus, "Ecclesiastes," vol. 5, col. 858D.

26. Ibid., col. 1012B–C.

27. Ibid., col. 1013C.

28. Ibid., col. 1035B.

29. Ibid., col. 1036E.

30. Ludham, *Practis*, fol. 9^r.

31. Cicero *De inventione* 1. 7. 9: "partes autem eae quas plerique dixerunt, inventio, dispositio, elocutio, memoria, pronuntiatio."

32. Ludham, *Practis*, fol. 9^v.

33. Ibid., fol. 10^v.

34. Ibid., fol. 51^r.
35. Ibid., fol. 22^r.
36. See ibid., fol. 18^r.
37. Ibid., fol. 53^v, fol. 57^v.
38. See Erasmus, "Ratio," vol. 5, col. 79A.
39. Erasmus, "Ecclesiastes," vol. 5, col. 920F.
40. Rudolf Agricola, *De inventione dialectica*, p. 15.
41. Ibid., pp. 17–18.
42. Ibid., p. 9.
43. Ibid., p. 197.
44. Ibid., p. 1.
45. Ibid., p. 180.
46. Peter Ramus, *Institutionum dialecticarum libri tres*, p. 348.
47. Cicero *Topica* 2. 6.
48. Ramus, *Institutionum*, p. 173.
49. Peter Ramus, *The Logike*, pp. 71–72.
50. Talon's notes to Ramus, *Institutionum*, p. 337, n. 4.
51. Ibid., p. 332.
52. Ibid., p. 311.
53. Ibid., p. 281.
54. Ibid.
55. Talon's notes to Ramus, p. 345, n. 1.
56. Ramus, *The Logike*, p. 100.
57. See Wilbur S. Howell, *Logic and Rhetoric in England, 1500–1700*, p. 206.
58. William Perkins, "The Art of Prophecying," in *Works*, 2:673^b.
59. Ibid., p. 645.
60. Ibid., p. 670^a.
61. Ibid.
62. Ibid., p. 651^b.
63. Ibid.
64. Ibid.
65. Ibid., p. 650^b.
66. See Augustine *De doctrina Christiana* 3. 30. 42–37. 56.
67. Perkins, "Art," 2:659^a.
68. Ibid., p. 662^a.
69. William Perkins, "A Godly and Learned Exposition of Christ's Sermon on the Mount," in *Works*, 3:104.
70. Perkins, "Art," p. 662^b.
71. Ibid.
72. Ibid., p. 663^a.
73. See Ramus, *The Logike*, bk. 1.
74. Perkins, "Art," p. 663^{ab}.
75. Ibid., p. 647^a.
76. Ibid., p. 664^a.
77. Ibid., p. 664^b.
78. Ibid., p. 665^a.
79. Ibid., p. 651^a.
80. Ibid., p. 646^b.

CHAPTER 3

Section B / Protestant Preaching of the English Reformation

1. For a representative collection see W. O. Ross, ed., *Middle English Sermons*.
2. Desiderius Erasmus, "Ecclesiastes," vol. 5, col. 860E.
3. John Calvin, "Responsio ad Sadoleti Epistolam," in *Opera selecta*, 1:468.

Translated as "Reply to Sadolet" in J. K. S. Reid, ed. and trans., *Calvin: Theological Treatises,* Library of Christian Classics series (Philadelphia: Westminster Press, 1954), p. 233.

4. William Tyndale, "Obedience of a Christian Man," in *Doctrinal Treatises, etc.,* p. 276.

5. Hugh Latimer, "Sixth Sermon before Edward VI," in *Sermons,* p. 199.

6. See André Wilmart, "Un répertoire d'exégèse," pp. 342–43, no. 6.

7. Luther, "In epistolam S. Pauli ad Galatas Commentarius," in *Werke,* vol. 40, pt. 1, 40:521. Translated in the American edition of *Luther's Works,* ed. Jarsolav Pelikan, (St. Louis: Concordia, 1963), 26:338–39.

8. Tyndale, "Obedience," p. 156.

9. Hugh Latimer, "Last Sermon before the King," in *Sermons,* p. 240.

10. John Stockewood, "A Very Fruitefull Sermon, preached at Paules Cross, May, 1579."

11. Ibid., Preface.

12. See John Jewel, "A Sermon Preached at Paul's Cross, 1560," in *Works,* 1:5.

13. James Brooks, "A Sermon Very Notable, Fruitful and Godlie," (1553).

14. Jewel, "A Sermon Preached at Paul's Cross, 1560," 1:20.

15. "a similitude not very agreeable, how the Scriptures be like a nose of wax." John Jewel, "An Apologie of the Church of England," in *English Reformers,* ed. T. H. L. Parker, Library of Christian Classics series (Philadelphia: Westminster Press, 1966), p. 37. See OED s.v. "nose" I. 4. For the phrase in Alan of Lille, see *PL* 210, col. 333A.

16. Hugh Latimer, "Sermon Preached on Septuagesima Sunday, 1552" in *Sermons and Remains,* p. 199.

17. John Jewel, "Sermon on Joshua 6, 1569," in *Works,* 2:983.

18. John Hooper, "A Funeral Sermon, 1549," in *Early Writings of John Hooper,* p. 568.

19. John Hooper, "An Oversight and Deliberation upon the Holy Prophet Jonas, 1550," ibid., p. 452.

20. Ibid., pp. 489–90.

21. Thomas Cartwright, *A Commentary upon the Epistle of St. Paul Written to the Colossians,* p. 1^a.

22. Ibid., pp. 2^b–3^a.

23. Thomas Cartwright, "Speech at Daughter's Betrothal," in *Cartwrightiana,* pp. 185–86.

24. Perkins, "A Godly and Learned Exposition," p. 248^b.

25. Ibid., p. 26^b.

26. Ibid., p. 241^b.

27. Ibid., p. 13^b.

28. Ibid., p. 23^b.

29. Ibid., p. 95^b.

30. Ibid.

31. Ibid., p. 48^b.

32. Ibid., p. 224^a.

33. Ibid., pp. 3^b–4^a.

34. Ibid., p. 4^a.

35. Ibid., p. 4^a.

36. Ibid., p. 241^b.

37. Ibid., pp. 21^b–22^a.

38. Ibid., p. 12^a.

39. Ibid., p. 12^b.

40. Ibid., p. 13^a.
41. Ibid., p. 5^a.
42. Ibid., p. 10^a.

CHAPTER 4

Section A / The Reaction of the High Church Party
1. Richard Hooker, "Of the Laws of Ecclesiastical Polity," in *Works*, 1:125.
2. The first "Admonition to Parliament," in *Puritan Manifestoes*, p. 5.
3. Hooker, "Of the Laws," 1:142.
4. Ibid., 1:287.
5. Ibid., 2:85–86.
6. Ibid., 2:20.
7. Ibid., 1:218–19.
8. Ibid., 1:147.
9. Ibid., 1:360.
10. The first "Admonition to Parliament," p. 11.
11. Hooker, "Of the Laws," 2:99.
12. Ibid., 2:84.
13. Ibid., 2:64.
14. See Mark H. Curtis, *Oxford and Cambridge in Transition*, pp. 220 ff.
15. Thomas Playfere, "The Meane in Mourning," in *The Whole Sermons of Thomas Playfere*, p. 4.
16. John Eachard ridicules Playfere's division of this sermon: "By reason what he did, was done by undoubted Art and absolute industry: but as for the other, the common report is that it was found out by mere foolish fortune" ("The Grounds and Occasions of the Contempt of the Clergy and Religion," p. 280). For mention of this procedure in the *Ars praedicandi*, see Robert de Basevorn, "Forma praedicandi," p. 255.
17. Playfere, "The Difference between the Law and the Gospel," in *Whole Sermons*, p. 231.
18. References to Henri de Lubac, "Symboles de la concorde," in *Exégèse médiévale*, 1:351, 346, 350; Nicholas of Lyra, *Glossa ordinaria*, 4:410^r.
19. Playfere, "Heart's Delight," in *Whole Sermons*, p. 2.
20. Playfere, "The Sick-man's Couch," ibid., p. 37, misnumbered as p. 39.
21. Garnier de Rochefort mistakenly attributed to Rhaban Maur *Allegoriae in Sacram Scripturam* (*PL* 112. 1069–70). 'Turtus' does not occur in the Vulgate reading of the Psalm text.
22. Lancelot Andrewes, "Sermon 10 of the Holy Ghost, Whit-Sunday, 1617" in *Sermons*, p. 272.
23. Andrewes's sermon is no. 3 in Story's collection, "Sermon 11 of the Nativity, 1616." See Bernard, *In Annun. Beatae Mariae* (*PL* 183. 383 ff.).
24. Lancelot Andrewes, "Sermon preached before the King on Christmas Day, 1614," in *Works*, 1:142.
25. Andrewes, "Sermon 12 of the Nativity, 1618," in *Sermons*, p. 85. For the Fathers on 'Verbum infans' see Augustine *Sermo* 190 (*PL* 38. 1008). Bernard, "In Vigilia Nativitatis," in *Opera* (Rome: Editiones Cistercienses, 1966), 4:198.
26. Andrewes, "Sermon 11 of the Resurrection, 1616," in *Sermons*, p. 183.
27. Andrewes, "Sermon 4 of Repentance, 1619," ibid., p. 122.
28. Andrewes, "Sermon 11 of the Nativitie, 1616," ibid., p. 71.
29. Andrewes, "Sermon 12 of the Nativitie, 1618," ibid., p. 77.
30. Andrewes, "Sermon 15 of the Nativitie, 1622," ibid., p. 101.
31. For Hooker and Andrewes, see David Novarr, *The Making of Walton's "Lives,"* p. 210. For Playfere and Andrewes, see Curtis, *Oxford and Cambridge*, p. 222. For Donne and Andrewes, see R. C. Bald, *John Donne: A Life*, pp. 307, 415.

CHAPTER 4

Section B | Donne on How the Preacher Should Deal with His Text
1. O.E.D. under *Rhapsoder* = *Rhapsodist*: (1) "A collector of literary pieces."
2. John Donne, "A litanie," in *The Divine Poems*, p. 19, l. 80.
3. See Vincent of Lerins *Commonitorium* (*PL* 50. 640). For the Tridentine canon, see H. Denzinger and A. Schönmetzer, eds., *Enchiridion symbolorum*, no. 1507. Donne owned a copy of the Council's proceedings: see Geoffrey L. Keynes, *A Bibliography of Dr. John Donne*, p. 214, L78.
4. John Donne, *Devotions upon Emergent Occasions*, pp. 125–26.
5. John Donne, *Essays in Divinity*, p. 8 = Nicholas of Lyra, *Glossa Ordinaria*, 1:C.
6. See for example, Donne, *Essays*, p. 67.
7. 9. 11. 125–26 = Augustine *Doctrina* 2. 40. 61.
8. Donne, *Essays*, p. 40.
9. Thomas Wilson, *The Arte of Rhetorique*, p. 162. O.E.D. under *Poetical*, (l.b) "Such as is found only in poetry or imaginative writing."
10. See for example Richard Bernard, *The Faithful Shepherd*, p. 246. O.E.D. under *Wanton*, (A. 8. a) "Of speech or imagination: extravagant."
11. Donne, *Essays*, p. 48.
12. Ibid., p. 13, refers to the "Expositio primae dictionis" at the end of Pico della Mirandola, "Heptaplus," in *De hominis dignitate, Heptaplus, De ente et uno*, pp. 374–83.
13. Pico della Mirandola, "Heptaplus," p. 192.
14. Donne, *Essays*, p. 91. Refers to Johann Reuchlin, "De arte cabalistica," in *Opera omnia of Pico*, p. 770.
15. Reuchlin, "De arte cabalistica," p. 772, misnumbered 872.
16. Donne, *Essays*, p. 14.
17. See 9. 2. 812–15; 9. 1 for dating.
18. Donne, *Essays*, pp. 23 ff.
19. See also, 2. 15. 281–83; 3. 5. 693–99; 5. 16. 219 ff; 7. 1. 541 ff; 7. 18. 427–37.
20. Donne, *Essays*, p. 45.
21. See on Cain and Abel (3. 1¹. 95–98), on Cain, Samuel, Matthew, and John (3. 1². 315–21), on Ishmael and Isaac (6. 9. 317–20), on the women at the tomb (9. 8. 140–51), etc.
22. Donne, *Essays*, p. 23.
23. See 2. 2. 240–41; 9. 2. 578–79; 9. 11. 233–37; 10. 9. 180 ff.
24. It may be that Donne differed from Hooker in his view of the efficaciousness of bare reading, but certainly his own procedures of exposition had more in common with Hooker's than with those of the extreme Puritans. But see Thomas F. Merrill, "John Donne and the Word of God," pp. 597–616.

CHAPTER 5

Section A | The Divisio
1. 8. 4. 171–73.
2. For mention of term *paraphrase* in the *divisio* of other sermons, see 3. 12. 76; 4. 1. 18; 8. 2. 19. For paraphrastic distribution in fact, without explicit mention of the term, see 2. 1; 3. 10; 9. 17; 10. 1; etc. (Here and elsewhere in this section where only two figures are given in a citation, the reference is to the *divisio* paragraph of that sermon.)
3. See 1. 6. 314; 4. 7. 909; 5. 1. 269.
4. See Mark H. Curtis, *Oxford and Cambridge in Transition*, p. 161.

5. *Praeterita, praesentia, ad futura.* See Th. M. Charland, ed. *Artes praedicandi,* p. 169.

6. See 2. 17. 49.

7. See 3. 8. 91–93; 3. 15. 13–14; 4. 3. 121–22; 7. 5. 125–28: 8. 15. 80–83; etc.

8. For Bernard, see "Sermo 45, De varia Trinitate," *PL* 183, coll. 667–69. The ultimate source is Augustine, *De Trinitate,* bk. x. For mention of this trinity of the soul elsewhere in Donne's sermons, see 3. 5. 395–403; 5. 6. 692–712; 9. 2. 596–620.

9. See later in this same sermon 7. 3. 136, 263, 268.

10. See 4. 3. 146 ff.; 4. 6. 40–41; 6. 15. 278, 285; 8. 5. 119, 279; etc.

11. Namely, Beza and Piscator: 7. 4. 16–20.

12. See Cicero *Topica* 21. 79; Boethius *De differentiis topicis* (*PL* 64. 1205C).

13. Bartholomaeus Keckermann, *Rhetoricae ecclesiasticae sive artis formandi et habendi conciones sacras libri duo,* p. 100. The British Museum copy, C.79.a.31, was bound for Henry, Prince of Wales. See also Perry Miller, *The New England Mind: The Seventeenth Century,* p. 336.

14. See John Sparrow, "John Donne and Contemporary Preachers," p. 164.

15. See also 2. 5. 3; 4. 6. 21–22; 5. 11. 44–45; 6. 9. 360; etc.

16. See Frances Yates, *The Art of Memory.*

17. See also 6. 11. 34–37.

18. See also 7. 10. 95–98; 7. 14. 109–113. For images of the journey, see 5. 14. 187–89; 7. 9. 18–26; 7. 17. 29–30; 8. 12. 203–7.

19. Donne, *Essays,* p. 74. For "rumination" in the sermons, see 6. 1. 470–76; 8. 5. 103.

20. See also 2. 11. 88–112.

21. "And be this enough for the Explication of the words, and their Application, and Complication to the celebration of the day." 8. 14. 805–6.

22. "And be this enough for the Explication, and Application, and Complication of these words, in all these three places." 8. 13. 709–10.

23. See Augustine *Confessiones* 12. 18. 27 ff.

24. See 3. 6. 371–73; 8. 10. 145–47; 8. 13. 465–66; 8. 15. 313–14.

25. See also 3. 6, 7; 6. 16 and 7. 8; 10. 11.

26. See also 2. 12; 3. 4; 4. 3; 8. 9; etc.

27. 8. 9. 33–37.

CHAPTER 5

Section B / Multiplying the Words of Scripture

1. See also 8. 5. 65–67.

2. See 2. 5. 37; 3. 10. 235.

3. See 3. 18. 379; 5. 2. 628; 9. 13. 242.

4. See also 7. 12. 230–34.

5. See also 5. 8. 108–11. Jerome *Epistula* (*CSEL* 54. 155). Quoted by Cassiodorus *Expositio psalmorum* (*CCSL* 97. 6).

6. See 1. 6. 43.

7. See also 9. 8. 614–19.

8. See 9. 11. 233–36.

9. See also 9. 9. 479–99.

10. See 1. 3. 1114–16; 7. 5. 528 ff.

11. See also 8. 16. 28–30.

12. See 5. 16. 348–54; 6. 8. 77–83; 9. 6. 468–75.

13. But see 3. 13. 76–77.

14. See 7. 17. 273–76; 9. 7. 67–70.

15. See 5. 18. 188–90; 7. 2. 524–30; 7. 9. 390–91.

16. 1. 2. 218; 1. 4. 309; 4. 11. 621; 8. 8. 191; etc.

17. See also 5. 17. 589–639; 7. 8. 367–403; 7. 17. 577 ff.; 9. 18. 546–64.

18. 9. 18. 327. Also, "Saint Bernard takes the word, 'poverty,' in that place, but he multiplies it" (4. 6. 339–40).

19. See 8. 11. 99–100.

20. See also 1. 1. 88–111; 7. 17. 473–91; 8. 12. 212–21.

21. See note 5 to Ch. 4, sect. B.

22. For Augustine, *Enarrationes in Psalmos* on Ps. 90. 1. 6.

23. See 5. 18. 135–36; 9. 7. 310.

24. See 1. 5. 442; 8. 13. 178.

25. See 3. 18. 378; 10. 6. 524–25.

26. See 4. 1. 120; 7. 12. 824–25.

27. See 7. 7. 235.

28. See note 25 to Ch. 1, sect. C.

29. See also 2. 1. 271 ff.; 2. 3. 79–91; 7. 11. 103–12; 8. 1. 156–210. For Augustine on Hyssop, see *In Psalmos* on Ps. 50. 12.

30. See John Donne, *Essays in Divinity*, p. 7.

31. See 10. 4. 241 ff.

32. See 7. 6. 769–804.

33. See note 32 to Ch. 1, sect. C.

34. See 7. 1. 583–633.

35. See also 3. 10. 294 ff.; 5. 2. 605–18; 5. 8. 251–91; 8. 7. 619–56; etc.

36. See also 3. 13. 73–116; 3. 15. 294–378; 4. 2. 109–18; 6. 4. 33 ff.; etc.

37. See also 9. 1. 576 ff.

38. See 2. 9. 118–24; 6. 8. 615–16; 4. 10. 10; 10. 8. 442–45.

39. See 2. 8. 432–33; 5. 15. 630–31.

40. See also 5. 15. 73–79.

41. See 4. 4. 212–19; 5. 17. 843–49.

42. See 4. 6. 468–70.

43. See also 2. 11. 169–74.

44. See 5. 11. 442–43.

CHAPTER 5

Section C / Donne's Sermon on Ps. 32:1-2

1. Donne has *"Davidis erudiens"*; the margin of his King James Version had "Psalm of David, giving instruction"; Calvin's commentary had *"Erudiens Davidis"* (CR 59. 314).

2. Wolfgang Musculus, "Ad lectorem," in *Davidis Psalterium sacrosanctum commentarii*.

3. Joannes Lorinus, *Commentarii in librum psalmorum*, 2:192B.

4. See 5. 14. 105; 5. 15. 305.

5. l. 40, see Augustine *De Trinitate* 10. 1. 1.

l. 124, see *De doctrina Christiana* 2. 40. 61.

l. 130, see *Confessiones* 3. 4. 7.

l. 260, see *De Trinitate* 13. 5. 8.

l. 295, see *Confessiones* 1. 13. 21.

l. 298, see *Confessiones* 13. 9. 10.

6. l. 678, see Augustine *Enarrationes in Psalmos* on Ps. 31. 2. 15.

l. 741, see ibid., 2. 9.

l. 771, see ibid.

7. Gregory the Great *In librum primum regum* (CCSL), 144:472.

8. "Primus hic post primum Psalmum inchoat a beatitudine," Lorinus, *Commentarii*, 1:435A.

9. Elsewhere on this text these same two senses for *Blessed* are distinguished: "Blessednesse includes all that can be asked or conceived in the next world,

and in this too. . . . He that hath peace in the remission of sinnes, is blessed already, and shall have those blessings infinitely multiplied in the world to come" (10. 2. 495–506).

10. For the six places where mention is made of the marginalia of the Authorized Version, the notes are to be found in such an edition as that of R. Barker, London, 1616. The places are: 7. 12. 207; 7. 15. 529; 7. 16. 546; 8. 5. 16; 9. 18. 273; 9. 18. 622.

11. Augustine *In Psalmos* on Ps. 31. 2. 1.

12. Martin Luther, "The Seven Penitential Psalms," in *Works*, ed. Jarsolav Pelikan, trans. A. Guebert (St. Louis: Concordia, 1958), 14:149.

13. *Enchiridion Symbolorum*, no. 1678.

14. John Calvin *In librum psalmorum commentarius* on Ps. 32:1 (*CR* 59. 316).

15. See Hugh of St. Cher, *Opera omnia in universum vetus et novum testamentum* (Venice: Apud Nicolaum Pezzana, 1732), 2:fols. 76ᵛ–77ʳ; Franciscus de Puteo, *Cathena aurea super psalmos* (Paris: 1530), fol. 43ʳ.

16. "Pondus meum amor meus." Augustine *Confessiones* 13. 9. 10.

17. See also 2. 4. 132–39.

18. See 2. 14. 478.

19. So the verse is given at the head of the sermon (5. 7). It is the reading of the Geneva Bible.

20. John Calvin *In librum psalmorum* on Ps. 32:1 (*CR* 59. 316).

21. See also 6. 2. 658–59; 9. 1. 104–5.

SELECTED BIBLIOGRAPHY

PRIMARY SOURCES

Abelard, Peter. *Dialectica*. 2d ed. Edited by L. M. de Rijk. Assen: van Gorcum, 1970.

Agricola, Rudolf. *De inventione dialectica*. Cologne, 1523.

Alan of Lille. *PL* 210.

Alcock, Simon. "De modo dividendi thema pro materia sermonis dilatanda." Edited by Mary B. Boynton. *Harvard Theological Review* 34 (1941): 201–6.

Andrewes, Lancelot. *Sermons*. Edited by G. M. Story. Oxford: Clarendon Press, 1967.

––––––. *Works*. Library of Anglo-Catholic Theology. 11 vols. Oxford: James Parker, 1878.

Aristotle. *Categories, De interpretatione*. *OCT*, 1961.

––––––. *Poetics*. *OCT*, 1965.

––––––. *Rhetoric*. *OCT*, 1959.

––––––. *Topics*. *OCT*, 1958.

Augustine, Aurelius. *Confessiones*. Bibliothèque Augustinienne. 2 vols. Paris: Desclée, 1962.

––––––. "De doctrina Christiana" in *CCSL* 32, pp. 1–167.

––––––. *Enarrationes in Psalmos*. *CCSL* 38–40.

––––––. "De magistro," in *CSEL* 77, pp. 3–55.

––––––. *De ordine*. Edited by W. M. Green, pp. 97–148. Stromata series. Utrecht: Spectrum, 1956.

––––––. *De Trinitate*. *CCSL* 50–50A.

––––––. "De utilitate credendi," in *CSEL* 25, pp. 3–48.

Basevorn, Robert de. "Forma praedicandi." In *Artes praedicandi*, edited by Th. M. Charland, pp. 231–323. Publications de l'institut d'études médiévales d'Ottawa, no. 8. Paris: Vrin, 1936.

Bernard, Richard. *The Faithful Shepherd*. London: For Thomas Pavier, 1621.

Boethius. *Opera*. *PL* 64.

Bonaventure. *Opera omnia*. 10 vols. Quaracchi: College of St. Bonaventure, 1882–1902.

––––––. *Opera theologica selecta*. vol. 5. Quaracchi: College of St. Bonaventure, 1964.

"Bonaventure." "Ars concionandi." In *Opera omnia*, vol. 9, pp. 8–21. Quaracchi: College of St. Bonaventure, 1901.

Bromyard, John. *Summa praedicantium*. Nuremberg: per Anthonium Koberger, 1485.

Brooks, James. *A Sermon Very Notable, Fruitful and Godlie*.
London: Imprinted by Robert Caly, 1553. *STC* n. 3838.
Calvin, John. *Opera*. *CR* 29–87.
_____. *Opera selecta*. Edited by Peter Barth and William Niesel.
5 vols. Munich: Kaiser, 1962.
Cartwright, Thomas. *Cartwrightiana*. Edited by Albert Peel and
Leland H. Carlson. London: George Allen and Unwin, 1951.
_____. *A Commentary upon the Epistle of St. Paul Written to the
Colossians*. Edinburgh: James Nichol, 1864.
Cassiodorus. *Expositio Psalmorum*. *CCSL* 97.
_____. *Institutiones*. Edited by R. A. B. Mynors. Oxford:
Clarendon Press, 1963.
Cicero. *De inventione* and *Topica*. Loeb Classical Library.
Cambridge, Mass.: Harvard University Press, 1949.
_____. *De oratore*. Loeb Classical Library. 2 vols. Cambridge,
Mass.: Harvard University Press, 1948.
"Cicero." *Rhetorica ad Herennium*. Loeb Classical Library.
Cambridge, Mass.: Harvard University Press, 1954.
Denzinger, H., and Schönmetzer, S., eds. *Enchiridion
Symbolorum*. Barcelona: Herder, 1963.
Dionysius Thrax. "Ars grammatica." In *Grammatici Graeci*,
edited by G. Uhlig, vol li, pp. 1–100. Leipzig: Teubner, 1883.
Donatus. "Ars grammatica." In *Grammatici Latini*, edited by H.
Keil, vol. 4, pp. 367–402. 1864. Reprint. Hildesheim, W.
Germany: Olms, 1961.
_____. *Commentum Terenti*. Edited by P. Wessner. 2 vols.
Stuttgart: Teubner, 1962.
Donne, John. *Devotions upon Emergent Occasions*. Ann Arbor:
University of Michigan Press, 1959.
_____. *The Divine Poems*. Edited by Helen Gardner. Oxford:
Clarendon Press, 1964.
_____. *Donne's Prebend Sermons*. Edited by Janel M. Mueller.
Cambridge, Mass.: Harvard University Press, 1971.
_____. *Essays in Divinity*. Edited by E. M. Simpson. Oxford:
Clarendon Press, 1952.
_____. *The Sermons of John Donne*. Edited by Evelyn M.
Simpson and George R. Potter. 10 vols. Berkeley: University
of California Press, 1953–62.
Eachard, John. "The Grounds and Occasions of the Contempt
of the Clergy and Religion." 1670. In *Critical Essays and
Literary Fragments*, edited by J. C. Collins, pp. 241 ff. English
Garner series. Westminster: Archibald Constable, 1903.
Erasmus, Desiderius. *Opera omnia*. Vols. 1, 5. Leyden, Nether-
lands: Batavi, 1703–6.
_____. Erasmus to Jodocus Jonas, June 1521. In *Opus epis-*

tolarum Erasmi, edited by P. S. Allen, vol. 4, pp. 507–27.
Oxford: Clarendon Press, 1922.

Eucherius. "Formulae spiritualis intelligentiae," in *CSEL* 31,
pp. 1–62.

Fisher, John. *The English Works of John Fisher*. EETS, 27, 1876.

Franciscus de Puteo. *Cathena aurea super Psalmos*. Paris: C.
Wechel, 1530.

Frere, W. H., and Douglas, C. E., eds. *Puritan Manifestoes*.
London: SPCK, 1907.

Garnier de Rochefort [Rhaban Maur]. "Allegoriae in univer-
sam Sacram Scripturam." *PL* 112, cols. 849–1088.

The Geneva Bible, A Facsimile of the 1560 Edition. Introduction by
L. E. Berry. Madison: University of Wisconsin Press, 1969.

Guibert de Nogent. "Liber quo ordine sermon fieri debeat." *PL*
156, cols. 21–32.

"Henry of Hesse." "On the Art of Preaching." Edited and
translated by H. Caplan. *PMLA* 48 (1933): 340–61.

Hooker, Richard. *Works*. 7th ed. Arranged by John Keble,
revised by R. W. Church and F. Paget. 3 vols. Oxford:
Clarendon Press, 1888.

Hooper, John. *Early Writings of John Hooper*. Edited by Samuel
Carr. Parker Society. Cambridge: At the University Press,
1843.

Humbert of Romans. *De eruditione praedicatorum*. Maxima
Bibliotheca Veterum Patrum, vol. 25, pp. 426–56. Lyons:
1677.

Hyperius. *De formandis concionibus sacris seu de intrepatione
Scripturarum populari*. Basil, 1579.

Isidore of Seville. *Etymologiarum sive originum libri XX*. Edited
by W. M. Lindsay. *OCT*, 1911.

———. *Opera*. PL 81–84.

Jewel, John. *Works*. Edited by John Ayre. Parker Society. 4 vols.
Cambridge: At the University Press, 1845–50.

John of Salisbury. *Metalogicon*. Edited by Clemens C. I. Webb.
Oxford: Clarendon Press, 1929.

Keckermann, Bartholomaeus. *Rhetoricae ecclesiasticae sive artis
formandi et habendi conciones sacras libri duo*. Hanover: William
Antonius, 1606.

Latimer, Hugh. *Works*. Edited by G. E. Corrie. Parker Society. 2
vols. Vol. 1, *Sermons*; vol. 2, *Sermons and Remains*. Cam-
bridge: At the University Press, 1844–45.

Leclerq., J. "Smaragde et la grammaire chrétienne." *Revue du
moyen âge latin* 4 (1948): 15–22.

Lorinus, Joannes. *Commentarii in librum psalmorum*. 3 vols.
Lyon: Horatius Cardon, 1619.

Ludham, John. *The Practis of Preaching*. London: T. East, 1577.

Luther, Martin. *Werke*. Weimar: Böhlaus, 1883–.

Macrobius. *Saturnalia*. Edited by J. Willis. Leipzig: Teubner, 1963.

Martianus Capella. *De nuptiis Mercurii et Philologiae*. Edited by A. Dick. Leipzig: Teubner, 1925.

Martin of Dacia. "De modis significandi." In *Opera*, edited by H. Roos, pp. 1–118. Corpus Philosophorum Danicorum Medii AEvi. Copenhagen: Gad, 1961.

Melanchthon, Philipp. "Commentarii in Psalmos," in *CR* 13, cols. 1017–245.

"Melitus of Sardis." "Clavis." In *Spicilegium Solesmense*, edited by J. B. Pitra. 2 vols. Paris: Apud Firmin Didot Fratres, 1855.

Musculus, Wolfgang. *Davidis Psalterium sacrosanctum commentarii*. Basil: S. Henricpetri, 1599.

Nicholas of Lyra. *Glossa ordinaria*. 7 vols. Paris, 1590.

Perkins, William. *Works*. Translated by Thomas Tuke. 3 vols. London: J. Legatt, 1631.

Peter Helias. "Summa super Priscianum." Edited by Leo Reilly. Ph.D. dissertation, University of Toronto, 1974.

Peter of Cornwall. Prologue to the *Pantheologus*. Edited by R. W. Hunt. *Transactions of the Royal Historical Society* 4th ser. 19 (1936): 38–42.

Peter of Spain. *Tractatus* (*=Summulae logicales*). Edited by L. M. de Rijk. Assen: van Gorcum, 1972.

Pico della Mirandola. "Heptaplus." In *De hominis dignitate, Heptaplus, De ente et uno*. Edited by E. Garin. Florence: Vallecchi, 1942.

Piscator, Johannes. *In librum psalmorum commentarius*. Herborn, Germany: C. Corvinus, 1611.

Plato. *Opera*. Vols. 2, 6. *OCT*, 1902.

Playfere, Thomas. *The Whole Sermons of Thomas Playfere*. London: J. Legatt, 1603. *STC* no. 20003.

Priscian. "Institutiones." In *Grammatici Latini*, edited by Keil. Vols. 2 and 3, 1855–59. Reprint. Hildesheim, W. Germany: Olms, 1961.

Quintilian. *Institutio oratorio*. Loeb Classical Library. 4 vols. London: William Heinemann Ltd., 1953.

Rainolde, Richard. *The Foundacion of Rhetorike*. New York: Scholars' Facsimiles and Reprints, 1945.

Ramus, Peter. *Grammatica*. Paris: Apud Andream Wechelum, 1564.

———. *Institutionum dialecticarum libri tres*. Paris: Matthaeus David, 1552.

_____. *The Logike*. Translated by M. R. Makylmain. 1574. Reprint. Leeds: Scolar Press, 1966.

Reuchlin, Johann. "De arte cabalistica." In *Opera omnia of Pico*, pp. 733–900. Basil, 1557.

Ross, W. O., ed. *Middle English Sermons*. EETS, o.s. 209, 1960.

Servius. "Commentarius in artem Donati." In *Grammatici Latini*, edited by Keil, vol. 4, pp. 403–48. 1864. Reprint. Hildesheim, W. Germany: Olms, 1961.

_____. *In Vergilii Aeneidos libros XII commentarius*. Edited by G. Thilo and H. Hagen. 3 vols. 1881–87. Reprint. Hildesheim, W. Germany: Olms, 1961.

Siger of Courtrai. "Summa modorum significandi." In *Les oeuvres de Siger de Courtrai*, edited by G. Wallerand, pp. 91–125. Les philosophes Belges. Louvain: Institut Superieur, 1913.

Smaragdus of St. Mihiel. "Liber in partibus Donati" (partial). In *Grammatici Latini*. Edited by H. Keil. Vol. 8, *Anecdota Helvetica*, edited by H. Hagen, 1870, pp. ccxxxix–ccxlvi. Reprint. Hildesheim, W. Germany: Olms, 1961.

_____. "Liber in partibus Donati" (partial). Edited by E. Kalinka. *Weiner Studien* 16 (1895): 113–15.

_____. "Liber in partibus Donati" (partial). In *Vetera analecta*, edited by Mabillon, p. 358. Paris: Apud Montalant, 1723.

Stockewood, John. "A Very Fruitefull Sermon, Preached at Paules Cross, May, 1579." *STC* no. 23285.

Suetonius. "On Grammarians." In *Works*, vol. 2, pp. 397–433. Loeb Classical Library. London: Heinemann, 1950.

Talon. *Rhetorica*. Paris: Apud Andream Wechelum, 1562.

Thomas Aquinas. "In psalmos Davidis expositio." In *Opera omnia*, vol. 14, pp. 148–353. Parma, Italy: Peter Fiaccadorus, 1863.

"Thomas Aquinas." "Tractatulus solemnis de arte et vero modo praedicandi." In *Studies in Rhetoric and Public Speaking in Honor of James A. Winans*, edited by H. Caplan, pp. 61–90. New York: Russell and Russell, 1962.

Thurot, M. Charles. "Notices et extraits de divers manuscrits latins pour servir à l'histoire des doctrines grammaticales au moyen âge." In *Notices et extraits des manuscrits de la bibliothèque nationale et autres bibliothèques*, vol. 22, pt. 2. Paris: Imprimerie Nationale, 1868.

Toal, M. F., trans. *The Sunday Sermons of the Great Fathers*. 4 vols. Chicago: Henry Regnery, 1964.

Tyndale, William. "Obedience of a Christian Man." In *Doctrinal Treatises, etc.* Edited by H. Walter. Parker Society. Cambridge: At the University Press, 1848.

Uhlfelder, Myra L., ed. *De proprietate sermonum vel rerum.*
Papers and Monographs of the American Academy in
Rome, no. 15, 1954.
Victorinus, Marius. "De definitionibus." In *Tulliana et
Mario-Victoriniana*, edited by Th. Stangl, pp. 17–48. Munich:
Max Wild'sche, 1888.
————. "Explanationum in rhetoricam M. Tulii Ciceronis libri
duo." In *Rhetores Latini minores*, edited by C. Halm, pp.
155–310. Leipzig: Teubner, 1863.
Waleys, Thomas. "De modo componendi sermones." In *Artes
praedicandi*, edited by Th. M. Charland, pp. 328–403.
Publications de l'institut d'études médiévales d'Ottawa, no.
8. Paris: Vrin, 1936.
Walton, Izaak. "The Life of Dr. John Donne." In *Donne's
Devotions*, pp. v–li. Ann Arbor: University of Michigan
Press, 1959.
————. "The Life of Mr. Richard Hooker." In *The Works of
Hooker*, 7th ed., arranged by John Keble, revised by R. W.
Church and F. Paget, vol. 1, pp. 1–87. Oxford: Clarendon
Press, 1888.
William of Auvergne. "De arte praedicandi." Edited by A. de
Poorter. *Revue neo-scolastique de philosophie*, 1923, pp.
192–209.
William of Sherwood. "Introductiones in logicam." Edited by
M. Grabmann in *Philosophisch-historische Abteilung*, vol. 10.
Munich: Bayerischen Akademie der Wissenschaften, 1937.
Wilson, Thomas. *The Arte of Rhetorique.* Edited by C. H. Mair.
Oxford: Clarendon Press, 1909.

SECONDARY SOURCES
Alfaric, Prosper. *L'évolution intellectuelle de Saint Augustin.* Paris:
Emile Nourry, 1918.
Allen, D. C. *The Legend of Noah.* Urbana: University of Illinois
Press, 1963.
————. "Dean Donne Sets His Text." *ELH* 10 (1943): 208–29.
Bald, R. C. *John Donne: A Life.* Oxford: Clarendon Press, 1970.
Baldwin, C. S. *Medieval Rhetoric and Poetic.* New York: Macmillan, 1928.
Bauer, Robert J. "John Donne and the Schoolmen." Ph.D.
dissertation, University of Wisconsin, 1967.
Bellissima, Giuseppina. "Sant' Agostino grammatico." In
Augustinus magister, vol. 1, pp. 35–42. Paris: Etudes Augustiniennes, 1954.
Bennet, H. S. *English Books and Readers, 1475–1557.* Cambridge:
At the University Press, 1952.

Blau, Joseph L. *The Christian Interpretation of the Cabala in the Renaissance.* Port Washington, N. Y.: Kennikat Press, 1944.
———. "The Diffusion of the Christian Interpretation of the Cabala in English Literature." *Review of Religion* 6 (1942): 146–65.
Blench, J. W. *Preaching in England in the Late Fifteenth and Sixteenth Centuries.* Oxford: Basil Blackwell, 1964.
Bochénski, I. M. *A History of Formal Logic.* Translated by Ivo Thomas. Notre Dame, Ind.: University of Notre Dame Press, 1961.
Bougerol, J. Guy. *Introduction à l'étude de S. Bonaventure.* Paris: Desclée, 1961.
Boyle, L. E. "The *Oculus sacerdotis* and some other works of William of Pagula." *Transactions of the Royal Historical Society* 5 (1955): 81–110.
Bredvold, Louis I. "The Religious Thought of Donne in Relation to Medieval and Later Traditions." In *Studies in Shakespeare, Milton and Donne* by Members of the English Department of the University of Michigan, vol. 1, pp. 193–232. New York: Macmillan, 1925.
Bruyne, D. de. "*Enarrationes in Psalmos* prêchées à Carthage." In *Miscellanea Agostiniana,* vol. 2, pp. 321–25. Rome: Tipographia Poliglatta Vaticana, 1931.
Bursill-Hill, G. L. *Speculative Grammars of the Middle Ages.* The Hague: Mouton, 1971.
The Cambridge History of the Bible. Vol. 1, edited by P. R. Ackroyd and C. F. Evans. Cambridge: At the University Press, 1970.
———. Vol. 2, edited by G. W. H. Lampe. 1969.
———. Vol. 3, edited by S. L. Greenslade. 1963.
Caplan, Harry. "Classical Rhetoric and the Medieval Theory of Preaching." *Classical Philology* 28 (1933): 73–96.
———. "The Four Senses of Scriptural Interpretation and the Medieval Theory of Preaching." *Speculum* 4 (1929): 282–90.
———. *Medieval artes praedicandi: A Handlist.* Cornell Studies in Classical Philology, no. 24. Ithaca, N.Y., 1934.
———. *Medieval artes praedicandi: A Supplementary Handlist.* Cornell Studies in Classical Philology, no. 25. Ithaca, N.Y., 1936.
———. "Rhetorical Invention in Some Medieval Tractates on Preaching." *Speculum* 2 (1927): 284–95.
Carrithers, Gale. *Donne at Sermons.* Albany: State University of New York Press, 1972.
Charland, Th. M., ed. *Artes praedicandi.* Publications de l'institut d'études médiévales d'Ottawa, no. 8. Paris: Vrin, 1936.

Chenu, M. D. *La Théologie au douzième siècle*. Paris: Vrin, 1957.

Colish, Marcia L. *The Mirror of Language*. New Haven: Yale University Press, 1968.

Collart, Jean. "Saint Augustin grammairien dans le *De magistro.*" *Revue des études Augustiniennes* 17 (1971): 279–92.

Comeau, Marie. *Saint Augustin: Exégète du quatrième évangile*. Paris: Gabriel Beauchesne, 1930.

Comparetti, D. *Vergil in the Middle Ages*. Translated by E. F. M. Benecke. London: Swan Sonnenschein, 1895.

Costello, William T. *The Scholastic Curriculum at Early Seventeenth-Century Cambridge*. Cambridge, Mass.: Harvard University Press, 1958.

Curtis, Mark H. *Oxford and Cambridge in Transition*. Oxford: Clarendon Press, 1959.

Davis, Barbara H. "Ruth Wallerstein's *Studies in Donne.*" Ph.D. dissertation, University of Wisconsin, 1962.

Deferrari, R. J. "St. Augustine's Method of Composing and Delivering Sermons." *American Journal of Philology* 43 (1922): 97–127; 193–219.

Delhaye, Ph. "Pour la fiche 'Alain de Lille.'" *Mélanges de science religieuse* 20 (1963): 39–51.

De Rijk, L. M. *The Place of the Categories of Being in Aristotle's Philosophy*. Assen: Van Gorcum, 1952.

Dodd, C. H. *According to the Scriptures*. London: Fontana Books, 1952.

———. *The Apostolic Preaching and Its Development*. London: Hodder and Stoughton, 1963.

Eliot, T. S. "Lancelot Andrewes." In *Essays Ancient and Modern*, pp. 11–29. London: Faber and Faber, 1936.

Empson, William. "Donne and the Rhetorical Tradition." *Kenyon Review* 11 (1949): 571–87.

Field, George C. "Donne and Hooker." *Anglican Theological Review* 48 (1966): 307–9.

Fontaine, Jacques. *Isidore de Seville et la culture classique dans L'Espagne Wisigothique*. 2 vols. Paris: Etudes Augustiniennes, 1959.

Gardner, Helen. *The Limits of Literary Criticism*. London: Oxford University Press, 1956.

Garin, Eugenio. *Giovanni Pico della Mirandola, Vita e Dottrina*. Florence: Felice le Monnier, 1937.

Gifford, William. "John Donne's Sermons on the 'Grand Days.'" *The Huntington Library Quarterly* 29 (1965–66): 235–44.

Gilbert, Neal W. *Renaissance Concepts of Method*. New York: Columbia University Press, 1960.

Gilson, Etienne. *The Christian Philosophy of St. Augustine.* Translated by L. E. M. Lynch. New York: Random House, 1960.

———. "Michel Menot et la technique du sermon médiéval." In *Les idées et les lettres,* pp. 93–154. Paris: Vrin, 1955.

Glunz, H. H. *History of the Vulgate in England from Alcuin to Roger Bacon.* Cambridge: At the University Press, 1933.

Greenslade, S. L. "The English Reformers and the Fathers of the Church." Inaugural Lecture. Oxford: Clarendon Press, 1960.

Grislis, Egil. "The Hermeneutical Problem of Richard Hooker." In *Studies in Richard Hooker,* edited by W. Speed Hill, pp. 159–206. Cleveland: Press of Case Western Reserve University, 1972.

Hadot, Pierre. *Marius Victorinus, Recherches sur sa vie et ses oeuvres.* Paris: Etudes Augustiniennes, 1971.

Hagendahl, Harald. *Augustine and the Latin Classics.* Goteborg, Sweden: Acta Universitatis Gothoburgensis, 1967.

Haller, William. *The Rise of Puritanism.* New York: Harper Torchbooks, 1957.

Hayward, John. "A Note on Donne the Preacher." In *A Garland for John Donne,* edited by Theodore Spencer, pp. 73–97. Gloucester, Mass.: Peter Smith, 1958.

Herr, A. F. *The Elizabethan Sermon: A Survey and Bibliography.* Philadelphia: 1940.

Hickey, Robert L. "Donne's Delivery." *Tennessee Studies in Literature* 9 (1964): 39–46.

———. "Donne's Art of Memory." *Tennessee Studies in Literature* 3 (1958): 29–36.

———. "Donne's Art of Preaching." *Tennessee Studies in Literature* 1 (1956): 65–74.

Hill, Dietrich Arno. "The 'Modus praedicandi' of John Donne." Ph.D. dissertation, University of Illinois, 1962.

Hödl, Ludwig. "Eine Unbekannte Predigtsammlung des Alanus von Lille . . . " *Zeitschrift für Katholische Theologie* 80 (1958): 516–27.

Howell, A. C. "'Res et Verba': Words and Things." *ELH* 13 (1946): 131–42.

Howell, Wilbur S. *Logic and Rhetoric in England, 1500–1700.* Princeton: Princeton University Press, 1956.

Hunt, R. W. "English Learning in the Late Twelfth Century." *Transactions of the Royal Historical Society* 4th series 19 (1936): 19–42.

———. "The Introduction to the Artes in the Twelfth

Century." In *Studia Mediaevalia in Honor of R. J. Martin*, pp. 85–112. Bruges, Belgium: De Tempel, 1948.

———. "Notes on the 'Distinctiones monasticae et morales.'" In *Liber Floridus, Festschrift P. Lehmann*, pp. 355–62. St. Ottilien: Eos Verlag der Erzabtei, 1950.

———. "Studies on Priscian in the Eleventh and Twelfth Centuries." *Medieval and Renaissance Studies* 1 (1941–43): 194–231; 2 (1950): 1–56.

Jackson, B. Darrell. "The Theory of Signs in St. Augustine's *De doctrina Christiana*." *Revue des études Augustiniennes* 15 (1969): 9–49.

Jacobs, Noah J. *Naming-Day in Eden*. New York: Macmillan, 1969.

Janton, Pierre. *L'éloquence et la rhétorique dans les sermons de Hugh Latimer*. Paris: Presses universitaires de France, 1968.

Jolivet, Jean. "Quelques cas de 'platonisme grammatical' du VIIᵉ au XIIᵉ siècle." In *Mélanges offerts à René Crozet*, edited by Gallais et Riou, vol. 1, pp. 93–99. Poitiers: Société d'études médiévales, 1966.

Kearney, Hugh. *Scholars and Gentlemen: Universities and Society in Pre-industrial Britain, 1500–1700*. Ithaca, N.Y.: Cornell University Press, 1970.

Kennedy, George. *The Art of Persuasion in Greece*. Princeton: Princeton University Press, 1963.

———. *The Art of Rhetoric in the Roman World*. Princeton: Princeton University Press, 1972.

Kevane, Eugene. "Augustine's *De doctrina Christiana*: A Treatise on Christian Education." *Recherches Augustiniennes* 4 (1966): 97–133.

Keynes, Geoffrey L. *A Bibliography of Dr. John Donne*. Cambridge: At the University Press, 1958.

Kneale, William and Martha. *The Development of Logic*. Oxford: Clarendon Press, 1971.

Kristeller, Paul O. *Eight Philosophers of the Italian Renaissance*. Stanford, Calif.: Stanford University Press, 1964.

Lacombe, Georges. *La vie et les oeuvres de Prévostin*. Kain, Belgium: Le Saulchoir, 1927.

Larkin, Miriam Therese. *Language in the Philosophy of Aristotle*. The Hague: Mouton, 1971.

Lechner, Joan M. *Renaissance Concepts of the Commonplaces*. New York: Pageant Press, 1962.

Leclerq, Jean. "L'art de la composition dans les sermons de S. Bernard." *Studi Medievali* 3. 8 (1966): 128–53.

_____. *The Love of Learning and the Desire for God.* Translated by C. Misrahi. New York: Mentor Omega Books, 1961.

_____. "Smaragde et la grammaire chrétienne." *Revue du moyen âge latin* 4 (1948): 15–22.

Lecoy de La Marche, A. *La chaire francaise au moyen âge.* Paris: Renouard, Laurens, 1886.

Lubac, Henri de. *Exégèse médiévale: les quatre sens de l'Ecriture.* 4 vols. Paris: Aubier, 1959–64.

McAdoo, H. R. *The Spirit of Anglicanism: A Survey of Anglican Theological Method in the Seventeenth Century.* London: A. and C. Black, 1965.

McKeon, Richard. "Renaissance and Method in Philosophy." In *Studies in the History of Ideas,* vol. 3, pp. 37–114. New York: Columbia University Press, 1935.

_____. "Rhetoric in the Middle Ages." *Speculum* 17 (1942): 1–32.

MacLure, Millar. *The Paul's Cross Sermons, 1534–1632.* Toronto: University of Toronto Press, 1958.

Mahood, M. M. *Poetry and Humanism.* Port Washington, N.Y.: Kennikat Press, 1950.

Markus, R. A. "St. Augustine on Signs." *Phronesis* 2 (1957): 60–83.

Marrou, H. I. *Saint Augustin et la fin de la culture antique.* 4th ed. Paris: Editions E. de Boccard, 1958.

Martz, Louis L. *The Poetry of Meditation.* New Haven: Yale University Press, 1962.

Merrill, Thomas F. "John Donne and the Word of God." *Neuphilologische Mitteilungen* 69 (1968): 597–616.

Miller, Perry. *The New England Mind: The Seventeenth Century.* Boston: Beacon Press, 1939.

Mitchell, W. F. *English Pulpit Oratory from Andrewes to Tillotson.* London: SPCK, 1932.

Mohrmann, Christine. "Saint Augustin prédicateur." In *Etudes sur le latin des chrétiens,* vol. 1, pp. 391–402. Rome: Edizioni di Storia e Letteratura, 1958.

Moloney, Michael F. *John Donne: His Flight from Medievalism.* Urbana: University of Illinois Press, 1944.

Moore, John F. "Scholasticism, Donne, and the Metaphysical Conceit." *Revue Anglo-Américaine* 13 (1936): 289–96.

Moore, Philip S. *The Works of Peter of Poitiers.* Notre Dame Publications in Medieval Studies. Notre Dame, Ind.: University of Notre Dame Press, 1936.

Mueller, Janel M. "Donne's 'Ars praedicandi': The Development of the Methods and Themes of His Preaching." Ph.D. dissertation, Harvard University, 1964.

Mueller, William R. *John Donne: Preacher*. Princeton: Princeton University Press, 1962.

Murphy, James J. *Rhetoric in the Middle Ages*. Berkeley: University of California Press, 1974.

Novarr, David. *The Making of Walton's "Lives."* Ithaca, N. Y.: Cornell University Press, 1958.

O'Donnell, J. Reginald. "The Sources and Meaning of Bernard Silvester's Commentary on the Aeneid." *Medieval Studies* 24 (1962): 233–49.

Ong, Walter J. *Ramus: Method, and the Decay of Dialogue*. Cambridge, Mass.: Harvard University Press, 1958.

————. "Wit and Mystery: A Revaluation in Medieval Latin Hymnody." *Speculum* 22 (1947): 310–41.

Owst, G. R. *Literature and Pulpit in Medieval England*. Cambridge: At the University Press, 1933.

————. *Preaching in Medieval England*. Cambridge: At the University Press, 1926.

Parker. T. H. L. *The Oracles of God: An Introduction to the Preaching of John Calvin*. London: Lutterworth, 1947.

Pelikan, Jarsolav. *Luther the Expositor*. St. Louis: Concordia, 1959.

Pepin, Jean. "Saint Augustin et la protreptique de l'allégorie." In *Recherches Augustiniennes*, vol. 1, pp. 243–86. Paris: Etudes Augustiniennes, 1958.

Pfander, H. G. "The Medieval Friars and Some Alphabetical Reference-books for Sermons." *Medium AEvum* 3 (1934): 19–29.

————. *The Popular Sermon of the Medieval Friar in England*. New York: New York University Press, 1937.

————. "Some Medieval Manuals of Religious Instruction in England and Observations on Chaucer's Parson's Tale." *JEGP* 35 (1936): 243–58.

Pontet, M. *L'exégèse de Saint Augustin prédicateur*. Paris: Aubier, n.d.

Quain, E. "The Medieval *accessus ad auctores*." *Traditio* 3 (1945): 215 ff.

Quinn, Dennis. "Donne's Christian Eloquence." *ELH* 27 (1960): 276–97.

————. "Donne's Principles of Biblical Exegesis." *JEGP* 41 (1962): 313–29.

————. "John Donne's Sermons on the Psalms and the Traditions of Biblical Exegesis." Ph.D. dissertation, University of Wisconsin, 1958.

Ramsay, M. P. *Les doctrines médiévales chez Donne*. 2nd ed. London: Oxford University Press, 1924.

Reidy, Maurice F. *Bishop Lancelot Andrewes, Jacobean Court Preacher*. Chicago: Loyola University Press, 1955.

Robins, R. H. *Ancient and Medieval Grammatical Theory in Europe*. London: G. Bell, 1951.

_____. *A Short History of Linguistics*. Bloomington: Indiana University Press, 1967.

Rooney, William J. J. "John Donne's 'Second Prebend Sermon'—a Stylistic Analysis." *Texas Studies in Literature and Language* 4 (1962): 24–34.

Rugoff, Milton A. *Donne's Imagery: A Study in Creative Sources*. New York: Corporate Press, 1939.

Schleiner, Winfried. *The Imagery of John Donne's Sermons*. Providence, R.I.: Brown University Press, 1970.

Secret, F. *Les Kabbalistes chrétiens de la renaissance*. Paris: Dunod, 1964.

Simpson, E. M. *A Study of the Prose Works of John Donne*. Oxford: Clarendon Press, 1924.

Smalley, Beryl. *English Friars and Antiquity in the Early Fourteenth Century*. New York: Barnes and Noble, 1960.

_____. *The Study of the Bible in the Middle Ages*. Notre Dame, Ind.: University of Notre Dame Press, 1964.

Smyth, Charles. *The Art of Preaching*. London: SPCK, 1940.

Sparrow, John. "John Donne and Contemporary Preachers, Their Preparation of Sermons for Delivery and for Publication." In *Essays and Studies by Members of the English Association*, no. 16, pp. 144–78. Oxford: Clarendon Press, 1931.

Thompson, Craig R. *Universities in Tudor England*. Ithaca, N.Y.: Cornell University Press, 1959.

Thompson, Sister Geraldine. "John Donne and the Mindes Indeavours." *Studies in English Literature* 5 (1965): 115–31.

_____. "'Water wonderfully clear': Erasmus and Figurative Writing." *Erasmus in English*, no. 5. Toronto: University of Toronto Press, 1972.

Thurot, M. Charles. "Notices et extraits de divers manuscrits latins pour servir à l'histoire des doctrines grammaticales au moyen âge." In *Notices et extraits des manuscrits de la bibliothèque nationale et autres bibliothèques*, vol. 22, pt. 2. Paris: Imprimerie Nationale, 1868.

Trachtenburg, Joshua. "The Formation of Magical Names." Appendix 1 to *Jewish Magic and Superstition*. New York: Behrman's Jewish Book House, 1939.

Tuve, Rosemond. *Elizabethan and Metaphysical Imagery*. Chicago: University of Chicago Press, 1947.

_____. *A Reading of George Herbert*. Chicago: University of Chicago Press, 1952.

Umbach, H. H. "The Merit of Metaphysical Style in Donne's Easter Sermons." *ELH* 12 (1945): 108–29.

_____. "The Rhetoric of Donne's Sermons." *PMLA* 52 (1937): 354–58.

Van der Meer, F. *Augustine the Bishop*. Translated by Battershaw and Lamb. New York: Harper Torchbooks, 1961.

Wallerstein, Ruth. *Studies in Seventeenth-Century Poetic*. Madison: University of Wisconsin Press, 1950.

Webber, Joan. "Celebration of Word and World in Lancelot Andrewes's Style." *JEGP* 64 (1965): 255–69.

_____. *Contrary Music: The Prose Style of John Donne*. Madison: University of Wisconsin Press, 1963.

White, Helen C. "John Donne and the Psychology of Spiritual Effort." In *The Seventeenth Century: Studies in the History of English Thought and Literature from Bacon to Pope by R. F. Jones and Others Writing in His Honor*, pp. 355–68. Stanford, Calif.: Stanford University Press, 1951.

Williams, Arnold. *The Common Expositor: An Account of the Commentaries on Genesis, 1527–1633*. Chapel Hill: University of North Carolina Press, 1948.

Wilmart, André. "Les allégories sur l'écriture attribuées à Raban Maur." *Revue Benedictine* 32 (1920): 47–56.

_____. "Un répertoire d'exégèse." In *Mémorial Lagrange*, pp. 307–46. Paris: Librairie Lecoffre, 1940.

_____. "La tradition des grands ouvrages de Saint Augustin." In *Miscellanea Agostiniana*, vol. 2, pp. 257–315. Rome: Tipografia Poliglatta Vaticana, 1931.

Woodward, William H. *Studies in Education during the Age of the Renaissance*. Cambridge: At the University Press, 1924.

Yates, Frances. *The Art of Memory*. London: Routledge and Kegan Paul, 1966.

INDEX

A

Abelard, Peter, 49, 54
Adam the Premonstratensian, 38
Admonitions to Parliament, 95, 97
Agricola, Rudolph, 68, 76–77
Alan of Lille, 45–46, 50, 56, 86, 121, 131
—*Distinctiones dictionum theologicalium*, 39; Sermon on Matthew 16:19, 40–42
Ambiguity: in classical grammatical treatise, 5; in Augustine, 20, 21, 24–26, 31, 129; in Smaragdus, 36; in Perkins, 81; in Donne, 119–20, 129
Application: in Perkins, 81, 82, 88, 90; in Hooker, 97–98; in Donne, 115
Andrewes, Lancelot, 98, 100–101, 102
Aristotle, x, 6; on topical invention, 69, 75–76
—*Categories*, 48–49, 54; *De interpretatione*, 78; *Prior Analytics*, 78; *Rhetoric*, 68; *Topics*, 68
Arminianism, 98
Augustine, Aurelius, 35, 42, 58, 80, 82, 88, 129; in Donne, 43, 104, 109–10, 116, 118–19, 126–29, 139–146 *passim*
—*De doctrina Christiana*, 6, 18–25, 29, 33, 42, 55, 70, 81, 104, 126–27, 140; *De magistro*, 15–17; *De musica*, 12; *De ordine*, 13, 17, 19; *De Trinitate*, 142; *De utilitate credendi*, 3, 19–20; *Enarrationes in Psalmos*, 29–33, 139, 143

B

Baro, Peter, 98–99
Bartholomaeus Anglicus, 58
Basevorn, Robert de, 46, 47, 49–50, 51, 55, 60
Bernard of Clairvaux, xi, 42, 100, 113, 116
Bonaventure, 112; as scholastic preacher, 59–65

Boethius, 45
—Commentary on Cicero's *Topics*, 52; Commentary on the *Categories*, 53; Commentary on the *De interpretatione*, 50, 54; *De differentiis topicis*, 69; *De divisione*, 47, 52
Brooks, James, 85

C

Cabalists, 105–7
Calvin, 84, 114, 145, 151
Calvinist doctrine, 90, 95, 98, 102, 143–44, 151
Capella, Martianus, x
Carrithers, Gale, xi–xii
Cartwright, Thomas, 87, 89, 95
Cassiodorus, 34–35, 37
Catena. See Chain of scriptural texts
Chain of scriptural texts, 58–59, 125–26, 133–34
Cicero, x, 7, 28, 29, 68, 75, 76
—*De inventione*, 73; *Topics*, 51–52, 69, 72, 77
Commonplaces: in Renaissance ecclesiastical rhetoric, 67–75, 83; in Donne, 113, 114, 139. *See also* Topics, logical
Complication, 117–18
Concordances: use of in preaching, 56, 124–26, 148; compilation of, 169 (n. 47)
Confirmation of division, 55–57, 62–65, 101, 113
Council of Trent, 103, 144

D

Definition: Aristotle on, 6, 52; rhetorical development of, 51–53, 55, 73
Differentiae, 10, 124; compilations of, 8, 15, 25, 34, 58
Differentiation by *in bono* and *in malo*: in Servius, 10, 25; in Augustine, 24–25, 31; in Eucherius, 37; in Donne, 128, 146–47, 150
Dilatation, ix, 57–58, 109–10
Dionysius Thrax, 4
Distinctiones, 48; compilations of, 36–40, 58, 100; in Alan of Lille,

41–42; in Bonaventure, 62–65; in
Donne, 118, 120, 128, 129–31
Division: of scholastic sermon,
46–57, 59, 60–62, 70, 83, 99, 101,
111–13; of sermon intrinsically and
extrinsically, 47, 51, 67; Boethius
on, 47–49; Abelard on, 49; of
Donne's sermon IX.11, 137–39,
153
Donatus, x
—Ars grammatica, 5, 9, 35; Commen-
tary on Terence, 10
Donne, John, 4, 18, 43, 45, 66, 83, 87,
91, 98, 102; response to Puritan
method of preaching, 102–3,
156–57; on the Fathers, 103–5, 110,
127–28, 140–41
—Devotions, 104; Essays, 104, 105–8,
116–17, 176 (n. 30); "A Litanie,"
174 (Ch. 4, n. 2); Sermons: I.1, 176
(n. 20); I.2, 175 (sect. B, n. 16); I.3,
127, 175 (sect. B, n. 10); I.4, 175
(sect. B, n. 16); I.5, 176 (n. 24); I.6,
102, 110, 174 (Ch. 5, n. 3), 175 (Ch.
5, n. 6); I.7, 129, 130, 131; I.9, 108;
II.1, 174 (Ch. 5, n. 2), 176 (n. 29);
II.2, 114, 117, 174 (n. 23); II.3, 146,
176 (n. 29); II.4, 148, 177 (n. 17);
II.5, 147, 175 (sect. A, n. 15), 175
(sect. B, n. 2); II.8, 120, 131, 132,
133, 134, 176 (n. 39); II.9, 176 (n.
38); II.11, 103, 115, 116, 131, 175
(n. 20), 176 (n. 43); II.12, 175 (n.
26); II.14, 103, 177 (n. 18); II.15,
122, 174 (n. 19); II.17, 175 (sect. A,
n. 6); III.1¹, 123, 174 (n. 21); III.1²,
174 (n. 21); III.3, 103; III.4, 103, 175
(n. 26); III.5, 174 (n. 19), 175 (sect.
A, n. 8); III.6, 175 (n. 24), 175 (n.
25); III.7, 108; III.8, 175 (sect. A, n.
7); III.10, 111, 174 (Ch. 5, n. 2), 175
(sect. B, n. 2), 176 (n. 35); III.12,
174 (Ch. 5, n. 2); III.13, 175 (sect.
B, n. 13), 176 (n. 36); III.15, 175
(sect. A, n. 7), 176 (n. 36); III.16,
102; III.17, 127; III.18, 175 (sect. B,
n. 3), 176 (n. 25); IV.1, 174 (Ch. 5,
n. 2), 176 (n. 26); IV.2, 121, 176 (n.
36); IV. 3, 112, 128, 175 (sect. A, n.
7), 175 (sect. A, n. 10), 175 (n. 26);
IV.4, 176 (n. 41); IV.6, 132, 140, 175
(sect. A, n. 10), 175 (sect. A, n. 15),
176 (n. 18), 176 (n. 42); IV.7, 115,
174 (Ch. 5, n. 3); IV.8, 122; IV.10,

116, 119, 176 (n. 38); IV.11, 175
(sect. B, n. 16); V.1, 123, 163
(intro., n. 1), 174 (Ch. 5, n. 3); V.2,
125, 135, 175 (sect. B, n. 3), 176 (n.
35); V.4, 131, 132, 135; V.6, 175
(sect. A, n. 8); V.7, 150, 177 (n. 19);
V.8, 108, 175 (sect. B, n. 5), 176 (n.
35); V.9, 121; V.11, 175 (sect. A, n.
15), 176 (n. 44); V.12, 116; V.14,
123, 124, 141, 175 (n. 18), 176 (n.
4); V.15, 127, 131, 176 (n. 39), 176
(n. 40), 176 (n. 4); V.16, 134, 174 (n.
19), 175 (sect. B, n. 12); V.17, 176
(n. 17), 176 (n. 41); V.18, 175 (sect.
B, n. 15), 176 (n. 23); VI.1, 126, 175
(n. 19); VI.2, 117, 134, 177 (n. 21);
VI.4, 176 (n. 36); VI.6, 122; VI.8,
175 (sect. B, n. 12), 176 (n. 38);
VI.9, 132, 174 (n. 21), 175 (sect. A,
n. 15); VI.10, 102; VI.11, 175 (n.
17); VI.15, 175 (sect. A, n. 10);
VI.16, 175 (n. 25); VII.1, 107, 113,
174 (n. 19), 176 (n. 34); VII.2, 175
(sect. B, n. 15); VII.3, 114, 152, 175
(sect. B, n. 9); VII.4, 105, 175 (sect.
A, n. 11); VII.5, 175 (sect. A, n. 7),
175 (sect. B, n. 10); VII.6, 176 (n.
32); VII.7, 176 (n. 27); VII.8, 175 (n.
25), 176 (n. 17); VII.9, 114, 175 (n.
18), 175 (sect. B, n. 15); VII.10, 175
(n. 18); VII.11, 115, 176 (n. 29);
VII.12, 175 (sect. B, n. 4), 176 (n.
26), 177 (n. 10); VII.13, 163 (n. 1);
VII.14, 175 (n. 18); VII.15, 177 (n.
10); VII.16, 115, 177 (n. 10); VII.17,
175 (n. 18), 175 (sect. B, n. 14), 176
(n. 17), 176 (n. 20); VII.18, 174 (n.
19); VIII.1, 176 (n. 29);VIII.2, 174
(Ch. 5, n. 2); VIII.3, 114; VIII.4,
110, 141, 174 (Ch. 5, n. 1); VIII.5,
103, 175 (sect. A, n. 10), 175 (n.
19), 175 (sect. B, n. 1), 177 (n. 10);
VIII.6, 114, 116; VIII.7, 108, 176 (n.
35); VIII.8, 175 (sect. B, n. 16);
VIII.9, 175 (n. 26), 175 (n. 27);
VIII.10, 175 (n. 24); VIII.11, 115,
176 (n. 19); VIII.12, 118, 124, 175
(n. 18), 176 (n. 20); VIII.13, 175 (n.
22), 175 (n. 24), 176 (n. 24); VIII.14,
114, 175 (n. 21); VIII.15, 175 (sect.
A, n. 7), 175 (n. 24); VIII.16, 175
(sect. B, n. 11); IX.1, 105, 132, 152,
174 (n. 17), 176 (n. 37), 177 (n. 21);
IX.2, 121, 174 (n. 17), 174 (n. 23),

175 (sect. A, n. 8); IX.3, 105, 119, 128; IX.5, 117; IX.6, 175 (sect. B, n. 12); IX.7, 175 (sect. B, n. 14), 176 (n. 23); IX.8, 174 (n. 21), 175 (sect. B, n. 7); IX.9, 175 (sect. B, n. 9); IX.11, 118, 137–54, 174 (n. 7), 174 (n. 23), 175 (sect. B, n.8); IX.13, 126, 175 (sect. B, n. 3); IX.15, 122; IX.16, 114; IX.17, 114, 174 (Ch. 5, n. 2); IX.18, 176 (n. 17), 176 (n. 18), 177 (n. 10); X.1, 129, 174 (Ch. 5, n. 2); X.2, 123, 177 (n. 9); X.4, 123, 176 (n. 31); X.6, 176 (n. 25); X.8, 176 (n. 38); X.9, 132, 133, 174 (n. 23); X.11, 175 (n. 25)

E

Eachard, John, 173 (n. 16)
Encyclopedists, 24, 34, 58
Erasmus, 68, 80, 84
—*Copia*, 72; *Ecclesiastes*, 72–74, 76; *Ratio*, 69–72
Etymology: in classical grammarians, 7, 10, 34; rhetorical use of, 7–8; in Donne, 108, 124, 147, 148
Etymology of proper names: in Augustine, 23, 31; in Bonaventure, 63; in Andrewes, 100, 101; in Donne, 107–8, 132, 136
Eucherius, 37

F

Figures of speech, 5, 79, 81
Fisher, John, 84
Fourth Lateran Council, 40

G

Garnier de Rochefort, 38, 100
Gerardus, Andreas. *See* Hyperius
God: as sustainer of language, 17–19, 157–58
Grammar: as an art, 4–5, 6–7, 12–14; classical treatise on, 5
Grammatical categories: as representing reality, 8–9, 15, 35–36, 141; in division of scholastic sermon, 49–51, 60–61
Grammatical commentary, 42, 97–98; classical examples of, 9–11; in Augustine, 3–4, 16, 20, 22, 28; in Donne, 109–11, 154
Gregory the Great, xi, 140
Guibert de Nogent, 39

H

Homonyms: in classical grammatical treatise, 5–6; in Augustine, 25; in Smaragdus, 36–37; in Adam the Premonstratensian, 38; in Playfere, 99–100; in Donne, 119
Hooker, Richard, 87, 95–98, 102
Hooper, John, 86–87, 91
Hyperius, 67–68, 74–75, 80, 82, 88, 97

I

Invention: exegetical, 18, 20–26 *passim*, 29, 102, 108, 131, 136; in Peter of Cornwall, 40; dialectical, 45, 51–55 *passim*, 59, 65; topical, 68–69, 72–77 *passim*, 80, 82, 83, 98; in Ramus, 78
Isidore of Seville
—*De proprietate sermonum*, 34; *Etymologiae sive origines*, 34

J

Jean de Galles, 44, 55
Jerome, St., 101, 122, 141
Jewel, John, 85–86
John of Salisbury, 47, 51, 53
Judgment: in rhetoric, 69, 77–80

K

Keckermann, Bartholomew, 115
Keys of division, 47, 52, 56, 61, 113, 138–39

L

Langton, Stephen, 40
Latimer, Hugh, 84, 85, 86, 91
Laudianism, 98
Lorinus, Johannes, 137, 141
Ludham, John, 67–68, 74–75
Luther, Martin, 84, 144

M

Macrobius, 9, 11
Marius Victorinus, 6–7, 14, 51
Martin of Dacia, 54
Mathematical arts: in comparison with arts of grammar and rhetoric, 4, 13–14, 53, 157
Melanchthon, Philipp, 74, 103
"Melitos of Sardis", 37–38, 40
Memory: in Augustine, 16–18, 26–28, 142; in Ramus, 79; in Perkins, 80; in Donne, 113, 115–18, 121, 144, 153

Mitchell, W. Fraser, x
Mueller, Janel M., xi
Musculus, Wolfgang, 137

N
Names, divine, 106–8
Natural history: as aid in reading
    Scripture, 22, 23, 32, 38, 58, 127
Nicholas of Lyra, 104, 126
Noun, derivation of, 7, 15, 157

O
Onomastica sacra. See Etymology of
    proper names
Oratio, 46, 53–54, 55. See also State-
    ment
Order of words in Scripture, 22, 31,
    101, 141
Origen, 70–71

P
Parallelism of expression, 42, 50,
    60–61, 70, 112, 167 (n. 39)
Pastoral manuals, 40, 84
Perkins, William, 97, 115
—The Art of Prophecying, 80–83, 88;
    Sermons on Matthew 5–7, 87–91
Peter the Cantor, 39, 40, 42
Peter of Cornwall, 40
Peter Helias, 54
Peter of Poitiers, 40
Pico della Mirandola, 105, 106
Piscator, 89, 103
Plato
—Cratylus, 4, 13; Gorgias, 4; Sophist,
    53; Timaeus, 106
Playfere, Thomas, 98–100, 102
Pliny, 23, 127
Porphyry, 48
Prepositinus, 40
Priscian, 51, 53–54
Prodicus, 8
Proposition, 73, 114
Puritan method of exposition, 91,
    96–98, 102

Q
Quinn, Dennis, xi
Quintilian, 71

R
Rainolde, Richard, 78
Ramism, 76, 91, 97; in Perkins, 80–82
Ramsay, M. P., x

Ramus, Peter, 68, 77–80, 82
Ratio: in classical grammatical
    treatise, 6; in Augustine, 12, 25–26
Regula: in classical grammatical
    treatise, 6. See also Rule of faith
Resolution: in Perkins, 81–82, 88, 90;
    in Donne, 115
Reuchlin, Johann, 105, 106–7
Richard of Thetford, 47–48, 58
Rule of faith, 19–20, 21, 24, 26, 35,
    119. See also Regula
Rumination, 16, 18, 26–28, 30, 116,
    165 (n. 40)

S
Schleiner, Winfried, xi
Servius: commentary on Donatus, 5,
    6, 7, 9; in Saturnalia, 9; on Vergil,
    10, 11
Siger of Courtrai, 50–51
Signification: in Augustine, 15–16
Signification, proper: in classical
    grammatical treatise, 5; in Augus-
    tine, 20–21; in Donne, 126–27
Signification, transferred: in Augus-
    tine, 20, 21–26, 30, 31, 32; in
    Cicero, 28; in Smaragdus, 36; in
    Perkins, 81; in Donne, 104, 111,
    120, 126–36, 146–48, 149–50, 152,
    154; in Pico, 106
Smaragdus of St. Mihiel, 35–36
Speculative grammar, 50–51, 54
Statement: scriptural text preached
    on as instance of, 45–47, 49, 55; as
    predication, 48, 50; as represent-
    ing reality, 53–55, 65. See also
    Oratio
Status, 69, 72, 73, 75
Stockewood, John, 85
Subdivision: in scholastic preaching,
    56–57; in Bonaventure, 62–65; in
    Donne, 145
Syncategoremata, 54, 55
Synonyms: in classical grammatical
    treatise, 5; in Augustine, 25; in
    Bonaventure, 62; in Playfere, 99; in
    Donne, 146

T
Talon, 78, 79
Topics. See Commonplaces; Topics,
    logical
Topics, logical: in Aristotle, 68; in
    Cicero, 69; in Agricola, 76; in

Ramus, 77–78; in Perkins, 81–82, 89; in Donne, 114–15, 142–44

Translations, use of in preaching: in Augustine, 21; in Donne, 118–19, 126, 149, 151–52

Travers, Walter, 95

Tyndale, William, 84–85

U

Understanding: in Donne, 113–14, 142–44

V

Varro, Marcus
—*Disciplinae libri IX*, x; *De lingua Latina*, 6

Vergil: in classical grammatical treatise, 5, 8; commented on by Servius, 10, 11; discussed in *Saturnalia*, 11; commented on by Augustine, 16

W

Waleys, Thomas, 46, 47, 50, 55, 56–57, 58

Wallerstein, Ruth, xi

Weaving: image of continuity in discourse, 29, 33, 38, 79, 81–82

Webber, Joan, xi

William of Auvergne, 58

Wilson, Thomas, 73, 105

Words, as representing reality: in classical grammatical treatise, 7; in Augustine, 14, 21–22; in Andrewes, 100; in Donne, 108, 123–24

DATE DUE

DEMCO 38-297